THE KARL MARX LIBRARY

EDITED AND TRANSLATED BY

SAUL K. PADOVER

Distinguished Service Professor of Political Science,
Graduate Faculty, New School for Social Research

ALREADY PUBLISHED

On Revolution
On America and the Civil War

TITLES IN PREPARATION

On the First International
On Religion
On Freedom of the Press and Censorship

Also by Saul K. Padover

THE REVOLUTIONARY EMPEROR: JOSEPH II

SECRET DIPLOMACY AND ESPIONAGE

(*with James Westfall Thompson*)

THE LIFE AND DEATH OF LOUIS XVI

JEFFERSON (*a biography*)

EXPERIMENT IN GERMANY

LA VIE POLITIQUE DES ÉTATS-UNIS

FRENCH INSTITUTIONS: VALUES AND POLITICS

THE GENIUS OF AMERICA

UNDERSTANDING FOREIGN POLICY

THE MEANING OF DEMOCRACY

THOMAS JEFFERSON AND THE FOUNDATIONS OF AMERICAN FREEDOM

. .

Edited by Saul K. Padover

THOMAS JEFFERSON ON DEMOCRACY

THE COMPLETE JEFFERSON

THOMAS JEFFERSON AND THE NATIONAL CAPITAL

A JEFFERSON PROFILE

THE WRITINGS OF THOMAS JEFFERSON

THE COMPLETE MADISON (also titled: THE FORGING OF AMERICAN FEDERALISM)

THE WASHINGTON PAPERS

THE MIND OF ALEXANDER HAMILTON

WILSON'S IDEALS

THE LIVING UNITED STATES CONSTITUTION

CONFESSIONS AND SELF-PORTRAITS

THE WORLD OF THE FOUNDING FATHERS

NEHRU ON WORLD HISTORY

TO SECURE THESE BLESSINGS

On America and the Civil War

KARL MARX (1818–1883)

THE KARL MARX LIBRARY
VOLUME II

On America and the Civil War

KARL MARX

ARRANGED AND EDITED, WITH AN
INTRODUCTION AND NEW TRANSLATIONS
by Saul K. Padover

McGraw-Hill Book Company

NEW YORK   ST. LOUIS   SAN FRANCISCO
DÜSSELDORF   LONDON   MEXICO   PANAMA
SYDNEY   TORONTO

Library of Congress Cataloging in Publication Data
Marx, Karl, 1818–1883.
    The Karl Marx library.
    Bibliography: v. 1, p. 641–643.
    CONTENTS: v. 1. On revolution.—v. 2. On America and the Civil War.
    1. Socialism—Collections. I. Title.
HX276.M2773   1972   335.43'08   78–172260
ISBN 0–07–048078–8
ISBN 0–07–048084–2 (pbk.)

Design: *Herb Johnson*
Art Direction: *Harris Lewine*

FIRST EDITION

123456789 BPBP *798765432*

Contents

The Civil War

Contents   ix

Photographs following pages 42 and 170

Introduction:
Karl Marx on America and
the Civil War

KARL MARX, the archetype European revolutionist, had a lifelong interest in the United States. As early as 1845, when he was twenty-seven
years old and living in exile in Brussels, he was thinking seriously of
emigrating to America. On October 17 of that year he wrote to
Franz Damian Görtz, the Oberbürgermeister of his native Trier, in
Rhenish Prussia, asking to be provided with an *Auswanderungsschein*
(Emigration Certificate) "to the United North American States." He
had in mind Texas, which had just been admitted into the Union. But
instead of emigrating in person, Marx maintained close contact with
many people in the United States, especially German immigrants
whom he knew. He followed American politics and movements with
acute interest and, during the Civil War, with passionate involvement.

Marx came to have an intimate knowledge of American conditions.
Even localized events, such as the Antirent War in upstate New
York in the 1840s, did not escape his attention. In preparation for his
economic works Marx also read, with a sharp and critical eye, leading
American theorists. Among them were three Philadelphians, one trans-
planted and two indigenous. In *Critique of Political Economy* (1859),
Marx discussed little-known economic essays of Benjamin Franklin,
paying him tribute as having "formulated the basic law of modern
political economy" in connection with the labor theory of value. Of
another Philadelphian, Charles Henry Carey, whose works[1] he studied
carefully, Marx said that he was "the only important American

---

1. *Essay on the Rate of Wages* (London, 1835); *Principles of Political Economy*
(Philadelphia, 1837); *The Past, the Present, and the Future* (Philadelphia, 1848);
The Harmony of Interests (Philadelphia, 1851); *The Slave Trade, Domestic and
Foreign* (London, 1853); *The Principles of Social Science* (3 vols., Philadelphia and
London, 1848–59).

economist." Carey was not a radical, but an American nationalist, an optimistic expansionist and a believer in *laissez-faire*.

But Marx had no such high opinion of the other Philadelphia-born economist, the radical Henry George. Copies of his *Progress and Poverty* (1880), which had created a sensation in the United States, were sent him by American friends. Marx dismissed George's advocacy of a single tax on land as a solution for all economic and social ailments, as a "last attempt to save the capitalist regime."[2] The single tax idea, Marx wrote, was neither original nor sound. It had been discussed by some of David Ricardo's older disciples and rejected by Marx himself years earlier in his first book, *The Poverty of Philosophy* (1847). Marx concluded that Henry George, although a talented writer of good intentions, was a presumptuous "panacea hatcher" and a "humbug" ignorant of both economic theory and basic American conditions:

> He should have asked himself: How did it happen that in the United States, where relatively, that is, compared to civilized Europe, land was accessible to the great mass of the people and still is to a certain degree (again relatively), capitalist economy and the corresponding enslavement have developed more *rapidly* and more *shamelessly* than in any other country?"[3]

It is interesting that Henry George reciprocated Marx's lack of admiration. America's oddest economic reformer had no use for Europe's forémost radical theorist. In 1884, the year after Marx's death, George wrote to an English socialist that the author of *Capital* was a "superficial thinker" who "lacked analytical power and logical habits of thought."[4] In another letter George repeated the statement that "Carl Marx" was a "superficial thinker . . . totally deficient in analytical powers."[5] This quaint view of the most formidably learned and profoundly philosophical social philosopher of the nineteenth century might be described as a "vagrant opinion," defined by the American satirist Ambrose Bierce as one that has no visible means of support; at the time Henry George passed his *outré* judgment on Marx, the latter's major writings, including *Capital*, were not available in English.

Marx's knowledge of the United States was extensive in range and detail. He obtained it by wide reading and by keeping abreast of published works, both general and specific. His reading included such books as *The War with Mexico* (1849), by Roswell Sabine Ripley

---

2. See his letter to John Swinton, page 47.
3. Marx to Friedrich Adolph Sorge, pages 47–49.
4. Henry George to Henry Mayers Hyndman, January 22, 1844: MS in N. Y. Public Library; photocopy in Tamamint Library, E50.
5. Henry George to Walker, June 26, 1884, *ibid*.

(later a Confederate brigadier general during the Civil War), and *Notes on North America* (1851) by the British traveler Alexander Keith Johnston, which Marx read as soon as it appeared. Both were two-volume works replete with comprehensive detail. Ripley's book, incidentally, helped convince Marx that Winfield Scott, the hero of the Mexican War and General-in-Chief of the U. S. Army at the outbreak of the Civil War, was a pompous and self-seeking commander—"a petty, untalented, nagging, envious dog and humbug." Scott, Marx wrote, "seems to be as much a great general as the many-sided Greeley is a great philosopher." Horace Greeley, who had founded the *New-York Daily Tribune* in 1841, was Marx's employer at the time.

An American correspondent who had several interviews with Marx in London for the *Chicago Tribune*, reported:

> During my conversations I was struck with his intimacy with American questions which have been uppermost during the past twenty years. His knowledge of them, and the surprising accuracy with which he criticized our national and state legislation, impressed upon my mind the fact that he must have derived his information from inside sources.[6]

Marx's "inside sources" consisted primarily of American publications, which he continued to read until the last three or four years of his life, when a succession of grave illnesses prevented him from doing sustained intellectual work. But his interest in the United States never flagged. On April 4, 1876, he asked his friend, the German socialist Friedrich Adolph Sorge, who lived in Hoboken, N.J., to send him catalogs containing the latest books on American agriculture, credit, finances, and other economic subjects. Sorge did his best to supply Marx with various American materials and reports on labor conditions in the industrial states, including Pennsylvania, Ohio, and Massachusetts. As late as August, 1879, some three and a half years before his death, the ailing Marx was pleased to write Frederick Engels that Carroll Davidson Wright, chief of the Massachusetts Bureau of Statistics of Labor, had sent him all the Reports from 1874 to 1879, as well as the Compendium of the Massachusetts Census. Commissioner Wright had also promised that he would be "pleased, in future, to send you our publications as soon as issued."

Marx was greatly impressed by American technological progress. In 1851, a decade before the outbreak of the Civil War, he noted in a letter to Engels that at the London Industrial Exhibition the Americans had carried off every technological prize—a noteworthy feat for the relatively young republic. The Americans won first prizes in

---

6. *Chicago Tribune*, January 5, 1879.

guttapercha rubber ("new stuff and new productions"); in arms; in machinery (reapers, sowers, sewing machines); in photography ("daguerreotypes applied on a large scale for the first time"); in navigation; in luxury articles ("a golden service of pure [California] gold"). *Capital* contains a subtle analysis of the reasons for the widespread use of machinery in America. In 1859, in his first book on economics, *Critique of Political Economy*, Marx observed that the United States was "the most modern form of bourgeois society."

For a time Marx entertained general notions about a proletarian revolution in the United States. He thought that such a possibility would exist after the Civil War, when the emancipated Negroes, in alliance with the disgruntled and exploited farmers of the West, would join the workers in forming a strong labor party in the States. The program of such a party, as developed by the First International, Marx told a correspondent of the *New York Herald*, was:

> . . . to emancipate the workingman from the rule of politicians, and to combat monopoly in all the many forms it is assuming there, especially that of the public lands. We want no more monstrous land grabs, no more grants to swindling railroad concerns, no more schemes for robbing the people of their birthright for the benefit of purse-proud monopolists. More than that, let these men be warned in time; their ill-gotten goods shall be taken from them, and their wealth shall vanish like the baseless fabric of a vision. We oppose also all protectionist measures, which make all the necessaries of life dear to the poor man merely to put money into the pockets of a few aristocrats who know how to buy over your corrupt politicians.[7]

Marx believed that a large American labor party would be able to attain power without the necessity of using violence. "We apprehend no violence or trouble there," Marx told the *Herald* correspondent, "unless, indeed, some of your great iron or other monopolists should take it into their hands to employ force to put down strikes, as they have done in one or two instances."

Marx expressed a similar view about the use of force to achieve labor's goals in a speech he delivered in Amsterdam on September 8, 1872, at the time he worked to move the First International's headquarters to America to keep it out of the hands of the anarchists. In that speech, published in various European radical newspapers, Marx conceded that violent revolution might not be necessary in democratic countries, where workers had access to the ballot. "You know," he said, "that the institutions, mores, and traditions of various countries must be taken into consideration, and we do not deny that

---

7. Published August 3, 1871.

there are countries—such as America, England, and if I were more familiar with your institutions, I would perhaps also add Holland—where the workers can attain their goal by peaceful means."

Marx's interest in America acquired a special acuteness when he became correspondent for the *New-York Daily Tribune*. He was aware that to be effective as a journalist he had to acquaint himself fully with the country where his new—and, in truth, his only—reading public now was. "You know, *mon cher*," he wrote to a German communist friend who had emigrated to the United States in 1851, "how difficult it is to contribute to a paper on the other side of the ocean, without a knowledge of that public, etc."[8]

Marx's connection with the *Tribune* was one of the crucial events in his life. For one thing, it provided him with an eagerly desired platform for his opinions and ideas, which he could express freely within the limitations of the factual requirements of journalism. For another, it kept him going financially in the decade 1851–61 during which he was the *Tribune*'s London correspondent. When the correspondenceship ended so did Marx's sole means of steady income, such as it was.

The *Tribune* was then, in Marx's words, "the foremost English-language American newspaper." With a circulation of about 200,000, and selling for two pennies, it was also the largest and probably the most influential paper in the United States. Its appeal was to educated people, and it provided its readers with substantial and serious journalistic fare, both domestic and foreign. Horace Greeley, who was to run as the Democratic candidate for the presidency in 1872,[9] was, in the time of Marx's correspondenceship, under the influence of the Fourierist Albert Brisbane, and lent his paper to the advocacy of utopian ideas. Among the *Tribune*'s outstanding editors were the Transcendentalists Charles Anderson Dana, who had spent five years at Brook Farm, and George Ripley.

Dana and Marx met in the summer of 1848, when Marx was editor and publisher of the radical *Neue Rheinische Zeitung*, in Cologne. Dana, only a year younger than Marx, was reporting to the *Tribune* on the various revolutions taking place in Austria, France, and Germany. Dana's reports show that he shared Marx's pro-revolutionary sympathies. Like Marx, he saw in the continental uprisings a natural and creative process, the purpose of which, he wrote, was "not simply to change the form of government, but to change the form of society."[10]

In August, 1851, Marx, then a poverty-stricken exile in London,

8. Marx to Weydemeyer, February 20, 1852.
9. See Chronology, pages xxxiii–liii.
10. *New-York Daily Tribune*, August 29, 1848.

received a letter from Dana inviting him to write for the *New-York Daily Tribune*. It was a welcome opportunity, but the problem was that Marx could not then write in English. As usual when in difficulties, he turned to his friend Frederick Engels for help. "If it were possible for you," Marx wrote Engels in Manchester (August 8, 1851), "to supply an article in English on German conditions . . . it would be a splendid beginning." Engels, a gifted linguist whose knowledge of the English language was impeccable, replied two days later that he was ready to help his friend in need, but that he needed further details. "Write me soon in what form it is to be—whether you want one suitable article or a series, and, secondly, how the material is to be handled, for I know nothing whatever about the politics of the *New-York Tribune* except that it is American Whig."

Marx replied on August 14: "Write a series of articles on Germany, from 1848 on. Clever and unceremonious. The gentlemen [of the *Tribune*] are *impudent* in the foreign department."

Engels complied. For a whole year he wrote articles on Germany —there were nineteen altogether—and sent them to Marx, who in turn dispatched them to New York under his own name. The *Tribune* printed them between October 25, 1851, and October 23, 1852. The articles were published in book form in 1896,[11] under the title, *Revolution and Counter-Revolution in Germany in 1848*. It was not until 1913 that Engels' authorship became known.

Marx's own contribution to the *Tribune* began in August, 1852, a year after he received Dana's invitation. Even then he wrote his reports in German, sent them to Engels for translation, and then forwarded them to New York. Marx's first article, which Engels divided for him into two parts—"The Elections in England: Tories and Whigs," and "The Chartists"—came out in the *Tribune* on August 21 and 25, 1852.

Marx made his first plunge into English writing six months later. "Yesterday," he informed Engels on January 29, 1853, "for the first time, I risked writing an article for Dana in English . . . If I could now obtain a decent grammar and stoutly plunge into the writing, it would go passably well." The *Tribune* featured the article, which covered "Capital Punishment—Mr. Cobden's Pamphlets—Regulations of the Bank of England," on February 18, 1853.

Soon Marx's English improved to such an extent that Engels was moved to compliment him. "Your English," he wrote to Marx on June 1, 1853, "is not only good, it is brilliant. Here and there a few

---

11. The book was brought out in English by Marx's daughter, Eleanor Marx-Aveling. A German translation also appeared in 1896, and a French one, by another daughter, Laura Lafargue, in 1900.

catchwords are not woven in fluently enough, but this is the worst that can be said."

Marx was flattered: "The praise you bestow on my 'young' English," he replied the next day, "has had a heartening effect on me. What I mainly lack is, first, grammatical sureness, and, secondly, a knack for certain secondary turnings of phrase, without which sharp writing is impossible."

For the next decade Marx continued to write for the *Tribune*, his style improving with the years. The early articles still showed evidence of ponderous Germanism, but the later ones tended to be terse and muscular. The words were chosen with precision, and the style was frequently eloquent.

As a correspondent Marx had his own established routine. In essence an interpretive journalist rather than an original investigator, he did not report from personal observation or interviews. His sources were almost entirely the printed word, primarily newspapers, of which he was an avid reader. For politics and international affairs Marx relied on continental and British papers, especially the influential and well-informed *Times,* from which he quoted extensively. Buying newspapers daily was his main financial outlay as a correspondent, and often he could hardly afford even that modest expenditure. When he did not have the money to buy a newspaper, he could not do his stint as correspondent for the *Tribune.* "I did not write the articles for Dana," he wrote Engels on September 8, 1852, "because I did not have the penny to read newspapers."

For economic and social materials Marx depended on the British Museum, where he often worked from ten in the morning to seven in the evening. There he read official reports and publications, making extensive notes of facts and figures which he wove into his reportage for the *Tribune.* Many of Marx's articles were so full of statistical data that they read like official reports themselves—with a special point of view.

After assembling his notes and clippings, Marx often worked late into the night on his articles—two a week for a long time—writing them in his cramped Germanic script that no English-language typesetter could possibly read. Jenny Marx, his wife, generally transcribed them. On Tuesdays and Fridays the articles, which Marx called "letters," were dispatched to New York. If an article missed the departing steamer, Marx would lose half a week's income. The pieces appeared in the *Tribune* on an average about two weeks after they were mailed, which was more or less the time it took a steamer to cross the Atlantic.

Marx was proud of being correspondent for what he considered

the most important English-language paper in America, but his relationship with the *Tribune* was not always smooth or happy. There
were both editorial and financial difficulties. Marx, as an honest and
hard-working journalistic craftsman, often felt that he and his products
were not treated properly, and he was often justified. Actually, Dana
did value Marx as a correspondent. Once, after Marx reported that
the Italian patriot, Giuseppe Mazzini, had eluded the continental
police and arrived safely in London, the *Tribune* printed a short editorial in praise of its London correspondent:

> In this connection we may properly pay a tribute to the remark-
> able ability of the correspondent by whom this interesting piece
> of intelligence is furnished. Mr. Marx has very decided opinions
> of his own, with some of which we are far from agreeing, but
> those who do not read his letters neglect one of the most instruc-
> tive sources of information on the great questions of current
> European politics.[12]

But the *Tribune* did not always treat Marx's "letters" respectfully.
The New York editors took liberties with the articles, using them
as it served their purpose, and often not printing them at all. Many of
the dispatches were published under Marx's name, but a large number
of others were printed anonymously, under a London dateline,
headed: "From Our Own Correspondent." Others were published
under trivial headlines. What particularly irked Marx was the way the
Tribune exploited his work and made it its own. "Recently," he told
Engels (April 22, 1854), "the *Tribune* has again appropriated all my
articles as leaders and published only trash under *my* name." Indeed,
at least eighty-four of Marx's articles—almost a fourth of his total
contributions—were published as leaders, that is, as unsigned *Tribune*
editorials, for which the author received no credit and little pay.

The money question was a source of almost constant irritation.
The *Tribune* paid per piece. If it chose not to print an article, Marx
did not get paid, and thus lost endless hours of work. At first the
compensation was £1, or $5, per article. Marx complained to Dana,
as he told Engels:

> The fellows must pay at least £3 per article. Thus they spent
> £500 to send [Bayard] Taylor to India, and the fellow writes
> worse and less from there—and what, after all, could he learn on
> a quick trip in such a country?—than I do from here on the same
> subject. With £3 per article, I could at last get out of the muck.

Dana agreed to pay £2 and to buy two a week. Under this arrange-
ment, which lasted about four years, Marx thus earned £4, or $20,

---

12. April 7, 1853.

per week. But this did not mean a regular flow of income. Money orders were not infrequently delayed, and Marx often had to scramble to find somebody in the City with enough cash to take his promissory note on money from the *Tribune* that might or might not arrive in time. In addition, there was always the difficulty of cashing foreign money orders or checks.

In March, 1857, Marx was informed that the *Tribune* would henceforth take only one article a week. This cut his already meager earnings in half. Furious, Marx reported the bad news to Engels, who was a constant help financially, commenting that he would dearly love to tell the "lousy Yankees" where to get off, but he was in desperate need of money and ceaselessly dunned by creditors. "I am," he wrote to Engels in that special brand of Germanish in which he sometimes indulged, "... from all sides gebothert."

In February, 1861, the month during which the seceded states organized their Confederate Government in Montgomery, Ala.,[13] the *Tribune* suspended all foreign correspondents except Marx. For the next eight months they printed none of his work, and did not pay. In April, when the Civil War opened with the bombardment of Fort Sumter, S.C., and President Lincoln declared a state of "insurrection," Dana quit the *Tribune* in disagreement over its policy of compromise with the South. After Dana had written Marx about his departure from the *Tribune*, Engels wrote his friend that he had read in the *Manchester Examiner* and *Times*, that Dana left the *Tribune* "on account of differences of opinion with Mr. Horace Greeley." He added, "This old jackass *with the face angelic*[14] thus seems to be responsible for everything."

Marx realized that with the Civil War breaking out in the United States, American interest in the kind of foreign affairs he had been reporting was bound to fade. The fratricidal conflict would unavoidably become the absorbing concern of the American people. "American conditions," Marx wrote to Lion Philips, his uncle (May 6, 1861), "are rather harmful for me personally, as for the time being transatlantic newspaper readers have eyes and ears *only* for their own affairs."

In the latter part of 1861 the *Tribune* temporarily resumed printing Marx's articles, but only because they were connected with the American struggle. Between October 11 and December 25, 1861, the *Tribune* published eight pieces by Marx, dealing with the effect of the Civil War on British commerce and public opinion.

Marx's last *Tribune* article, which marked the end of his career as an American correspondent, appeared March 10, 1862. "The

---

13. See Chronology, pages xxxiii–liii.
14. Engels wrote these four words in English.

Mexican Imbroglio," was a sharp criticism of Britain's cynical diplomacy, a subject he had treated in a previous dispatch, in which he warned against the planned intervention of the European powers in Mexico while the United States was busy fighting the Civil War.[15]

The year 1861 was a particularly desperate one for Marx and his family. The income from the *Tribune* was all but irreplaceable. Debt-ridden and tormented by illness—he signed one of his letters to Engels: "Your Hemmorrhoidarius"—Marx did not know where to turn. On August 20, 1862, he wrote to Engels with bitter humor, "*Dear boy,*[16] no matter what you may say, it is in reality painful to make so much *bother* for you with my miseries. If only I knew how to start some *business!* Grey, dear friend, is all theory, and only *business* is green.[17] Alas, I came to this insight too late."

The eight articles the *Tribune* printed in 1861 brought Marx a total of £16, or $80, for the year. This barely sufficed to pay his most pressing debts. In November, 1861, with a gift of £5 from Engels, Marx paid £18 of debts to the butcher, baker, tea grocer, green grocer, oil man, and milkman; he spent ten shillings for coal. But he had no money left to pay the landlord, to whom he owed a year's rent and who constantly threatened him with eviction; or for school fees for his children, or for the cobbler, or the family's approaching winter needs, including food. He was at least £100 in debt. The situation, he said, was desperate enough to drive a man crazy.

It was under this pressure that Marx agreed to accept an invitation to write for *Die Presse*, a middle-class Vienna daily, which he had previously turned down because of its conservative politics. The *Presse*, with a circulation of 30,000, was Austria's largest newspaper. It would pay only half of what the *Tribune* paid—£1 per article and ten shillings per newsletter. Marx thought such a low honorarium was demeaning, but he accepted it because, as he said resignedly, "*il faut vivre.*" Considering the amount of time and work he put into his writing, it was indeed a miserable wage.

The *Presse* treated Marx's correspondence even more shabbily than the *Tribune* had done. It either ignored his articles or at best printed only what and when it chose. Most of the *Presse*'s choices were on the American Civil War, in which there was widespread interest even in Central Europe. Marx said the *Presse* published only about one out of every four articles he sent in, and of course he was paid only for what was printed.

---

15. "The contemplated intervention in Mexico by England, France, and Spain, is, in my opinion, one of the most monstrous enterprises ever chronicled in the annals of international history" (see page 102).

16. The words in italics were written in English.

17. Cited after Goethe's *Faust*, Scene 4, Part 1.

Altogether the *Presse* published fifty-two articles, two of them written in collaboration with Engels. Of the fifty-two, thirty-five were on the Civil War and are included in this volume. At the end of July, 1862, Marx wrote Engels that his total income from the *Presse* in the past three months had amounted to £6, or $30, just enough to pay his debt to the butcher. That, he said, "puts me deeply below the penny-a-liner."

By the end of 1862, completely fed up with his treatment at the hands of the "lousy fellows" in Vienna, he stopped writing for them. His last *Presse* article, primarily on the situation in the Confederate States, appeared December 4, 1862. His opinions on the later stages of the Civil War can be found in the Addresses to Presidents Lincoln and Johnson, which he wrote in the name of the First International, and in the personal letters included in this volume.

As a revolutionary radical, Marx was naturally concerned with the question of human enslavement, including serfdom, everywhere in the world. Before the outbreak of the American Civil War he followed with keen interest such events as John Brown's raid on Harpers Ferry, Va., for which Brown was executed in December, 1859, and the slave uprising in Bolivar, Mo., which occurred the same month. Both coincided with antiserfdom agitation in Russia. Marx was convinced, as he wrote Engels on January 11, 1860, that the movement of these slaves, black and white, in such widely separated parts of the globe, marked the beginning of the emancipation of the working class and was "the biggest thing now happening in the world." He also anticipated a similar "downbreak" in Central Europe.

In June, 1861, Marx began a serious study of the background of the Civil War.[18] He did this with his usual thoroughness and attention to detail, as can be seen from his *Presse* articles of October 25 and November 7, 1861, which contain a remarkably comprehensive account of the outbreak of the great American tragedy. His succeeding articles on the subject were no less thorough, all of them showing a detailed knowledge and mastery of materials, both military and political, that many a historian might envy.

Marx derived his information and data from two principal American sources: authoritative books and the press, including southern newspapers. Among the books he consulted were *The Rebellion Record*, edited by Frank Moore (Vol. I, 1861), on the background of the Secession; James Kent's *Commentaries on American Law* (1826–28, 1830), James Spence's *The American Union* (2d ed., 1862), and Timothy Walker's *Introduction to American Law* (4th ed., 1860), on

---

18. The extent of Marx's specific information on the subject can be seen in his letter to Engels of July 5, 1861 (see page 250).

legal and constitutional aspects; and Thomas Jefferson's *Memoir, Correspondence and Miscellanies*, edited by Thomas Jefferson Randolph (4 vols., 1829) and Henry Wheaton's *Elements of International Law* (1st ed., 1836), on problems connected with the blockade and contraband, such as were involved in the *Trent* affair.

For the details and the politics of the war itself, Marx relied on newspapers. He read as many as he could find in the British Museum and in the "American coffeehouse" in London, among them, in addition to the *Tribune*, four other New York dailies—the *Herald*, the *Evening Post*, the *Times*, and the *World*. Information he found in daily and even weekly newspapers from all over the Confederacy gave a special and authentic flavor to his dispatches.

But to Marx the Civil War was more than a subject of journalism. It was a cause, a gigantic struggle between the forces of freedom and of oppression. On the one side a small plantation aristocracy living on the labor of millions of slaves; on the other, a democratic republic fighting for survival and, as a consequence, for the ultimate elimination of slavery. Like those of millions of other Europeans, especially the poorer classes, all Marx's sympathies were on the side of the Union, and against the Confederacy. Marx was so emotionally engaged in the struggle on the other side of the Atlantic that he infected his whole family as he followed the political and military news from America with passionate concern. In the Marx home Abraham Lincoln, the humble-born and sad-faced President, became a household name as a fumbling battler for freedom. In later years Marx's youngest child, Eleanor ("Tussy"), a girl of six when the Civil War began, wrote of her father at that time:

> With what patience and gentleness Mohr[19] answered all my questions regarding American battle reports and Blue Books, which for a time replaced Marryat and Scott. For days I brooded over English Government reports, over American maps . . . At that time, I well recall, I had the unshakable conviction that Abraham Lincoln could not succeed without my advice, and so I wrote him long letters, which Mohr had to read and take to the post office. Many years later he showed me the childish letters which had so amused him that he had preserved them all that time.

For Marx, the final outcome of the Civil War was never in doubt. Provided the North persisted in the struggle and was not betrayed by its own generals (Marx suspected some of them, including McClellan, of treason), it had to prevail, no matter how long it took. This was not mere wish fulfillment. It was a view based on hard material realities. Marx made, in this sense, a "Marxist" calculation of the physical and

---

19. Mohr—"Moor"—was a nickname used by Marx's family and close friends.

human elements involved on both sides of the Civil War and came to the conclusion that the South did not have a chance.

To begin with, geography itself militated against the Confederacy. The South had few ports. If these were captured or blockaded, as they were quite early in the war, vitally important imports and exports would be choked off. This was aggravated by a primitive railroad system which gradually disintegrated in the course of the war. In addition, the South's great rivers, the Mississippi and the Tennessee, offered handy invasion routes through the heartland of the Confederacy, of which the Union forces took full advantage.

Economically, too, the South was at a disadvantage. Primarily an agricultural economy, it depended for its livelihood on the production and sale of such staples as tobacco, cotton, naval stores, rice, and sugar cane. It had few sizable cities and its banking system was inadequate. Despite great natural resources, Southern industry was undeveloped. The South had to rely largely upon imports for manufactured goods.

The North, on the other hand, had a balanced economy, with a diversified agriculture and a prosperous industry. Its large cities were also great Atlantic ports, and it had a big merchant marine. A wide-branching railroad system connected the cities of the East with those of the Middle West, which were burgeoning centers of commerce and manufacturing.

From an economic point of view, indeed, the Civil War presented an almost classic "Marxist" picture. Here was a huge conflict between two competing types of civilization. On one side, in the South, was a static society, where a rural population of "poor whites," whose lot could be compared to that of "the Roman plebeians in the period of Rome's extreme decline," was ruled by a plantation oligarchy of some 300,000 slaveowners. On the other side, in the North, there was a dynamic capitalist economy, dominated by a large bourgeois class, using free labor. On one side, the predominant need was for more agricultural land; on the other, for more markets.

"The present struggle between the South and the North," Marx wrote in the *Presse* of November 7, 1861, "is, therefore, nothing but a conflict between two social systems, the system of slavery and the system of free labor. The struggle broke out because the two systems can no longer live peacefully side by side on the North American Continent. It can only terminate with the victory of one system or the other."

Just as in economics, so also in population the advantage was on the side of the North. According to the census of 1860, the U.S. population was 31,513,000. Of this number, 11,133,360 were in the southern states. But if one deducts the border states, which were soon lost to the South, the total population of the Confederacy was only about 9,000,000, of whom nearly 4,000,000 were Negro slaves. Altogether, therefore, the North, preponderantly white and free, outnumbered the white South by at least four to one.

The northern population, moreover, was constantly replenished by European immigration, while that of the Confederacy was declining by loss of territory and desertion or emancipation of Negroes. In the five years of the Civil War more than 800,000 European immigrants entered the United States. The bulk of this immigration consisted of British (around 247,000), Germans (about 233,000), and Irish (over 196,000). They filled the North's labor and military ranks. A total of some 400,000 foreign-born persons, including immigrants, served in the Union ranks—well over one-fourth of the total Union enlistments.

As Marx pointed out in his *Presse* article of March 26, 1862, the "considerable mass of military experience that emigrated to America" was of great help to the Union armies. Many immigrant officers recruited, organized, trained and commanded Northern troops. A considerable number of them attained high rank.

Among the foreign-born officers who were breveted Union generals, there were at least ten Scots, six Canadians, five Hungarians and five French, and one each from Italy, Poland, Russia, Spain, Sweden, and Switzerland. There were also twenty-four generals born in England and Wales, and twenty-seven in Ireland.

But it was the Germans who contributed the largest contingent to the Union forces. Many of the German-born officers were radicals whom Marx knew personally. Among them were the Union colonels Friedrich Anneke, Friedrich Franz Hecker, and Joseph Weydemeyer —the latter, who commanded in St. Louis, Mo., an especially close friend of Marx. Among the generals whom Marx had known in their days as German revolutionists were Louis Blenker, who commanded a division in the Army of the Potomac; Alexander Schimmelfennig, who fought at Bull Run, Chancellorsville, and Gettysburg; Carl Schurz, who commanded a division at Bull Run and an Army Corps at Nashville; Franz Sigel, who saw service at Bull Run and in Missouri; and August Willich, who commanded a brigade in Ohio. Marx was later to become a comrade of the French-born General Gustave Paul Clusseret, a Paris Communard in 1871, who served under both McClellan and Frémont. Altogether, at least forty German-born officers, among them a number of German Jews, saw war duty on the side of the North and attained the rank of brevet general.

The Confederacy, fighting in defense of slavery, had no such appeal to Europeans. In the Southern armies, with a total enlistment of something over one million, there were not many immigrants and only about ten foreign-born generals. Two of them, Prince de Polignac and Pierre Soulé, were Frenchmen who served on the staff of Louisiana-born General Pierre Gustave Toutant Beauregard.

In spite of the North's overwhelming advantages, the war at first dragged on indecisively. In many early engagements superior Northern forces were defeated and even routed by smaller numbers of Confederates. Friends of the Northern cause, such as Frederick Engels in Manchester, were disconcerted by such a situation and grew pessimistic about the outcome. Engels, who had made what he called "militaria" a life specialty, wrote to Marx on November 5, 1862, "I must say I cannot work up any enthusiasm for a people which on such a colossal issue allows itself to be continually beaten by a fourth of its own population, and which after eighteen months of war has achieved nothing more than the discovery that all its generals are asses and all its officials rascals and traitors."

Marx agreed that the Northern politicians were inept or venal and that the early crop of Union generals, mostly civilians until quite recently, were appallingly incompetent, and perhaps even worse. But, as he saw it, this was an unavoidable condition of the society in which they operated. They were a product of the capitalist system, just as the Confederates were a product of an oligarchical society.

"The manner in which the North wages war," he wrote to Engels in September of 1862, "is only to be expected from a bourgeois republic, where fraud has so long reigned supreme. The South, an oligarchy, is better adapted thereto, particularly as it is an oligarchy where the whole of the productive labor falls on the Negroes, and the four millions of 'white trash' are filibusters by profession."

But all the same, he wrote, "I would wager my head" that the Southerners would come off second best. In Marx's view, no amount of Northern blundering and fumbling could change the final outcome. The preponderance of strength on the Northern side was such that in the long run the South could not possibly win. Northern incompetence and foot-dragging could only prolong the war and unnecessarily increase the dreadful slaughter, but could not affect the ultimate result. The growing shortage of manpower alone was bound to end in the South's defeat. Thus the bloody Battle of Antietam, fought in September, 1862, nearly three years before the Civil War ended, convinced Marx that it was "decisive" and a "graveyard" for the Confederacy. At Antietam the Southerners suffered 13,724 casualties—26% of their effectives—and Marx saw clearly that the Confederacy simply did not have the human resources to replenish such casualties.

The Preliminary Emancipation Proclamation, which Lincoln issued in September, 1862, after the Battle of Antietam, signified to Marx the beginning of the end of "Secessia." Emancipation was bound inevitably to disintegrate the slavery foundation of the Confederacy and bring about its doom. Marx considered the Proclamation "the most significant document in American history," which made its author a major figure. Marx's article in the *Presse* on October 12, 1861, discussing Lincoln, whom the pro-Confederate London *Times* called a "respectable buffoon," is a gem of character analysis and a memorable piece of historical writing:

> The figure of Lincoln is *"sui generis"* in the annals of history. No initiative, no idealistic eloquence, no buskin, no historic drapery. He always presents the most important act in the most insignificant form possible. Others, when dealing with square feet of land, proclaim it as a "struggle for ideas." Lincoln, even when he is dealing with ideas, proclaims their "square feet." Hesitant, resistant, unwilling, he sings the bravura aria of his role as though he begged pardon for the circumstances that force him "to be a lion." The most awesome decrees, that will always remain historically remarkable, which he hurls at the enemy, all resemble, and are intended to resemble, the trite summonses that one lawyer sends to an opposing lawyer, the legal chicaneries and pettifogging stipulations of an *actiones juris* [court case]. . . . Lincoln is not the product of a people's revolution. The ordinary play of the electoral system, unaware of the great tasks it was destined to decide, bore him to the summit—a plebeian . . . a man without intellectual brilliance, without special greatness of character, without exceptional importance—an average man of good will. Never has the New World scored a greater victory than in the demonstration that with its political and social organization, average men suffice to do that which in the Old World would have required heroes!

Marx correctly foresaw that Lincoln, then a burlesque figure to much of the London press, would take his place "directly next to Washington" in the history of the United States and of humanity.

This volume contains virtually everything known that Marx wrote about the United States. Except for minor details of modernizing spelling and punctuation, the selections in English are given as they were first published. All the translations from the German are by the editor. Footnotes and explanatory material in brackets are the editor's, except when otherwise indicated.

Chronology:
Marx as Journalist and Writer[1]

1842

MAY 5, 8, 10, 12, 15, 19 — *Publishes a series of articles in* Rheinische Zeitung *in Cologne.*

MID OCTOBER — *Becomes editor of* Rheinische Zeitung *at the age of twenty-four.*

1843

MARCH 17 — *Resigns from* Rheinische Zeitung.

LATE OCTOBER — *Moves to Paris and becomes coeditor (with Arnold Ruge) of* Deutsch-Französische Jahrbücher.

1844

LATE FEBRUARY — *Publishes first double issue of* Deutsch-Französische Jahrbücher.

MARCH 26 — Deutsch-Französische Jahrbücher *suspended.*

APRIL–AUGUST — *Works on* Economic and Philosophical Manuscripts *(first published in Berlin, 1932).*

1845

FEBRUARY 5 — *Moves to Brussels.*

FEBRUARY 24 — *Publishes, in collaboration with Frederick Engels,* The Holy Family, *a polemic against Bruno Bauer and his associates.*

SEPTEMBER — *Begins work on* The German Ideology.

---

1. For a full chronology of Marx's life, see Karl Marx *On Revolution*, Karl Marx Library, Vol. I.

1847

JULY   Publishes, in French, the anti-Proudhon book, The
                Poverty of Philosophy.
SEPTEMBER   Publishes a number of articles in the Brussels Ger-
    12–   man-language newspaper Deutsche-Brüsseler Zeit-
FEBRUARY 13,   ung.
    1848

1848

LATE JANUARY   Completes, in collaboration with Engels, the Mani-
                festo of the Communist Party.
FEBRUARY   The Manifesto is published anonymously in London
                in the German language.
JUNE 1   Publishes first issue of Neue Rheinische Zeitung in
                Cologne.
NOVEMBER   Meets Charles A. Dana, who will later (1852) ap-
                point him London correspondent of the New-York
                Daily Tribune.

1849

MAY 19   Publication of last issue of Neue Rheinische Zeitung.
JUNE 3   Moves to Paris.
AUGUST 24   Arrives in London after expulsion from France.
                (Marx was to live in London until his death in 1883.)

1850

MARCH 6   Publishes first issue of Neue Rheinische Zeitung.
                Politisch-Ökonomische Revue.
MARCH–   Publishes The Class Struggles in France, 1848–50, as
NOVEMBER 29   a series of articles in the Revue.
NOVEMBER 29   Publication of the last—Fifth-Sixth—issue of the
                Revue.
NOVEMBER 30   First publication of The Communist Manifesto in
                English (translated by Helen Macfarlane).

1852

JANUARY–   First publication of The Eighteenth Brumaire of
    MAY   Louis Bonaparte, in the New York German-language
                weekly Die Revolution.

AUGUST 21   *Publishes his first article—"The Elections in Eng-land: Tories and Whigs"—in the* New-York Daily Tribune. (*Engels translated it into English for him.*)

1855

JULY 28–   *Publishes a series of six articles—"Lord John Russell"*
AUGUST 15   *—in the* Neue Oder Zeitung *of Breslau.*

1856

APRIL 5–26   *Publishes a series of four articles—"The Fall of Kars" —in the London* People's Paper.

1857

SEPTEMBER–   *Publishes sixteen articles, mostly biographical (eight*
APRIL, 1858   *of them in collaboration with Engels) in* The New American Cyclopaedia.

1859

JUNE 11   *Publishes* Critique of Political Economy, *in German, in Berlin.*

JULY 3   *Becomes editor of* Das Volk, *a German-language weekly published in London from May 7 to August 20.*

1861

JANUARY–   *The* New-York Daily Tribune *suspends Marx's cor-*
OCTOBER 11   *respondenceship after nearly a decade, printing none of his articles.*

OCTOBER 11–   *The* Tribune *prints eight of Marx's articles, six of*
DECEMBER 25   *them on the Civil War.*

OCTOBER 25   *Marx begins his correspondenceship for the Vienna daily,* Die Presse, *with his article "The North American Civil War."*

1862

MARCH 10   *His last* Tribune *article, "The Mexican Imbroglio," is published.*

DECEMBER 4   *His last* Presse *article, "English Neutrality . . ." is published.*

1864

SEPTEMBER 28 *Attends the founding meeting of the International Working Men's Association (First International), of which, for the next eight years, he is to be the leader and the draftsman of its public papers.*

1867

SEPTEMBER 14 *Publication of* Capital, *Vol. I, in German, in Hamburg.*

1869

JULY *Publication in book form, in German, of* The Eighteenth Brumaire, *in Hamburg.*

1871

MAY *Publication of* The Civil War in France, *a pamphlet defending the Paris Commune.*

1873

JUNE *Publication of the second German edition of* Capital.

1883

MARCH 14 *Marx dies at his home in London.*

1885

Publication of Capital, *Vol. II, in German, under Engels' editorship; the second German edition came out in 1893.*

1887

Publication of English edition of Capital, *Vol. I, in London; it was translated by Samuel Moore and Edward Aveling under Engels' supervision.*

1894

Publication of Capital, *Vol. III, in German, under Engels' editorship.*

1909

Publication of Capital, *Vol. II, in English, by Charles H. Kerr & Co., Chicago.*

1966

Publication of Capital, *Vol. III, in English, by Prog-ress Publishers, Moscow.*

1963–71

Publication of Capital, *Vol. IV, Parts I–III* (Theories of Surplus Value), *in English, by Progress Publishers, Moscow.*

Chronology:
The Civil War and Reconstruction

Civil War

1860

NOVEMBER 6 *In the American presidential election, in which the Republican standard bearer, Abraham Lincoln, runs against three other candidates, he receives 39.8 percent of the total vote. Of the thirty-three states in the Union, he carries eighteen, but not a single southern one, with a total of 180 electoral votes as against 123 for his three rivals combined. With a clear majority of the electoral vote, Lincoln and his running mate, Hannibal Hamlin, win the presidency and vice-presidency.*

Candidate	Political Party	Popular Vote*	Electoral Vote*
Abraham Lincoln	Republican	1,865,593 (39.8%)	180
Stephen A. Douglas	Democratic	1,382,713 (29.4%)	12
John C. Breckinridge	National Democratic	848,356 (18.2%)	72
John Bell	Constitutional Union	592,906 (12.6%)	39

* All the election figures here and in the following pages are from *Historical Statistics of the United States, Colonial Times to 1957* (Washington, D.C., 1960), p. 682.

DECEMBER 20 *In protest against Lincoln's election, South Carolina Legislature unanimously adopts Ordinance of Secession, declaring the "Union now subsisting between South Carolina and the other States, under the name of 'United States of America,' is hereby dissolved."*

1861

JANUARY 9   *Mississippi secedes from the Union.*

JANUARY 10   *Florida secedes.*

JANUARY 11   *Alabama secedes*

JANUARY 19   *Georgia secedes.*

JANUARY 26   *Louisiana secedes.*

FEBRUARY 1   *Texas secedes.*

FEBRUARY 4   *Delegates of the seven seceded states meet in Montgomery, Ala., and form a provisional government, with the name, Confederate States of America.*

FEBRUARY 8   *Confederates adopt constitution, modeled after U. S. Constitution, with provisions for protection of slavery, but prohibiting the "importation of Negroes of the African race from any foreign country."*

FEBRUARY 9   *Jefferson Davis, Kentucky-born Mississippi planter and politician, is elected Provisional President, and Alexander H. Stephens, Georgia lawyer and politician, Vice-President of the Confederate States of America (later confirmed by the Confederate elections of November 6 of that year).*

FEBRUARY 18   *Davis and Stephens are inaugurated in Montgomery.*

MARCH 4   *Inaugurated sixteenth President of the U. S. in Washington, D. C., Lincoln makes conciliatory speech, "I have no purpose directly or indirectly to interfere with the institution of slavery in the States where it exists," but insists: "We cannot separate."*

APRIL 12   *Civil War opens with Southern bombardment of Fort Sumter, S. C.*

APRIL 13   *Fort Sumter is surrendered by its Union commander, Major Robert Anderson.*

APRIL 15   *Lincoln declares state of "insurrection" and calls for 75,000 volunteers to serve for three months.*

APRIL 17   *A Virginia convention votes, 103 to 46, to secede.*

APRIL 19   *Lincoln proclaims blockade of Confederate ports.*

APRIL 20   *Lieutenant Colonel Robert E. Lee, former Superintendent at West Point (1852–1855), resigns from U. S. Army to assume command of Virginia troops as major general.*

MAY 6   *Arkansas secedes.*

MAY 7   *Tennessee secedes.*

MAY 13   Great Britain recognizes Confederate States as belligerents.

MAY 20   North Carolina secedes.

MAY 21   Richmond, Va., is chosen as Confederate capital; government moves there from Montgomery early in June.

MAY 25   Union Major General Benjamin F. Butler, in command of Fortress Monroe, Va., rules that slaves escaping to his lines are "contraband of war," not to be returned to their masters.

JUNE 3–
SEPTEMBER 11   After prolonged contests in their legislatures, four slave states—Delaware, Kentucky, Maryland, and Missouri—vote to remain in Union.

JUNE 11   In Wheeling, a convention representing mountainous western Virginia organizes a Union government; it is admitted into the Union as West Virginia June 20, 1863.

JULY 21   In first Battle of Bull Run, near Manassas Junction, Va., poorly trained Union forces under Brigadier General Irvin McDowell and Major General Robert Patterson are routed by Confederates commanded by Brigadier General Pierre Gustave Toutant Beauregard and Major General Joseph E. Johnston, as well as Colonel (later Major General) Thomas Jonathan ("Stonewall") Jackson; Union forces stampede back to Washington in panic.

	Casualties*	
	Union	Confederate
Troops engaged	28,452	32,232
Killed	418	387
Wounded	1,011	1,582
Missing	1,216	12
Total losses:	2,645 (11%)	1,981 (16%)

* Estimates given in Mark Mayo Boatner, *The Civil War Dictionary* (N.Y., 1959), p. 101, citing Thomas L. Livermore, *Numbers and Losses in the Civil War in America, 1861–65* (Boston, 1901).

JULY 24   The defeated General McDowell is replaced by Major General George B. McClellan as commander of the Division of the Potomac.

AUGUST 6   Congressional confiscation act provides for emancipation of slaves employed in arms or labor against U. S.

AUGUST 16   *Lincoln issues order forbidding trade with seceded states.*

AUGUST 28–
29   *Union forces capture Forts Clark and Hatteras on North Carolina coast.*

AUGUST 30   *Union Major General John Charles Frémont, in command of newly created Western Department, proclaims that slaves of Missourians fighting against U. S. are free.*

SEPTEMBER 18   *Kentucky Legislature takes steps to oust Confederate forces.*

NOVEMBER 1   *General McClellan is appointed General-in-Chief of Union forces upon resignation of General-in-Chief Winfield Scott.*

NOVEMBER 8–
DECEMBER 25   *The* Trent *affair. See editorial note, pages 112–13.*

1862

JANUARY 15   *Edwin M. Stanton is appointed Secretary of War, replacing Simon Cameron's corrupt and inefficient administration.*

FEBRUARY 16   *Fort Donelson, main defense of Nashville, Tenn., surrenders to Brigadier General Ulysses S. Grant with some 14,000 Confederate troops.*

FEBRUARY 25   *Nashville, evacuated by General Albert Sidney Johnston, falls to Union forces.*

MARCH 8   *The frigate* Merrimac, *made over by the Confederates into an ironclad and renamed* Virginia, *sinks the ship* Cumberland *and burns the ship* Congress *off Hampton Roads, Va.*

MARCH 9   *Merrimac is engaged by Union ironclad* Monitor *(with revolving gun-turret amidships), the first battle between armored ships in naval history; after five-hour engagement,* Merrimac *withdraws to Norfolk for repairs.*

MARCH 11   *Major General Henry W. Halleck becomes commander of Union armies in the West.*

MARCH 14   *Union forces occupy New Bern, N. C., to form base from which to threaten Richmond, Va.*

MARCH 23–
JUNE 9   *General "Stonewall" Jackson opens Shenandoah Valley campaign with force of 18,000 men; he strikes Union Major General Nathaniel P. Banks at Front*

Royal (May 23), and routs Union troops at Winchester (May 25), posing threat to Washington.

APRIL 6–7   *At Shiloh, Tenn., in struggle for control of Upper Mississippi, General Grant, supported by Major General Don Carlos Buell's Army of the Ohio and a division under Major General Lewis ("Lew") Wallace, defeats Confederates under General Beauregard.*

	Casualties*	
	Union	Confederate
Troops engaged	62,682	40,335
Killed	1,754	1,723
Wounded	8,408	8,012
Missing	2,885	959
Total losses:	13,047 (20%)	10,694 (26.7%)

* Boatner, *op. cit.*, p. 757, citing Livermore.

APRIL 16   *Confederate Congress conscripts all white males eighteen to thirty-five, for three years' service; the age is raised to forty-five in September.*

APRIL 16   *Slavery is abolished, with compensation to owners, in District of Columbia.*

APRIL 24–25   *A Union force of seventeen ships and 15,000 troops under Flag Officer (later Admiral) David G. Farragut and General Benjamin F. Butler, bombards New Orleans, which is taken on May 1.*

MAY 5   *General McClellan occupies Yorktown, Va.*

MAY 9   *Union Major General David Hunter, commander of the Department of the South (including Georgia, Florida, and South Carolina), proclaims emancipation of slaves in his Department, but order is disavowed by President Lincoln (May 19).*

MAY 10   *Union forces occupy Norfolk; Confederates burn Merrimac (May 11) to keep it out of Union hands.*

MAY 14   *General McClellan's Army of the Potomac reaches Pamunkey River, twenty miles from Richmond, but despite preponderant forces moves no further, waiting for reinforcement from General McDowell.*

MAY 30   *Confederates evacuate Corinth, in northeast Mississippi.*

MAY 31–
JUNE 1   *At Seven Pines (Fair Oaks), along the Chickahominy River, only a few miles from Richmond, General Mc-*

Clellan's forces fight those of Joseph E. Johnston to
a draw.

| | Casualties* | |
	Union	Confederate
Troops engaged	41,797	41,816
Total losses:	5,031 (12%)	6,134 (14%)

* Boatner, op. cit., p. 273, citing Livermore.

JUNE 1   *General Lee succeeds General Albert Sidney Johnston,
fatally wounded at Shiloh (April 6), as commander
of the Army of Northern Virginia.*

JUNE 6   *Confederates surrender Memphis, Tenn.*

JUNE 19   *Slavery is abolished, without compensation to owners,
in territories of U. S.*

PENINSULAR CAMPAIGN:

JUNE 26–
JULY 2   *In struggle for control over strategic Virginia peninsula (between James and York rivers), forces of Generals Lee and McClellan fight a series of battles for
seven days.*

JUNE 26–27   *Mechanicsville.*

JUNE 27   *Gaines' Mill.*

JUNE 29   *Savage's Station.*

JUNE 30   *Frayser's Farm (White Oak Swamp).*

JULY 1   *Malvern Hill.*

JULY 2   *Confederates withdraw toward Richmond. Union
forces withdraw to Harrison's Landing on the James.*

| | Casualties* | |
	Union	Confederate
Killed	1,734	3,478
Wounded	8,062	16,261
Missing	6,053	875
Total losses:	15,849	20,641

* Richard B. Morris, ed., *Encyclopedia of American History* (New York, 1953), p. 237.

JULY   *New Confederate raider,* Alabama, *joins sister ship*
Florida, *which, together with other Southern raiders,
ultimately destroy 257 Union vessels.*

JULY 11   *General Halleck becomes General-in-Chief of U. S. Army.*

JULY 11   *General Grant is promoted to command of Army of West Tennessee.*

JULY 17   *Second congressional confiscation act liberates slaves owned by persons who have committed treason or supported rebellion against U. S.*

AUGUST 3   *Union Major General John Pope, defeated by Confederate Major General James Longstreet at Thoroughfare Gap, Va., withdraws to the outer defenses of Washington, D. C.*

AUGUST 5   *General McClellan becomes commander of the Army of the Potomac.*

AUGUST 9   *General "Stonewall" Jackson defeats Union General Banks at Cedar Mountain, Va.*

AUGUST 26   *General Jackson destroys General Pope's headquarters and supply bases at Manassas Junction, Va.*

AUGUST 29–30   *Confederates under General Jackson defeat General Pope in second Battle of Bull Run.*

SEPTEMBER 4   *General Lee's forces cross Potomac and invade Maryland, with aim of cutting railroad lines to Washington and ultimately taking Harrisburg, Pa.*

SEPTEMBER 14   *Union forces defeat Confederates at South Mountain and Crampton's Gap, Md., but lose Harpers Ferry, West Va., with its 11,000-man garrison and supplies, to General Jackson.*

SEPTEMBER 17   *At Antietam, near Sharpsburg, western Maryland, Confederates under General Lee fight Union troops under General McClellan in a bloody battle, which Karl Marx considered "decisive" and a "graveyard" of the Confederacy.*[1]

	Casualties*	
	Union	Confederate
Troops engaged	75,316	51,844
Killed	2,108	2,700
Wounded	9,549	9,024
Missing	753	*ca.* 2,000
Total losses:	12,410 (16.5%)	13,724 (26%)

* Boatner, *op. cit.*, p. 21, citing Livermore.

1. See Marx's letter to Engels October 29, 1862, page 262.

SEPTEMBER 18   *Having lost over a fourth of his forces at Antietam,*
                General Lee withdraws to Virginia.

SEPTEMBER 23   *Encouraged by Antietam—a technical victory for the*
                North—President Lincoln issues Preliminary Eman-
                cipation Proclamation, freeing (as of January 1, 1863)
                all slaves in areas held by Secessionists.

OCTOBER 8   *Confederate force under General Braxton Bragg (who*
                had succeeded Beauregard), advancing north of Chat-
                tanooga toward Louisville, is defeated by General
                Buell at Perryville, Ky.

| | Casualties* | |
	Union	Confederate
Troops engaged	36,940	16,000
Killed	845	510
Wounded	2,851	2,635
Missing	515	251
Total missing:	4,211 (11.4%)	3,396 (21%)

* Boatner, *op. cit.,* p. 644, citing Livermore.

NOVEMBER 7   *President Lincoln replaces General McClellan with*
                Major General Ambrose E. Burnside.

DECEMBER 13   *General Burnside pushes advance into Virginia and is*
                crushed at Fredericksburg, Va.

| | Casualties† | |
	Union	Confederate
Troops engaged	106,000	72,500
Killed or wounded	12,700 (12%)	5,300 (7.3%)

† Boatner, *op. cit.,* p. 313.

DECEMBER 31–
JANUARY 3,
1863   *In battle of Murfreesboro (Stones River), Tenn.,*
                Union General William S. Rosecrans defeats Confed-
                erates under General Bragg and checks their advance
                on Nashville.

| | Casualties* | |
	Union	Confederate
Troops engaged	41,400	34,739
Killed or wounded	12,906 (31%)	11,739 (34%)

* Boatner, *op. cit.,* p. 808, citing Livermore.

1863

JANUARY 1   *Lincoln's Emancipation Proclamation declares all slaves in areas under rebellion "then, thenceforward, and forever free."*

JANUARY 21   *Union General Fitz-John Porter is dismissed as scapegoat for General Pope's defeat at Bull Run (August 29–30, 1862).*

JANUARY 25   *General Burnside, the loser at Fredericksburg (December 13, 1862), is replaced by General Joseph ("Fighting Joe") Hooker.*

FEBRUARY 3   *Emperor Napoleon III's offer to mediate in the Civil War is rebuffed by Secretary of State Seward (February 6) and by concurring congressional resolution (March 3) which calls mediation "foreign intervention."*

MARCH 3   *First Union Conscription Act makes all men twenty to forty-five liable to military service, but by payment of $300 or procuring a substitute, draft can be avoided.*

MARCH 29   *General Grant leaves supply base at Memphis and crosses Mississippi above Vicksburg.*

APRIL 30–
MAY 17   *General Grant, with 20,000 men, advances northeastward on rear of Vicksburg, fights victorious battles—Port Gibson, May 1; Big Black River, May 13; Champion's Hill, May 16—and forces Confederates under Lieutenant General John C. Pemberton into Vicksburg perimeter.*

MAY 2–4   *In Virginia, General Hooker's Army of the Potomac, having crossed Rappahannock River, is defeated by Generals Lee and Jackson at Chancellorsville.*

	Casualties*	
	Union	Confederate
Troops engaged	133,868	60,892
Killed, wounded, and missing	17,278 (12.8%)	12,821 (21%)

* Boatner, *op. cit.*, p. 140, citing John Bigelow, *The Campaign of Chancellorsville* (New Haven, 1910).

MAY 22   *On the Mississippi, General Grant begins siege of Vicksburg.*

JUNE–JULY 4   *GETTYSBURG CAMPAIGN:*

EARLY JUNE   *General Lee's Army of Northern Virginia begins invasion of North, by way of Shenandoah Valley into southern Pennsylvania.*

JUNE 13–15   *Confederate General Richard S. Ewell defeats Union garrison at Winchester, Va.*

JUNE 15   *President Lincoln calls for 100,000 volunteers for six months' service.*

JUNE 17   *General Ewell crosses Potomac.*

JUNE 23   *General Ewell nears Chambersburg, Pa.*

JUNE 25   *In move against General Lee, General Hooker crosses Potomac, coming between Lee's forces and those of his cavalry chief, General James E. B. ("Jeb") Stuart.*

JUNE 27   *General Hooker establishes headquarters at Frederick, Md., before General Lee, at Chambersburg, Pa., knows about it.*

JUNE 27–28   *Confederate General Ewell captures Carlisle and York, Pa.*

JUNE 28   *Union General Hooker, in conflict with General-in-Chief Halleck, resigns command and is replaced by General George G. Meade.*

JUNE 29   *General Ewell's cavalry comes within ten miles of Harrisburg.*

JUNE 30   *Chance encounter between Confederate General Ambrose P. Hill and Union General John Buford, both in search of boots and saddles, at Gettysburg, opens the great battle.*

JULY 1   *Confederates drive Union forces back through Gettysburg to strong defensive positions on Cemetery Hill and Culp's Hill. Confederates occupy Seminary Ridge, a partially wooded rise running parallel north and south to Union position.*

JULY 2   *General Meade, with numerical superiority of 15,000 men, drives Confederate General Jubal A. Early off Seminary Ridge—a decisive action.*

JULY 3   *Confederate General Ewell is driven down Culp's Hill. General Lee orders reluctant General James Longstreet to make direct attack on powerfully fortified Cemetery Hill; his troops are mowed down by withering Union artillery and musketry.*

JULY 4   *General Lee withdraws to position west of Sharps-*

burg, where his retreat is blocked by flooded Potomac; despite Lincoln's orders, he is not pursued by Union troops, but escapes to Virginia July 13.

	Casualties*	
	Union	Confederate
Troops engaged	88,289	75,000
Killed	3,155	3,903
Wounded	14,529	18,735
Missing	5,365	5,425
Total losses:	23,049 (26%)	28,063 (37%)

* Boatner, *op. cit.*, p. 339, citing Livermore.

Gettysburg, where President Lincoln dedicates national cemetery November 17, marks beginning of end of Confederacy; crippled in manpower, it is henceforth compelled to fight on the defensive.

JULY 4   *Vicksburg is starved into surrender to General Grant.*

JULY 8   *Port Hudson, farther down the Mississippi, surrenders, thereby giving the Union control of the entire river and cutting off Arkansas, Louisiana, and Texas from rest of Confederacy.*

JULY 13–16   *Four-day rioting, primarily by poor Irish, in New York City, in protest against inequity of the draft.*

SEPTEMBER
19–20   *In struggle over Tennessee, Union Major General William S. Rosecrans is defeated by Confederate Major General Braxton Bragg at Chickamauga, forcing him to fall back to Chattanooga.*

	Casualties*	
	Union	Confederate
Troops engaged	58,222	66,326
Killed	1,657	2,312
Wounded	9,756	14,674
Missing	4,757	1,468
Total losses:	16,170 (28%)	18,454 (28%)

* Boatner, *op. cit.*, p. 152, citing Livermore.

NOVEMBER
23–25   *General Grant, reinforced by troops from Vicksburg under Major General William T. Sherman and from*

the Potomac under General Hooker, defeats Confed-
erates in Battle of Chattanooga (Lookout Mountain,
November 24; Missionary Ridge, November 25), driv-
ing them out of Tennessee, and opening road to Geor-
gia, whose invasion by General Sherman the following
year is to split Confederacy into two halves.

	Casualties*	
	Union	*Confederate*
Troops engaged	56,359	64,165
Killed	753	361
Wounded	4,722	2,160
Missing	349	4,146
Total losses:	5,824 (10.3%)	6,667 (10.3%)

* Boatner, *op. cit.,* p. 147, citing Livermore.

1864

FEBRUARY 25   *Confederacy changes age of conscription; instead of*
eighteen to forty-five it is now seventeen to fifty.

MARCH 9   *Grant is promoted to lieutenant general.*

MARCH 12   *Grant becomes General-in-Chief of the Armies of the*
United States. General Sherman succeeds him in com-
mand of the Military Division of the Mississippi.

MAY 5–6   *General Grant's Army of the Potomac begins system-*
atic drive against General Lee in Virginia, fighting in-
decisive Battle of the Wilderness.

	Casualties*	
	Union	*Confederate*
Troops engaged (exclusive of cavalry)	101,895	61,025
Killed	2,246	—
Wounded	12,073	—
Total losses:	14,319 (14%)	7,750 (12.6%)

* Boatner, *op. cit.,* p. 925, citing Livermore.

MAY 5   *Farther south, General Sherman leaves Chattanooga*
with 100,000 men to begin his march through Georgia.

MAY 8–12   *Despite losses, General Grant proceeds against Gen-*
eral Lee, vainly attempting to dislodge him at Spot-
sylvania Court House, eleven miles from Fredericks-
burg, Va. After five days of trench warfare, and some

12,000 casualties, Grant informs General Halleck: "I propose to fight it out along this line if it takes all summer" (May 11).

JUNE 1–3   *At Cold Harbor, ten miles from Richmond, General Grant fights another bloody battle, losing 12,000 men in one day (June 3). By June 12, Grant's losses for the past thirty days amount to 60,000 men (about the same as Lee's total strength), as against 25,000–30,000 Confederate casualties.*

JUNE 15–18 *Grant makes vain assault on Petersburg, twenty-three miles below Richmond, and begins siege of Richmond which is to last nine months.*

	Casualties*	
	Union	Confederate
Troops engaged	63,797	41,499
Killed	1,688	not known
Wounded	8,513	not known
Missing	1,185	not known
Total losses:	11,386 (17.6%)	not known

* Boatner, *op. cit.*, p. 646, citing Livermore and William F. Fox, *Regimental Losses in the . . . Civil War* (Albany, 1898).

JULY 17   *General Sherman crosses Chattahoochee River, Ga., while his Confederate opponent, General Joseph E. Johnston, refuses to give him battle.*

JULY 22   *General Sherman defeats Confederate Lieutenant General John B. Hood, after General Johnston has been removed, in Battle of Atlanta.*

SEPTEMBER 2 *Confederates evacuate Atlanta.*

NOVEMBER 8 *Lincoln is reelected President, with Andrew Johnson as Vice-President, winning 55 percent of popular vote and 212 electoral votes:*

Candidate	Political Party	Popular Vote	Electoral Vote
Abraham Lincoln	Republican	2,206,938 (55%)	212
George B. McClellan	Democratic	1,803,787 (45%)	21
(Not voted)[2]	—	—	81

NOVEMBER 16 *General Sherman begins his march to the sea, ravaging Georgia.*

2. Votes of Southern states still outside the Union.

DECEMBER 20   *General Sherman reaches the sea at Savannah, Ga., which is abandoned by Confederates.*

1865

JANUARY 16–
MARCH 21   *General Sherman turns north to march through South Carolina, ravaging it as he did Georgia.*

FEBRUARY 17   *Columbia, capital of S. C., is burned on April 4, 1865, either by Union or, as General Sherman claimed, by Confederate soldiers: "I charge [Confederate General] Wade Hampton with having burned his own city of Columbia, not with a malicious intent . . . but from folly and want of sense, in filling it with lint, cotton, and tinder."*

FEBRUARY 18   *Union fleet occupies Charleston, S. C.—in whose harbor, at Fort Sumter, the Civil War had started nearly four years earlier.*

MARCH 4   *In his Inaugural Address, President Lincoln appeals for reconciliation: "With malice toward none, with charity for all . . . let us strive on . . . to bind up the nation's wounds . . . to do all which may achieve and cherish a just and lasting peace among ourselves and with all nations."*

MARCH 13   *Confederate Government authorizes military conscription of Negroes.*

APRIL 1   *In Virginia the war is coming to an end; Union Major General Philip H. Sheridan defeats Confederate Major General George E. Pickett at Five Forks, forces evacuation of Petersburg, and cuts off General Lee's retreat.*

APRIL 2   *General Lee abandons Richmond; President Davis and most of his cabinet leave by train for Danville, Va., where they remain for a week, then go farther south; Confederate Government ceases to exist.*

APRIL 3   *Richmond is occupied by Union Major General Godfrey Weitzel; a fire destroys most of the downtown district.*

APRIL 4   *From Danville, President Jefferson Davis issues his last message to the people of the Confederacy, refusing to admit defeat: ". . . let us meet the foe with fresh defiance, with unconquered and unconquerable hearts."*

APRIL 5   *President Lincoln visits Richmond, walks streets un-molested, confers with General Weitzel in Confed-erate White House abandoned by President Davis.*

APRIL 7   *With less than 30,000 troops left and few rations, General Lee is requested by General Grant to sur-render, and asks for terms.*

APRIL 9   *General Lee meets General Grant at Appomattox Court House, in central Virginia, and surrenders on terms permitting his men to return home, officers to retain side arms, and all soldiers to keep their own horses and mules. Union army issues 25,000 rations to Confederates.*

APRIL 10   *General Lee issues farewell to his army: "... the Army of Northern Virginia has been compelled to yield to overwhelming numbers and resources ... I have con-sented to this result ... from feeling that valor and devotion could accomplish nothing that could com-pensate for the loss that would have attended the continuation of the contest ... I earnestly pray that a merciful God will extend to you His blessing and protection ... I bid you an affectionate farewell."*

APRIL 11   *President Lincoln, in his last public address, given from balcony of White House, speaks of reconcilia-tion and reconstruction: "Let us all join in doing the acts necessary to restore the proper practical relations between these States and the Union."*

APRIL 14   *Attending a play in Ford's Theatre, in Washington, Lincoln is mortally wounded by assassin John Wilkes Booth.*

APRIL 15   *President Lincoln dies at 7:30 A.M., and Vice President Johnson takes oath of office as President three hours later.*

APRIL 26   *Confederate General Joseph E. Johnston, with 37,000 men, surrenders to General Sherman, on terms similar to those of Appomattox, near Durham Station, N. C.*

MAY 10   *President Davis is captured at Irwinville, Ga., and imprisoned for two years at Fortress Monroe; never brought to trial, he later makes his home in Beauvoir, Miss., and writes* The Rise and Fall of the Confederate Government *(1881).*

JUNE 2   *Last Confederate army under General (Edmund) Kirby Smith surrenders to Union Major General Edward R. S. Canby at Shreveport, La.*

Reconstruction

1865

MAY 29–
JULY 13   *President Johnson issues proclamation of amnesty, granting pardon to Confederates on taking oath of allegiance; proceeds to organize provisional governments of Southern states on condition of their abolition of slavery and repudiation of state war debts.*

DECEMBER 4   *Newly convened Thirty-ninth Congress refuses to endorse President Johnson's policies and appoints a Joint Committee of Fifteen, under leadership of Congressman Thaddeus Stevens, a Radical Republican, to examine Southern issues; the Committee assumes almost dictatorial powers.*

DECEMBER 6   *In his First Annual Message to Congress, President Johnson declares the Union restored, but delegates of former Confederate states still await admission to Congress.*

DECEMBER 18   *Thirteenth Amendment to the U. S. Constitution, abolishing slavery, is ratified: "Neither slavery nor involuntary servitude . . . shall exist within the United States, or any place subject to their jurisdiction."*

1866

FEBRUARY 19   *Congress passes New Freedmen's Bureau Bill for protection of civil rights of Negroes in South (a Freedmen's Bureau, to take care of Negroes in South, had been established by Congress March 3, 1865). Vetoed by President Johnson, who is in increasingly bitter conflict with Congress, the bill is passed over his veto July 16.*

APRIL 9   *Over President Johnson's veto Congress passes Civil Rights Act, guaranteeing equal treatment of Negroes in South, declaring all persons born in U. S. to be citizens and entitled to equality before the law.*

JUNE 13   *Fourteenth Amendment to U. S. Constitution, incorporating principles of the Civil Rights Act, is sent to states for ratification; it provides for representation according to numbers (to encourage enfranchisement of Negroes), repudiation of state war debts, prohibi-*

tion of financial compensation for liberated slaves, and, in terms of the future, the highly significant clauses: "Nor shall any state deprive any person of life, liberty, or property without due process of law; nor deny to any person . . . the equal protection of the law."

JUNE 20 *Report of Joint Committee of Fifteen recommends that former Confederate states are not entitled to representation in Congress, and that Congress, rather than the President, has authority over Reconstruction.*

JULY 19 *Tennessee ratifies Fourteenth Amendment and is admitted into Union July 24. The other Southern states reject the Amendment upon advice of President Johnson.*

1867

MARCH 2 *After President Johnson is repudiated in congressional elections of November, 1866, Congress, controlled by Radical Republicans, passes First Reconstruction Act, dividing the South into five military districts subject to martial law, and providing conditions for restoration to Union: new constitutional state conventions, universal manhood suffrage, Negro suffrage, and ratification of Fourteenth Amendment.*

MARCH 23,
JULY 19, AND
MARCH 11,
1868 *Supplementary Reconstruction Acts require military commanders to initiate voter enrollment, with power to discriminate between voters and officeholders, and to declare that a majority of votes cast, regardless of numbers participating, is sufficient to insure legality of new state constitutions.*

Later in the year, Southern states vote to call conventions, which meet in 1868 and, under domination of Radical Republicans, with Negroes participating (they are a majority in S. C.), adopt new constitutions similar to those of the North.

1868

FEBRUARY 24 *A House of Representatives resolution, 126 to 47, calls for impeachment of President Johnson on eleven charges, among them violation of Tenure-of-Office Act (which he vetoed March 4, 1867) and high misdemeanor.*

MARCH 30   *Salmon P. Chase, Chief Justice of U. S. Supreme Court, presides over impeachment proceedings in Senate.*

MAY 26   *President Johnson is acquitted, the vote being thirty-five for conviction and nineteen against (seven Republicans and twelve Democrats)—one vote short of the two-thirds required for impeachment.*

JUNE 22–25   *Seven Southern states—Arkansas, Alabama, Florida, Georgia, Louisiana, North Carolina, South Carolina— satisfy requirements under Reconstruction Acts and are readmitted into the Union by Congress.*

JULY 28   *Fourteenth Amendment, ratified by the requisite number of states, is declared in force.*

NOVEMBER 3   *In presidential election General Ulysses S. Grant defeats Democratic candidate Horatio Seymour, in a campaign in which Republican main issue is the "bloody shirt of the rebellion."*

Candidate	Political Party	Popular Vote	Electoral Vote
Ulysses S. Grant	Republican	3,013,421 (52.7%)	214
Horatio Seymour	Democratic	2,706,829 (47.3%)	80
(Not voted)	—	—	23

1869

FEBRUARY 26   *Congress, fearing Southern whites, once in power, will repeal Negro suffrage in their states, adopts Fifteenth Amendment: "The right of citizens of the United States to vote shall not be denied or abridged by the United States or by any state on account of race, color, or previous condition of servitude."*

MARCH 4   *Ulysses S. Grant is inaugurated eighteenth President of U. S.*

1870

MARCH 30   *Fifteenth Amendment, ratified by the requisite number of states, is declared in force.*

JULY 15   *Georgia is readmitted into the Union after being* compelled to reinstate expelled state legislators and to adopt Fifteenth Amendment.

1871

MAY 8   *Treaty of Washington with Great Britain provides, among other things, for settlement of* Alabama *claims by an international commission in Geneva.*

1872

MAY 22   *Amnesty Act removes final disabilities from all but a few prominent former Confederates.*

AUGUST 25   *International commission in Geneva awards $15,500,-000 to U. S., to be paid by British, in compensation for damages inflicted by the* Alabama *and other Confederate raiders that had use of British ports during Civil War.*

NOVEMBER 5   *In presidential election, President Grant, running against Horace Greeley of the* New-York Daily Tribune *(of which Karl Marx was London correspondent for a decade) and five other Democratic candidates, in a campaign marked by protests against corruption in Washington, proposals of liberal reform, and confusion about treatment of the South—wins reelection by carrying every Northern state, as well as a few in the South.*

Candidate	Political Party	Popular Vote	Electoral Vote[3]
Ulysses S. Grant	Republican	3,596,745 (55.5%)	286
Horace Greeley	Democratic	2,843,446 (43.8%)	—
Charles O'Conor	"Straight-out" Democrats	29,489 —	—
Thomas A. Hendricks	Independent Democratic	— —	42
B. Gratz Brown	Liberal Democratic	— —	18
Charles J. Jenkins	Democratic	— —	2
David Davis	Democratic	— —	1
(Not voted)			17

3. Greeley died November 29, 1872, and the presidential electors divided their votes among four Democratic candidates, as listed above; there were three votes for the deceased Greeley, which were not counted.

1876

NOVEMBER 7–
FEBRUARY 28,
   1877   *In the confused presidential election the Democratic candidate, Samuel J. Tilden, wins the popular vote, but finally loses the presidency to Republican candidate Rutherford B. Hayes, owing to bitterly disputed Southern electoral votes.*[4]

Candidate	Political Party	Popular Vote	Electoral Vote
Samuel J. Tilden	Democratic	4,284,020 (50.9%)	184
Rutherford B. Hayes	Republican	4,036,572 (47.9%)	185
Peter Cooper	Greenback	81,737 (1.0%)	—

1877

MARCH 5   *Having been declared elected March 2, Hayes is inaugurated nineteenth President of the U. S.*

APRIL 10   *Following Republican promise, Federal troops are withdrawn from South Carolina.*

APRIL 24   *Federal troops are withdrawn from Louisiana.*
     This ends "Black Reconstruction" or "carpetbag rule" by Radical Republicans in South. Henceforth, Southern whites, in full control of their states, proceed systematically to nullify in practice Negro civil rights as guaranteed in Fourteenth and Fifteenth amendments; the successful nullification lasts well past mid-twentieth century, despite continuous struggles against it.

---

4. The disputed electoral votes (19) were those of South Carolina, Florida, and Louisiana. On January 29, after months of controversy, Congress appointed an Electoral Commission (five Senators, five Representatives, five Justices of the U. S. Supreme Court), which, by straight party vote—eight to seven—awarded the disputed electoral votes to Republican candidate Hayes, thus making him President. Republican victory in the Electoral Commission was due to promises made to Southern Democrats that federal troops would be withdrawn from the South, appropriations would be made for Southern economic improvements, and at least one Southerner would be appointed to the cabinet. President Hayes kept the promises.

Cost of the Civil War

	(1) *Financial** Amount	*Per Capita*
Federal Debt: 1860	$64,844,000	$2.06
1866	$2,677,929,000[5]	$75.42
	(2) *Human*	
Union casualties:†	364,511 deaths (140,414 in battle, 224,097 other) 281,881 wounded	
Confederate casualties:‡	258,000 (94,000 in battle) ca. 100,000 wounded	

* *Historical Statistics of the United States, op. cit.,* p. 721, which does not give Confederate figures.
† *Historical Statistics of the United States, op. cit.,* p. 735, which does not list Confederate casualties.
‡ Estimate in Morris, *op. cit.,* p. 245.

---

5. Not counting paper "greenbacks" (authorized as legal tender February, 1862) or debts incurred by states and municipalities.

VIEWS OF AMERICA

American Soil and Communism*

WE FULLY recognize the movement of the American National Reformers in its historical justification. We know that this movement strives for a result that, to be sure, for the time being would further the industrialism of the modern bourgeois society, but that as a result of the proletarian movement, as an attack on land ownership altogether, and especially under the existing conditions in America, its own consequences must drive it toward communism. Kriege, who, together with the German communists in New York, has joined the anti-rent movement, glosses over this thin fact with his usual high-flown communistic rhetoric without going into the positive content of the movement, and shows thereby that, to the highest degree, he is unclear about the connection between young America and American conditions. In addition to the passages already cited occasionally, we want to give another example of how he overwhelms an agrarian-based parceling of land on the American scale with his humanitarian enthusiasm.

The article *"Was wir wollen"* ["What We Want"], in No. 10, says: "They"—that is, the American National Reformers—"call the soil the common heritage of all people . . . and through the legislative power of the people they want to find means to preserve the fourteen hundred million acres of land that have not yet fallen into the hands of thieving speculators, as inalienable common property for all humanity."

---

* "The Economics of the *Volks-Tribun* and Its Attitude Toward Young America," in *Circular Against Kriege*, by Marx and Engels, Section 2, May, 1846. *Der Volks-Tribun*, a German-language weekly of the "true" socialists in New York, was edited by Hermann Kriege, and appeared from January 5 to December 31, 1846.

In order to "preserve for all humanity" this "inalienable common property" he adopts the plan of the National Reformers: "to put at the disposal of every farmer, for his subsistence, 160 acres of American earth, no matter whose land it may be," or as stated in No. 14, *"Antwort an Conze"* ["Reply to Conze"]: "From this as yet untouched land, nobody is to take possession of more than 160 acres, and then only if he farms them himself."

Thus the soil is to remain "inalienable common property," and for all of humanity at that, by *dividing* it up without delay. Kriege fancies that he can prohibit by law the necessary consequences of this parcelization: concentration, industrial progress, etc. For him, 160 acres remain a constant proportion, as if the value of such a superficies did not differ according to its quality. The "farmers" would have to exchange with each other the products of their soil, if not the soil itself, and if that comes to pass it will soon be seen that one farmer, even without capital, by his mere labor and the greater original productivity of his 160 acres, would again reduce another one to his vassal. And then, is it not the same as if "the soil" or the *products* of the soil fell "into the hands of thieving speculators"?

Let us take seriously Kriege's gift to humanity.

Fourteen hundred million acres are to be preserved for all humanity as inalienable common property. And specifically, each farmer is to get 160 acres. From this one can calculate the size of Kriege's "all humanity"—precisely eight and three-quarter million "farmers," each the head of a family of five, hence representing a total of forty-three and three-quarter million people. We can likewise calculate how long "all eternity" lasts, for which duration "the proletariat in its capacity as humanity" can "lay claim to the whole earth," at least the United States. If the population of the United States is to grow at the same rate as hitherto (that is, doubling every twenty-five years), then this "all eternity" will last not quite forty years; in that period, the fourteen hundred million acres would be occupied, and *nothing* is left for posterity to lay claim to. But since the generous distribution of land would greatly multiply immigration, Kriege's "eternity" would soon be "all." Particularly if one considers that land for forty-four million would hardly suffice to serve as a sufficient outlet for presently existing European pauperism—since in Europe every tenth man is a pauper and the British Isles alone could supply seven million of them. A similar economic naïveté is to be found in No. 13, *"An die Frauen"* ["To the Women"], in which Kriege believes that if the city of New York would give away its fifty-two thousand acres on Long Island, it would suffice to rid New York of all pauperism, misery, and crime in one stroke.

If Kriege had seen the Free-Soil movement as a first form of proletarian movement necessary under certain conditions, as a movement that, owing to the life circumstances of the class from which it springs, must necessarily develop further into a communist one; if he had shown how the communist tendencies in America[1] had to appear originally in this agrarian form that seemingly contradicts all communism, one would have nothing to say against it. But he declares a movement of specific people, one that is, indeed, in a still subordinate form, to be a matter of *humanity*, and against his better judgment presents it as the final, highest goal of all movements in general; he transforms the specific aims of the movement into pure, extravagant nonsense.

In the meantime, in the same article (No. 10) he continues undisturbed to sing his song of triumph:

"Thus the old dreams of Europeans were fulfilled at last; on this side of the ocean there was prepared for them a homestead which they had only to take up and to fructify with their own hands so as to be able proudly to call out to all the tyrants of the world:

> This is *my* cottage
> which you did not build;
> This is *my* hearth
> whose embers you envy me."[2]

He should have added: This is my manure pile, which I and my wife, child, servant, maid, and cattle have produced. Which Europeans are those whose "dreams" have been fulfilled here? Not the communist workers, but bankrupt shopkeepers and artisans or ruined dirt farmers who strive for the good fortune of becoming petty bourgeois or farmers again in America. And what kind of "wish" is it that is to be realized through fourteen hundred million acres? No other than to transform *all people into private property owners*, a wish that is as realizable and communistic as the one that would transform all people into emperors, kings, and popes. As final proof of Kriege's insight into communist-revolutionary movements and economic conditions, the following passage may serve: "Every person should learn from every

---

1. Hermann Kriege to Johann Werner Detering (in Osnabrück), October 12, 1845: ". . . America is the country of movement, of revolution; there is not one minute of Austrian-type placidity here; popular sovereignty is the majority here, no matter what the gentlemen professors may say. All the statesmen are not a bit more than the playthings of this gigantic people . . . You should see these highly celebrated statesmen once, how they sneak among the workers to hear what the latter want for the future, and how they then take the position they must take if they are not to be cast aside. Van Buren remained at the head of the Democrats for such a long time only because he cleverly knew how to sense whither the mass movement was tending . . . Now that agrarianism has begun . . . it will not be long before the world-historical, practical-revolution movement of communism begins here. . . ."

2. A paraphrase of Goethe's *Prometheus*, I, strophe 10.

trade at least so much that, in case of necessity, he could get along for a time by himself, if an unfavorable chance should separate him from human society."

It is, to be sure, much easier to gush about "love" and "devotion" than to occupy oneself with the development of real conditions and practical questions.

American Pauperism and
the Working Class*

THE MORE developed a society, and the more the bourgeoisie is developed in a country where the power of the state has a bourgeois aspect, the more glaringly does the *social* question emerge—in France more glaringly than in Germany, in England more glaringly than in France, in a constitutional monarchy more glaringly than in an absolute one, in a republic more glaringly than in a constitutional monarchy. For example, conflicts over the credit system, speculation, etc., are nowhere more acute than in North America. Also, nowhere does social inequality appear more harshly than in the eastern states of North America, because nowhere else is it less whitewashed by political inequality. If pauperism has not yet developed there as extensively as in England, it is due to economic relationships which will not be gone into here. Nevertheless, pauperism is making the most gratifying progress.

"In this country, where there are no privileged classes, where all classes of society have equal rights [the difficulty, however, is in the existence of *classes*[1]], and where our population is a long way from pressing on the means of subsistence, it is in fact alarming to see pauperism growing with such rapidity."[2]

"It is proven that in Massachusetts pauperism has increased by 60 percent in twenty-five years."[3]

Thomas Cooper, one of the most famous North American economists, who is a radical to boot, proposes: (1) that the propertyless

* From "Moralizing Criticism and Criticizing Morality," in *Deutsche-Brüsseler Zeitung*, November 11, 1847.

1. The words in brackets are Marx's.

2. Report by William Morris Meredith, in *The Register of Pennsylvania*, August 16, 1828.—K. M.

3. From *Niles' Weekly Register* [no date given].—K. M.

should not be allowed to marry, and (2) that universal suffrage be abolished. Then he exclaims: "Society is established for the protection of property. What reasonable claim can be made by those who, according to eternal economic laws, will always be propertyless, to legislate over the property of others? What common motive and interest exists between these two classes of inhabitants?

"Either the working class is not revolutionary, in which case it represents the interests of the employers, on whom its existence depends—thus in the last elections in New England the factory owners, to assure themselves of votes, had the names of candidates printed on calico, and every one of their workers wore such a piece of calico on his breeches flap—or the working class becomes revolutionary in consequence of its common living together, etc., in which case the political power of the country must sooner or later come into its hands, and property would no longer be safe under such a system."[4]

As in England under the name of Chartists, so in North America under the name of National Reformers, the workers have formed a political party whose battle slogan in no way includes republic or principality, but *rule of the working class* against *rule of the bourgeois class.*

---

4. Thomas Cooper, *Lectures on the Elements of Political Economy* (Columbia, S. C., 1826).

The American Budget and
the Christian-German One*

Cologne, January 6

DURING the past few days we have finally had in black and white what the Prussian Government costs the country. The *Preussische Staats-Anzeiger*, in the financial report for the year 1849, has at last shown us how we have been deceived in the previous budgets. This splendid New Year's bundle has surprised only those to whom every word of the divinely favored government has so far appeared as holy truth and the whole government-finance humbug since 1820 as proof of the excellence of our police-state budget.

Prussia is a country of approximately 50,000 square miles and a little over 16,000,000 inhabitants.

The United States of North America embraces an area about the size of all of Europe and the number of its inhabitants amounts to more than 21,000,000.

There is no more fitting introduction to a consideration of the Prussian budget of 1849 than the budget of the free North American States.

A comparison of both budgets shows how dearly the Prussian bourgeoisie has to pay for the pleasure of being ruled by a government-by-the-grace-of-God, of being manhandled by its mercenaries whether in a state of siege or not, and of being treated *en canaille* [with contempt] by a horde of arrogant officials and *Krautjunkers* [country-bumpkin squires]. At the same time it shows how a courageous bourgeoisie, conscious of its power and determined to use it, can arrange its own government.

The two budgets are already sufficient proof by themselves of the cowardice, narrow-mindedness, and philistinism of the one country, and of the self-reliance, intelligence, and energy of the other.

---

* *Neue Rheinische Zeitung*, January 7, 1849.

The total expenditures of the United States during the year 1846 amounted to $42,811,970. This includes the cost of the Mexican War, a war that was waged 2,000 miles away from the seat of the federal government. One can imagine what enormous expenses were entailed in the transportation of the army and its necessary supplies.

The income of the Union amounted to $35,436,750, and of this $31,757,070 were customs revenue, $3,328,642 came from the sale of public lands, and $351,037 were miscellaneous receipts. As the ordinary income did not suffice to cover the cost of the war, the deficit was covered by a loan, made *al pari* [at par]. One could ask whether the "Christian-German" government could raise even 1,000 Taler on such favorable terms in the money markets here!

In the United States, the fiscal year begins on July 1. Because of the Mexican War, expenditures will still be high until July, 1849, although not high compared with Prussia's. On the other hand, President Polk, in his Message to Congress, projects the usual peacetime budget for the fiscal year ending July 1, 1850.

How high are the expenditures of this powerful state—the North American bourgeois republic—in peacetime?

They amount to $33,213,152, including interest ($3,799,102) on the public debt and the $3,540,000 debt to Mexico to be paid on July 30, 1850.

If one deducts the last two sums, which are extraordinary budget items, the cost of the whole government and administration of the United States amounts to hardly $26,000,000 annually.[1]

And how much do the Prussian citizens pay to the State annually in *peacetime?*

The answer is a bitter one. It is given to us by the Preussische Anzeiger. It is *more than 94,000,000 [Taler] annually!*

Hence while the 21,000,000 inhabitants of the North American republic, with their prosperity, yea, their wealth, paid scarcely $26,000,000—that is, *38,000,000 Prussian Taler at course*—to the national treasury, the 16,000,000 Prussians, with their comparative poverty, had to throw 94,000,000 Taler into the jaws of the government exchequer, which is not satisfied even with that.

But are we not unjust?

The North American republic possesses nothing more than a President elected for four years, who naturally works harder for the country than a dozen kings and emperors together. But for this

---

1. Marx left out the fact that, unlike Prussia, the United States had a federal system in which (except for national defense) the states and localities, and not Washington, paid for the maintenance of government and its services. In 1848 there were thirty states in the United States, each with its own separate budget.

he gets a shabby annual salary of 37,000 Prussian Taler.[2] In this paltry sum of 37,000 Taler can be comprehended the whole pathos of a Christian-Prussian spirit with its God for King and Junkerdom. No chamberlains, no court jewelers, no racing down the highway to Charlottenburg for court ladies, no game preserve maintenance at the cost of the citizen. Oh, it is terrible! But the most terrible thing about it is that these North Americans do not even seem to understand this horrible thing—this desolation, this God-forsakenness.[3]

How entirely different it is with us! If we pay three or four times more, we also enjoy things which they [the Americans] do not have, and could not have for 37,000 Taler. We enjoy and are invigorated by the glitter of a divinely graced court which costs the people—one does not know exactly, but at an approximate estimate—from four to five millions annually.

While the Americans are such silly owls as to keep their money for their own glitter and their own use, we Christian-Germans feel obliged to throw away our own glitter—that is, our money—so that others may glitter. And apart from the glitter, what favors does not the court, richly endowed from the pockets of the people, bestow on the mass of poor counts, barons, knights, and simple vons? Many of these people, who are equipped to be only consumers, and not producers, would end in wretched deterioration if they did not receive public alms in a fine way. We could not even begin to enumerate all these benefits.

And in what other respects are the Americans, with their small budget, behind us?

Over there, for example, Herr *Oberpräsident* [Provincial Governor] Boetticher would not receive a gift of 3,000 from the national treasury. There they would think he should be satisfied with his salary. There they don't contribute much for the education of the children of counts and barons. The North American republic would say to such gracious gentlemen: *Alors il faut s'abstenir d'avoir des enfants* [Then don't have children]! There a "Hüser" would be cheated out of his annual gratuity of 6,000 Taler and would have to be satisfied with his salary, perhaps less by 3,000 Taler. And a man, a Prussian man, a Christian-German general, should live on that? Infamous thought! Begone!

When it comes to money questions, the Americans, like Herr

---

2. The President's annual salary was then $25,000. Beginning in 1969 it was $200,000.

3. For Marx's view of religion in the United States, see his "On the Jewish Question," *Karl Marx on Religion,* to be published in the Karl Marx Library in 1973.

Hansemann, lose all their good nature. At most they would give Don Carlos a few whippings, but never 700,000 Taler so he could do *bene* [well] by himself and his grandees and monks, and fight for the Metternichean legitimacy. This can be done only by a kingdom-by-the-grace-of-God, to whom the pockets of the people must, by rights, always remain open.

If the taxes paid by the Americans to their government are quite insignificant, they have, on the other hand, a standing army of only 10,000 men, which can be rapidly augmented to a fighting force of 2,000,000 in wartime. They do not even begin to know the good fortune of spending the greatest portion of taxes on an army which in peacetime besieges, mistreats, wounds, and kills us—all for the glory and honor of the Fatherland.

But what can you do? These bourgeois republicans are so stubborn that they know nothing about our Christian-German institutions, and yea, would rather pay low taxes than high ones.

Equally stubborn, the German bourgeois insists that the Grace-of-God-ship, with its armies of warriors and officials, its hordes of pensioners, its gratuities, its extraordinaries, etc., cannot be too highly paid.

The moneybag republicans of North America and the bourgeois in Prussia have the same relationship to each other as their budgets—37,000,000 to 94,000,000. The one is self-favored and the other is favored by the grace of God. This is the essential difference.

What Is a Negro Slave?*

WHAT is a Negro slave? A man of the black race. The one explanation is as good as the other.

A Negro is a Negro. He becomes a *slave* only in certain relationships. A cotton-spinning machine is a machine for spinning cotton. Only in certain relationships does it become *capital*. Torn from these relationships, it is no more capital than gold in and by itself is *money* or sugar the *price* of sugar.

---

* From "Wage Labor and Capital," in *Neue Rheinische Zeitung*, April 7, 1849.

The Global Consequences of the Discovery of Gold in California*

WE NOW come to *America*. The most important thing that has occurred there, even more important than the February Revolution [in
Europe], is the discovery of gold in California. Even now, hardly
eighteen months later, it can be foreseen that this discovery will have
much grander results than the discovery of America itself. For three
hundred and thirty years the whole trade of Europe with the Pacific
Ocean was carried on, with the most touching patience, via the Cape
of Good Hope or Cape Horn. All attempts to cut across the isthmus
of Panama were wrecked on the narrow-minded jealousy of the
trading nations. California's gold mines were discovered only eighteen
months ago, and the Yankees have already started a railroad, a great
highway, and a canal from the Mexican Gulf; steamers from New York
to Chagres, from Panama to San Francisco, are already in regular
service; trade with the Pacific Ocean is already concentrating in
Panama, and the trip around Cape Horn is obsolete. A coast of 30
degrees longitude, one of the most beautiful and fertile in the world,
hitherto practically uninhabited, is being visibly transformed into a
rich and civilized land, thickly populated with people of all races, from
Yankees to Chinese, from Negroes to Indians and Malays, from
Creoles and mestizos to Europeans. California gold is flowing in
streams over America and the Asian coast of the Pacific Ocean, drawing recalcitrant barbaric peoples into world commerce, into civilization. For the second time, world trade acquires a new direction. New
York, San Francisco, San Juan de Nicaragua [Greytown], Chagres,
and León are now becoming what Tyre, Carthage, and Alexandria
were in antiquity, what Genoa and Venice were in the Middle Ages,

* From Marx and Engels, "Revue," in *Neue Rheinische Zeitung. Politisch-
Ökonomische Revue*, Second Issue, January–February, 1850.

and what London and Liverpool have been hitherto—the emporia of world commerce. The center of gravity of world trade—in Italy in the Middle Ages and in England in modern times—is now the southern half of the North American hemisphere. The industry and commerce of Old Europe must make a mighty effort not to fall into the same decline as the industry and commerce of Italy have since the sixteenth century, if England and France are to avoid becoming what Venice, Genoa, and Holland are today. In a few years we will see a regular steamship service from England to Chagres, from Chagres and San Francisco to Sydney, Canton, and Singapore. Thanks to California gold and the untiring energy of the Yankees, both coasts of the Pacific Ocean will soon be as populated, as open to commerce and as industrialized as the coast from Boston to New Orleans is now. Then the Pacific Ocean will play the same role as the Atlantic Ocean does now and as the Mediterranean did in antiquity and in the Middle Ages—the role of a great water highway of world commerce—and the Atlantic Ocean will decline to the level of an inland sea, as the Mediterranean is now. The one chance the civilized European countries have of not falling into the same dependence as Italy, Spain, and Portugal today lies in a social revolution which, while there is still time, makes possible new productive forces through the means of production and communication arising from modern industrial needs —means that will insure the superiority of European industry and thus compensate for the geographic disadvantages.

Carey's Economic Harmonies[*]

IT IS IN this form that Mr. Bastiat has welded together his economic theodocy, *Harmonies Économiques*. . . .[1] But Bastiat is not the discoverer of this economic idea; he has, rather, borrowed it from the American [Henry Charles] Carey, in whose view the New World, of which he is a member, functions only as historical background; he has demonstrated, in his multi-volume works on its first epoch, that the economic "harmony" which is everywhere still only the reduction of the abstract conditions of the simple exchange process, that he lets these simple conditions everywhere be falsified by the state on the one side and by the influence on the world market on the other. By themselves, harmonies do exist. But within the non-American states—even in America itself in their most developed form—wherever these conditions appear, they are falsified, in their world-market reality, in the development of England. Carey, in order to restore them, ultimately finds no other means than to call upon the *diabolus*, the state, which he denounces, as a guardian angel to place at the gate of the harmonious paradise—a protective tariff. But since he is a scholar, and not a belletrist like Bastiat, in his latest work [*The Slave Trade, Domestic and Foreign* (Philadelphia, 1853)] he had to go further. The development of America in the last eighteen years has given his harmony views such a push that he no longer sees in the influence of the state the falsification of the "natural harmonies" which he still clings to, but in—commerce! Wonderful result, this—to celebrate exchange value as the foundation of harmonious production, and then to let it be repealed by the developed form of ex-

---

[*] From *Grundrisse der Kritik der politischen Ökonomie*, written 1857–58 and published in Moscow, 1939, Berlin, 1953, pp. 917–18, footnote p. 918.
1. Frédéric Bastiat, *Harmonies Économiques* (2d ed., Paris, 1851).

change, commerce, in its immanent laws![2] It is in this desperate form that he pronounces the dilatory judgment that the development of the harmonious exchange value is disharmonious.

---

2. Carey is in reality the only original economist of America, and what gives his works great importance is that his material is everywhere based on bourgeois society in its freest and widest reality. He expresses the great American conditions in abstract form, and, moreover, in contrast to the Old World. The only real background of Bastiat's [work] is the pettiness of French economic conditions, which everywhere stretch out their long ears from his harmonies, and, in contrast to the idealized English and American conditions of production are formulated as "Demands of Practical Reason." Carey, on the other hand, is rich in independent, so to say, bona fide researches on specific economic questions. Where, exceptionally, Bastiat proceeds to descend from his coquettishly polished commonplaces to real categories—for example, ground rents—he simply copies Carey. While the latter combats the opposition to his harmony views in the form that they are themselves developed by the classic English economists, Bastiat pleads the cause against the socialists. The deeper views of Carey find their contradiction in the economy itself, which he, as a harmonizer, has to combat, whereas the vain, dogmatic grumbler sees them only from the outside.—K. M.

Benjamin Franklin's Economic Theory*

THE FIRST CONSCIOUS, clear and almost trite analysis of exchange value into labor value is found in the writings of a man of the New World—where bourgeois relations of production, imported together with their representatives, sprouted rapidly in a soil in which the lack of historic tradition was compensated by a superabundance of humus. The man is Benjamin Franklin, who formulated the basic law of modern political economy in an early work, written in 1729 and published in 1731.[1] He declares it necessary to seek another measure of value than precious metals. This measure is labor:

> By labor may the value of silver be measured as well as other things. As, suppose one man is employed to raise corn, while another is digging and refining silver; at the year's end, or at any other period of time, the complete produce of corn, and that of silver, are the natural price of each other; and if one be twenty bushels, and the other twenty ounces, then an ounce of that silver is worth the labor of raising a bushel of that corn. Now if by the discovery of some nearer, more easy or plentiful mines, a man may get forty ounces of silver as easily as formerly he did twenty, and the same labor is still required to raise twenty bushels of corn, then two ounces of silver will be worth no more than the same labor of raising one bushel of corn, and that bushel of corn will be as cheap at two ounces, as it was before at one, *caeteris paribus* [other things being equal]. Thus the riches of a country are to be valued by the *quantity of labor* its inhabitants are able to purchase.

* From *Critique of Political Economy* (1859), Chapter I.
1. Benjamin Franklin, "A Modest Inquiry into the Nature and Necessity of a Paper Currency," in *The Works of Benjamin Franklin*, ed. by Jared Sparks (Boston, 1836), vol. II, p. 265.

From the outset, Franklin regards labor time from a one-sided economic viewpoint as the measure of value. The transformation of actual products into exchange values is taken for granted, and it is only a question of finding a measure of their value.

Franklin writes: "Trade in general being nothing else but the exchange of labor for labor, the value of all things is, as I have said before, most justly measured by labor."[2]

If in this sentence the term labor is replaced by actual labor, one immediately discovers that labor in one form is being confused with labor in another form. Since commerce, for example, consists in the exchange of the labor of a shoemaker, miner, spinner, painter, etc., is, therefore, the labor of the painter the best measure of the value of boots? Franklin, on the contrary, considers that the value of boots, minerals, yarn, paintings, etc., is determined by abstract labor which has no particular quality and can thus be measured in terms of mere quantity.[3] But since he does not explain that the labor contained in exchange value is abstract universal social labor, which comes out of the universal alienation of individual labor, he necessarily mistakes money for the direct embodiment of this alienated labor. He therefore does not see the intrinsic connection between money and the exchange value posited by labor, but on the contrary regards money as a rather technical convenience which has been introduced from the outside as an instrument of exchange.[4] Franklin's analysis of exchange value had no direct influence on the general course of the science, because he dealt only with isolated questions of political economy for definite practical purposes.

---

2. *Loc. cit.*, p. 267.
3. Franklin, "Remarks and Facts Relative to the American Paper Money" (1704).
4. Franklin, "Papers on American Politics," and "Remarks and Facts Relative to the American Paper Money" (1764).

The Eight-Hour Working Day*

In the United States of North America, every independent workers' movement was paralyzed so long as slavery disfigured a part of the Republic. Labor in white skin cannot emancipate itself where it is branded in black skin. But out of the death of slavery a new, rejuvenated life sprouted immediately. The first fruit of the Civil War was the eight-hours' agitation that strode with the seven-league boots of the locomotive from the Atlantic to the Pacific, from New England to California. The General Labor Congress at Baltimore[1] declared:

"The first and great necessity of the present, to free the labor of this country from capitalistic slavery, is the passing of a law by which eight hours shall be the normal working day in all states of the American Union. We are resolved to put forth all our strength until this glorious result is attained."

---

* From *Capital*, Vol. I, Part III, Chapter VIII, Sec. 3. In the English edition, edited by Engels, Chapter VIII ("The Working-Day") is Chapter X, and the above selection is in Sec. 7.

1. The Congress met August 20–25, 1866, and was attended by sixty delegates representing 60,000 trade-union members. It resolved, among other things, to establish a National Labor Union, as a political arm of the working class.

The Life-Destroying Toil of Slaves[*]

THE SLAVEOWNER buys his laborer as he buys his horse. If he loses his slave, he loses capital, which can only be replaced by new outlay in the slave market. But:

"The rice-grounds of Georgia, or the swamps of the Mississippi, may be fatally injurious to the human constitution; but the waste of human life which the cultivation of these districts necessitates is not so great that it cannot be repaired from the teeming preserves of Virginia and Kentucky. Considerations of economy, moreover—which, under a natural system, afford some security for humane treatment by identifying the master's interest with the slave's preservation—once trading in slaves is practiced, become reasons for racking the toil of the slave to the uttermost; for when his replacement can immediately be supplied from elsewhere, the duration of his life becomes a matter of less moment than its productiveness while it lasts. It is accordingly a maxim of slave management, in slave-importing countries, that the most effective economy is that which takes out of the human chattel in the shortest space of time the utmost amount of exertion it is capable of putting forth. It is in tropical culture, where annual profits often equal the whole capital of plantations, that Negro life is most recklessly sacrificed. It is the agriculture of the West Indies, which has been for centuries prolific of fabulous wealth, that has engulfed millions of the African race. It is in present-day Cuba, whose revenues are reckoned by millions and whose planters are princes, that we see in the servile class the coarsest fare, the most exhausting and unremitting toil, and even the absolute destruction of a portion of its numbers every year."[1]

---

[*] From *Capital*, Vol. I, Part III, Chapter VIII, Sec. 5. Translated from the fourth German edition.

1. John Elliot Cairnes, *The Slave Trade* (London, 1862), p. 110-11.

Mutato nomine de te fabula narratur.[2] For slave trade, read labor market; for Kentucky and Virginia, Ireland and agricultural districts of Scotland, and Wales; for Africa, Germany.

---

2. This could be thy story under a different name: Horace, *Satires,* Book I.

Immigration and Capitalism*

It is highly characteristic that for years the English Government has practiced this method of "primitive accumulation" prescribed by Mr. Wakefield[1] expressly for the use of the colonies. The fiasco was, of course, as ignominious as that of Peel's Bank Act.[2] The stream of emigration was only diverted from the English colonies to the United States. In the meantime, the progress of capitalist production in Europe, accompanied by growing governmental pressure, has made Wakefield's recipe superfluous. On the one hand the enormous and continuing stream of humanity, year after year driven to America, leaves behind stagnant sediments in the east of the United States, while the wave of immigration from Europe throws men on the labor market there more rapidly than the wave of immigration to the west can wash them away. On the other hand, the American Civil War brought in its train a colossal national debt,[3] and with it, pressure of taxes, the growth of the vilest financial aristocracy, the relinquishment of a huge portion of the public lands to speculative companies for the exploitation of railroads, mines, etc.—in short, the most rapid centralization of capital. Thus the great republic has ceased to be the Promised Land for emigrating workers. Capitalist production there advances with giant strides, even though the lowering of wages and the dependence of the wage worker are still far from being brought down to the normal European level.

---

* From *Capital*, Vol. I, Part VII, Chapter XXIV. Translated from the fourth German edition.

1. Edward Gibbon Wakefield, *England and America. A Comparison of the Social and Political State of Both Nations* (London, 1833).

2. Introduced by Sir Robert Peel in 1844, to reform the Bank of England.

3. For the size of the debt, see Chronology, p. liii.

Slavery as a General System[*]

IN THE slave system, money capital invested in the purchase of labor power plays the role of the money form of fixed capital, which is only gradually replaced after the expiration of the active life period of the slave. Among the Athenians, therefore, the gain realized by a slaveowner directly through the industrial employment of his slave, or indirectly by hiring him out to other industrial employers (for example, for mining), was regarded merely as interest (plus amortization) on the advanced money capital, just as in capitalist production the industrial capitalist places a portion of surplus value plus the depreciation of his fixed capital to the account of interest and replacement of his fixed capital; as it is also the rule with capitalists offering fixed capital (houses, machinery, etc.) for rent. Mere household slaves, whether they serve in the performance of necessary duties or simply as luxuries for display, do not come into consideration here: they correspond to our servant class. But the slave system too—so long as it is the dominant form of productive labor, in agriculture, manufacturing, navigation, etc., as it was in the developed states of Greece and Rome—preserves an element of natural economy. The slave market itself maintains a constant supply of its labor-power commodity by war, piracy, etc., and this rapine, for its part, is not promoted by a process of circulation but by the natural appropriation of outside labor power through direct physical compulsion. Even in the United States, after the transformation of the buffer territory between the wage-labor states of the North and the slave states in the South into a slave-breeding region for the South, where the slave

* From *Capital*, Vol. II, Chapter XX, Sec. 12. Translated from the German edition published by Engels in 1893.

thrown on the slave market thus became himself an element of the annual reproduction, this did not suffice for a long time, so that the African slave trade was continued as long as possible to satisfy the market.

Master, Slave, and Overseer*

THE WORK of management and supervision, insofar as it is not a special function arising from the nature of all combined social labor, but rather from the antithesis between the owner of the means of production and the owner of mere labor power—regardless of whether the latter is purchased with the purchase of the laborer himself, as in the slave system, or whether the laborer himself sells his labor power, so that the production process appears at the same time as the process by which capital consumes his labor—this function arising out of the servitude of the direct producer has often enough been cited as grounds for justification of this relationship; and the exploitation, the appropriation of unpaid labor of others, has quite as often been represented as the wage justly due the owner of capital for his work. But never better than by a defender of slavery in the United States, a lawyer named O'Conor, at a meeting held in New York on December 19, 1859, under the banner: "Justice for the South":

"Now, gentlemen," he said amid thunderous applause,

> "to that condition of bondage the Negro is assigned by Nature. He has strength, and has the power to labor; but the Nature which created the power denied to him either the intellect to govern, or willingness to work. [Applause.] Both were denied to him. And that Nature which deprived him of the will to labor gave him a master to coerce that will, and to make a useful servant in the clime in which he was capable of living, useful for himself and for the master who governs him. I maintain that it is not injustice to leave the Negro in the condition in which Nature placed him, to give

* From *Capital*, Vol. III, Part 5, Chapter XXIII. Translated from the first German edition, published by Engels in 1894.

him a master to govern him; nor is it depriving him of any of his rights to compel him to labor in return, and afford to that master just compensation for the labor and talent employed in governing him and rendering him useful to himself and to the society.[1]

Now the wage laborer, like the slave, must have a master to make him work and to rule him. And presupposing the existence of this domination-and-bondage relationship, it is proper that the wage laborer be forced to produce his own wages and also the wages of supervision, as compensation for the labor of ruling and supervising him, "and afford to that master just compensation for the labor and talent employed in governing him and rendering him useful to himself and to the society."

---

1. *New-York Daily Tribune*, December 20, 1859, pp. 7–8.—K.M.

Colonial Land, Farming, and Capitalism*

A SOMEWHAT analogous development takes place in the colonies, even where, *legally*, landed property exists, insofar as the government gives [land] gratis, as happened originally in the colonization from England; and even where the government actually institutes landed property by selling the land, though at a negligible price, as in the United States, at a dollar or something of the sort per acre.

Two different aspects must be distinguished here.

Firstly: There are the colonies proper, such as in the United States, Australia, etc. Here the mass of the farming colonists, although they bring with them a larger or smaller amount of capital from the motherland, are not *capitalists*, nor do they carry on *capitalist* production. They are more or less peasants who work themselves and whose main object, in the first place, is to produce *their own livelihood*, their means of subsistence. Their main product therefore does not become a *commodity* and is not intended for trade. They sell or exchange the excess of their products over their own consumption for imported manufactured commodities, etc. The other, smaller section of the colonists, who settle near the sea, navigable rivers, etc., form trading towns. There is no question of capitalist production here either. Even if capitalist production gradually comes into being, so that the sale of his products and the profit he makes from this sale

---

* From *Theories of Surplus Value* (Vol. IV of *Capital*), Part II, Chapter XII. *Theories of Surplus Value* was written between January, 1862, and July, 1863; it remained as unpublished notes (twenty-three notebooks, numbering 1,472 pages), until 1963, when it was published in Moscow as Vol. XXVI, Parts I and II, of the *Marx-Engels Werke*. Unlike the three preceding volumes of *Capital*, which were theoretical, Marx planned *Theories of Surplus Value* to be historical and critical, in connection with economic literature. The English translation used here and in the following three selections is by Progress Publishers, Moscow, 1968.

becomes decisive for the farmer who himself works and owns his land; so long as, compared with capital and labor, land still exists in elemental abundance providing a practically unlimited field of action, the first type of colonization will continue as well and production will therefore never be regulated according to the needs of the market—at a given market value. Everything the colonists of the first type produce over and above their immediate consumption, they will throw on the market and sell at any price that will bring in more than their wages. They are, and continue for a long time to be, competitors of the farmers who are already producing more or less capitalistically, and thus keep the market price of the agricultural product constantly *below* its value. The farmer who therefore cultivates land of the worst kind will be quite satisfied if he makes the average profit on the sale of his farm, i.e., if he gets back the capital invested; this is not the case in very many instances. Here therefore we have two essentially different conditions competing with one another: capitalist production is not as yet dominant in agriculture; secondly, although landed property exists legally, in practice it only exists as yet sporadically, and strictly speaking there is only possession of land. Or, although landed property exists in a legal sense, it is—in view of the elemental abundance of land relative to labor and capital—as yet unable to offer resistance to capital, to transform agriculture into a field of action, which in contrast to nonagricultural industry offers specific resistance to the investment of capital.

In the second type of colony—plantations—where commercial speculations figure from the start and production is intended for the world market, the capitalist mode of production exists, although only in a formal sense, since the slavery of Negroes precludes free wage labor, which is the basis of capitalist production. But the business in which slaves are used is conducted by *capitalists*. The method of production which they introduce has not arisen out of slavery but is grafted onto it. In this case the same person is capitalist and landowner. And the *elemental* existence of the land confronting capital and labor does not offer any resistance to capital investment, hence none to the competition between capitals. Neither does a class of farmers as distinct from landlords develop here. So long as these conditions endure, nothing will stand in the way of cost price regulating market value.

Fertile and Unfertile Colonial Land*

. . . RICARDO himself goes on to formulate his *assumption* thus: "If all land had the same properties, if it were unlimited in quantity, and uniform in quality, no charge could be made for its use."[1]

He does not say and cannot say, if it "were rich and fertile," because this condition would have absolutely nothing to do with the law. If instead of being rich and fertile the land were poor and sterile, then each colonist would have to cultivate a greater proportion of the whole land, and thus, even where the land is unappropriated, they would, with the growth of population, more rapidly approach the point where the practical abundance of land, its actual unlimitedness in proportion to population and capital, would cease to exist.

It is of course quite certain that the colonists will not pick out the least fertile land, but will choose the most fertile, i.e., the land that will produce most, with the means of cultivation at their disposal. But this is not the sole limiting factor in their choice. The first deciding factor for them is the *situation*, the situation near the sea, large rivers, etc. The land in West America, etc., may be as fertile as any; but the settlers of course established themselves in New England, Pennsylvania, North Carolina, Virginia, etc., in short, on the east coast of the Atlantic. If they selected the most fertile land, then they only selected the *most fertile land in this region.* This did not prevent them from cultivating *more fertile* land in the West, at a later stage, as soon as growth of population, formation of capital, development of means of communication, building of towns, made the more fertile land in this more distant region accessible to them. They do not look

---

* *Theories of Surplus Value*, Part II, Chapter XIII
1. David Ricardo, *On the Principles of Political Economy, and Taxation* (3d ed., London, 1821), p. 56.

[30]

for the most fertile region, but for the most favorably situated region, and within this, of course—given *equal* conditions so far as the situation is concerned—they look for the most fertile land. But this certainly does not prove that they progress from the more fertile region to the less fertile region, only that within the same region—provided the situation is the same—the more fertile land is naturally cultivated before the unfertile.

The Use of Machinery in America*

"IN AMERICA and many other countries, where the food of man is easily provided, there is not nearly such great temptation to employ machinery" (nowhere is it used on such massive scale and also, so to speak, for domestic needs as in America) "as in England, where food is high, and costs much labor for its production."[1]

How little the employment of machinery is dependent on the price of food is shown precisely by America, which employs relatively much more machinery than England, where there is always a redundant population. The use of machinery *may*, however, depend on the relative scarcity of labor, as, for instance, in America, where a comparatively small population is spread over immense tracts.[2] Thus we read in the *Standard*[3] of September 19, 1862, in an article on the Exhibition:

> "Man is a machine-making animal" . . . if we consider the American as a representative man, the definition is . . . perfect. It is one of the cardinal points of an American's system to do nothing with his hands that he can do by a machine. From rocking a cradle to making a coffin, from milking a cow to clearing a forest, from sewing on a button to voting for President, almost, he had a machine for everything. He has invented a machine for saving the trouble of masticating food . . . The *exceeding* scarcity of labor and its con-

---

* From *Theories of Surplus Value*, Part II, Chapter XVIII. The remarks in parentheses are by Marx, the ellipses and words in brackets are by the translator (see source note page 28n.).

1. Ricardo, *op. cit.*, p. 479.

2. According to the Census of 1860, the U.S. had a population of 31,443,321, living in a territory of 3,022,387 square miles, or approximately 10 persons per square mile.

3. A London Tory daily.

sequent value (despite the low value of food), as well as a certain innate "cuteness" have stimulated this inventive spirit . . . The machines produced in America are, generally speaking, inferior in value to those made in England . . . they are rather, as a whole, makeshifts to save labor than inventions to accomplish former impossibilities. (And the steamships?) . . . [at the Exhibition] in the United States department [. . .] is Emery's cotton gin. For many a year after the introduction of cotton to America the crop was very small; because not only was the demand rather limited, but the difficulty in cleaning the crop by manual labor rendered it anything but remunerative. When Eli Whitney, however, invented the saw cotton gin there was an immediate increase in the breadth planted, and that increase has up to the present time gone on almost in arithmetical progression. In fact, it is not too much to say that Whitney made the cotton trade. With modifications more or less important and useful, his gin has remained in use ever since; and until the invention of the present improvement and addition Whitney's original gin was quite as good as most of its would-be supplanters. By the present machine, which bears the name of Messrs. Emery of [. . .] Albany, N.Y., we have no doubt that Whitney's gin, on which it is based, will be almost entirely supplanted. It is simple and more efficacious; it delivers the cotton not only cleaner, but in sheets like wadding, and thus the layers as they leave the machine are at once fit for the cotton press and the bale . . . In [the] American Court proper there is little else than machinery. [. . .] *The cow milker . . . a belt shifter . . . a hemp carding and spinning machine*, which at one operation reels the cliver direct from the bale . . . *Machines* [. . .] *for the manufacture of paper bags,* which it cuts from the sheet, pastes, folds, and perfects at the rate of 300 a minute . . . Hawes's clothes wringer, which by two India rubber rollers presses from clothes the water, leaving them almost dry, [. . .] saves time, but does not injure the texture . . . *Bookbinders' machinery . . . machines for making shoes.* It is well known that the uppers have been for a long time made up by machines in this country, but here are machines for putting on the sole, others for cutting the sole to shape, and others again for trimming the heels . . . A *stone-breaking machine* is very powerful and ingenious, and no doubt will come extensively into use for ballasting roads and crushing ores . . . A system of *marine signals* by Mr. W. H. Ward of Auburn, New York . . . *Reaping and mowing machines* are an American invention coming into very general favor in England. [. . .] McCormick's [machine is] the best . . . Hansbrow's California Prize Medal *Force Pump* is in simplicity and efficiency the best [. . .] in the Exhibition . . . it will throw more water with the same power than any pump in the world . . . *Sewing machines.* . . .[4]

---

4. "America in the Exhibition," the *Standard*, September 19, 1862. The World Exhibition had opened in London on May 1, 1862.

The Transportation of Cotton to Liverpool*

FOR EXAMPLE, cotton is an illustration of how transport and communications affect the emptying of the reservoir. Since ships continually ply between Liverpool and the United States—speed of communications is one factor, continuity another—all the cotton supply is not shipped at once. It comes on to the market gradually (the producer likewise does not want to flood the market all at once). It lies at the docks in Liverpool, that is, already in a kind of circulation reservoir, but not in such quantities—in relation to the total consumption of the article—as would be required if the ship from America arrived only once or twice a year, after a journey of six months. The cotton manufacturer in Manchester and other places stocks his warehouse roughly in accordance with his immediate consumption needs, since the electric telegraph and the railway make the transfer from Liverpool to Manchester possible at a moment's notice.

* From *Theories of Surplus Value*, Part III, Chapter XXI.

The Program of the First International in the United States*

CORRESPONDENT: Have you a strong organization in the United States?

Dr. Marx: Yes, but we apprehend no violence or trouble there, unless, indeed, some of your great iron or other monopolists should take it into their hands to employ force to put down strikes, as they had done in one or two instances, in which case they will be swept away like chaff before the wind.

Correspondent: What are the principal aims of the society in the United States?

Dr. Marx: To emancipate the workingman from the rule of politicians, and to combat monopoly in all the many forms it is assuming there, especially that of the public lands. We want no more monstrous land grabs, no more grants to swindling railroad concerns, no more schemes for robbing the people of their birthright for the benefit of a few purse-proud monopolists. More than that, let these men be warned in time; their ill-gotten goods shall be taken from them, and their wealth shall vanish like the baseless fabric of a vision. We oppose also all protectionist measures, which make all the necessaries of life dear to the poor man merely to put money into the pockets of a few aristocrats, who know how to buy over your corrupt politicians.

---

* From an interview in the *New York Herald*, August 3, 1871. The interview had taken place in London on July 20, 1871.

Personal Letters

From letter written in French to Pavel Vassilyevich Annenkov (in Paris)
BRUSSELS, DECEMBER 28, 1846

My Dear Mr. Annenkov:

. . . *Liberty* and *slavery* constitute an antagonism . . . We are not dealing here with indirect slavery, the slavery of the proletariat, we are dealing with direct slavery, the slavery of the Blacks in Surinam, in Brazil, in the southern states of North America.

Direct slavery is the pivot of our industrialism today as much as machinery, credit, etc. Without slavery you have no cotton, without cotton you have no modern industry. It is slavery that has given value to the colonies; it is the colonies that created world trade; it is world trade that is the necessary condition for large-scale machine industry. Also, before the slave trade in Negroes, the colonies supplied the Old World with but very few products and did not visibly change the face of the world. Slavery is thus an economic category of the highest importance. Without slavery, North America, the most progressive country, would be transformed into a primitive country. You have only to erase North America from the map of nations and you will have anarchy, the total decay of commerce and of modern civilization. But to let slavery disappear is to erase North America from the map of nations. And thus slavery, because it is an economic category, is found among all nations since the world began. Modern nations have known how to disguise the slavery in their own countries and how to import it openly into the New World. . . .

Entirely yours,
CHARLES MARX

From letter to Frederick Engels (in Manchester)
LONDON, OCTOBER 13, 1851

Dear Engels!

. . . *Qu'est ce que fait la crise commerciale?* [How is the business crisis?] The *Economist* contains the consolations, protestations, and appeals that regularly precede crises. Nevertheless, one senses its fear, while it tries to chatter away the fear of others. If you should come across the following book, *Notes on North America*, 2 vols., 1851, you will find all kinds of interesting notes in it. For this Johnston is the English Liebig. . . .

The English admit that the Americans carried off the prize in the Industrial Exhibition and that they won in everything. (1) Gutta-percha: new stuff and new productions. (2) Arms: revolvers. (3) Machinery: reapers, sowers, sewing machines. (4) Daguerreotypes applied on a large scale for the first time. (5) Navigation, with its yacht. Finally, to show that they can supply luxury articles also, they showed a colossal lump of California gold ore and, alongside, a golden service of pure gold.

Salut!

Yours,

K. M.

From letter to Joseph Weydemeyer (in New York)
LONDON, MARCH 5, 1852

Dear Weywy!

. . . How little bourgeois society has developed intellectually in regard to understanding the class struggle is most brilliantly illustrated by H. C. Carey (of Philadelphia),[1] the only important North American economist. He attacks Ricardo, the classical representative of the bourgeoisie and the most stoical opponent of the proletariat, as a man whose work is the arsenal for anarchists, socialists, and all other enemies of the bourgeois order. He not only reproaches him but also Malthus, Mill, Say, Torrens, Wakefield, MacCulloch, Senior, Whately, R. Jones, etc.—these economic dancing masters of Europe—for tear-

---

1. Henry Charles Carey's work included *Essay on the Rate of Wages* (1835); *Principles of Political Economy* (1837, 1838, 1840); *Past, Present and Future* (1848); *The Harmony of Interests, Agricultural, Manufacturing and Commercial* (1851).

ing up society and spreading civil war by their demonstration that the economic foundations of various classes must give rise to a necessary and ever growing antagonism among them. He attempts to refute them, but not . . . by linking the existence of classes with the existence of political privileges and monopolies, rather by attempting to show that economic conditions—rents (landed property), profit (capital), and wages (wage labor)—instead of being conditions of struggle and antagonism, are rather conditions of association and harmony. Naturally, all he proves is that the "undeveloped" conditions in the United States are, for him, "normal conditions." . . .

Yours,

K. Marx

From letter to Frederick Engels (in Manchester)
LONDON, AUGUST 19, 1852

Dear Engels!

. . . Finally, in North America, as I see in the *New York Herald,* the most frantic speculation in railways, banks, house building, unheard-of expansion in the credit system, etc. Is this not approaching a crisis? The revolution may come sooner than we wish. Nothing is worse than for revolutionists to have to worry about bread.

Yours,

K. M.

From letter to Engels (in Manchester)
LONDON, JUNE 14, 1853

Dear Frederic!

. . . Carey, the American economist, has published a new book: "slavery at home and abroad."[1] Under "slavery" are comprehended all forms of servitude, wage slavery, etc. He has sent me his book, wherein he often refers to me (from the *Tribune*[2]) variously as "a recent English writer" and as "Correspondence of the *New-York*

---

1. Henry Charles Carey, *The Slave Trade, Domestic and Foreign: Why it Exists, and How it may be Extinguished* (1853).
2. Carey cited from Marx's article "The Elections—The Gloomy Financial Situation—The Duchess of Sutherland and Slavery" in the *New-York Daily Tribune,* February 9, 1853.

Tribune." As I have told you before, in this man's previous works the economic bases of the bourgeoisie are developed as "harmony" and every mischief is viewed as being due to superfluous government intervention. The state has been his *bête noire*. Now he whistles a different tune. Everything evil is caused by the centralizing activities of big industry. This is especially the fault of England, which has made itself the workshop of the world and brutally throws all other countries back to a nonmanufacturing, agricultural economy. England's sins, in turn, are the result of the Ricardo-Malthus theory and especially Ricardo's ground rent theory. The necessary consequence of Ricardo's theory, as well as of industrial centralization, will be communism. And to avoid all this—to oppose the centralization of the union of factory and farm scattered throughout the entire land—our ultra Free-Trader finally recommends—*protective tariffs.* To avoid the effects of bourgeois industry, for which he holds England responsible, he takes refuge, as a true Yankee, in the artificial acceleration of industrial development in America. For the rest, his opposition to England throws him into Sismondian praise of the petty bourgeoisie in Switzerland, Germany, China, etc. This is the same bloke [*Kerl*] who was formerly in the habit of ridiculing France for its resemblance to China. The only positive and interesting thing in the book is the comparison between the former English Negro slavery in Jamaica, etc., and Negro slavery in the United States. He shows how the main stock of Negroes in Jamaica, etc., always consisted of newly imported barbarians, since the English treatment of Negroes was such that their numbers not only failed to remain steady but actually declined to two-thirds of the annual slave import; whereas the present generation of Negroes in America is a native product, more or less Yankeeized, English-speaking, etc., and therefore *capable of emancipation.*

The *Tribune* naturally blows the trumpet for Carey's book with puffed cheeks. Both, of course, have this in common: that under the form of Sismondian-philanthropic-socialistic-antiindustrialism they represent the pro–protective tariff, that is, the industrial bourgeoisie, of America. This is also the secret of why the *Tribune,* for all its "isms" and socialistic pretenses, can be the "leading journal" in the United States. . . .

Yours,

K. M.

From letter to Engels (in Manchester)
LONDON, NOVEMBER 30, 1854

Dear Engels:

. . . The day before yesterday I finally received the two volumes of Ripley's *Mexican War*,[1] approximately 1,200 pages, large format. Ripley seems to me—a pure layman's judgment—to have fashioned himself *plus ou moins* [more or less] after Napier as a military historian. The book is sensible and, as it seems to me, not uncritical. Dana has surely not read it. Otherwise he would have seen that its [the *Tribune's*] hero, General Scott, by no means appears in a favorable light either as a commander-in-chief or as a gentleman. I was especially interested in the history, as I recently read about the campaign of Fernando Cortez in Antonio de Solis, *Conquista de Mexico*.[2] Very interesting comparisons can be made between the two *conquistas* [conquests]. Moreover, although the two commanders—Taylor as well as Scott—appear to me to be very mediocre, the whole war is surely a worthy overture to the war history of the great Yankee land. The enormous spaces in which the action takes place, and the small number of men with which it is waged (among them more volunteers than regular army), give it an "American" originality. As regards Taylor and Scott, their entire merit consists in their being convinced that Yankees will extricate themselves no matter how deep they are bogged down in the muck. Early next week I will send you the two volumes. Let me know whether—since they are massive—by post (I am not sure about the recent rates) or parcel co.

Addio.

Yours,

K. M.

From letter to Engels (in Manchester)
LONDON, DECEMBER 2, 1854

Dear Engels!

. . . On Monday I will send you by the indicated parcel co. Ripley and also Solis' *Conquista de Mexico*. The latter to be returned as soon as you no longer need it, since the Solis does not belong to me. I have now read all of Ripley (of course hastily, which suffices for my pur-

1. Roswell Sabine Ripley, *The War with Mexico* (2 vols., New York, 1849).
2. *Historia de la Conquista de Méjico* (new ed., Paris, 1844).

pose). It is now entirely clear in my mind—and Ripley conveys it often in flat and "restrained" sarcastic form—that the great Scott was a quite ordinary, petty, untalented, nagging, envious dog and humbug, who, conscious that he owed everything to the bravery of his troops and the skill of his divisional commanders, pulled cheap tricks to assure himself of fame. He seems to be as much a great general as the many-sided Greeley is a great philosopher. The fellow blundered and made so many fumbles throughout the whole campaign that he deserved to be shot by any court-martial. But he is the *first* (according to *rank*) general of America. This is probably why Dana believes in him. Taylor is surely always worth more than Scott, which is what the American public seems to have sensed, in that it made the former President of the United States and let the latter, despite all his efforts, drop again and again. To me, General Worth seems to be the most outstanding, a matter on which you must give me your opinion as soon as you have read the thing. Is it not curious that Scott is always two to ten miles removed from active operations, *never* appears on the battlefield *himself*, but is always merely "observing the progress of events" from his safe headquarters? He does not even show up, as Taylor does, when the appearance of the commander-in-chief is necessary for the "morale" of the Army. After the very hot battle of Contreras, he comes riding out with his whole staff when the thing is over. During the fluctuating battle of Molino del Rey, he let the "gallant" men know that they should persevere, that he might perhaps show up himself. Wherever he shows mistrust, it is always of his more talented divisional commanders, but never of Santa Anna, who leads him by the nose as if he were an elderly child. The characteristic aspect of the war seems to me to be that each division and each small corps of troops, despite deceptive or nonexistent orders from the chief, always stubbornly pursues its objective and uses every incident spontaneously, so that in the end something complete comes of it. It is the Yankee sense of independence and individual efficiency, perhaps even greater than among the Anglo-Saxons. The Spaniards are already degenerated. But now a degenerate Spaniard, a Mexican, is an ideal. All encumbrances, braggings, loudmouthedness, and quixoticisms of the Spaniards here raised to cubic power, but far from having the solidity of the latter. The Mexican guerrilla war is a caricature of the Spanish one, and even the running away of the regular armies is endlessly surpassed. But for that, the Spaniards do not have the kind of talent shown by Santa Anna.

Vale.

Yours,

K. M.

From letter to Friedrich Adolph Sorge (in Hoboken)
LONDON, APRIL 4, 1876

My Dear Sorge:

... And now I have several requests to make to you:

1. Could I get the *Tribune* articles which were preserved by my prematurely deceased friend Meyer (from Weydemeyer's legacy, I believe)? I have none of them.

2. Could I get from New York (at my expense, of course), the 1873 American book catalogs that have appeared to date? For me it is a question (for the second volume of *Capital*) of seeing for myself what useful things have been published on American agriculture and land conditions, ditto on credit (panic, money, etc., and everything connected with this).

3. From the English newspapers it is not possible to form an intelligent idea about the current scandals in the United States.[1] Did you preserve any American papers on this subject?

With warmest regards for your whole family and you.

Totus tuus [*Entirely yours*],

KARL MARX

From letter to Engels (in Ramsgate)
LONDON, JULY 25, 1877

Dear Fred:

... What do you say about the workers in the United States? This first outbreak since the Civil War against the associated oligarchy of capital will, of course, be beaten down, but could serve as a point of departure for the organization of a serious labor party.[1] Two favorable circumstances are there. The policy of the new President[2] and the large land expropriations (of precisely the fertile land) in favor of the railway, mining, etc., companies will make the Negroes and the farmers in the West, who already grumble very strongly, the allied troops of the workers. ...

Salut.

Yours,

MOHR[3]

---

1. The Western railroad land scandals under the Grant Administration.

1. A railroad strike, which began on July, 1877, soon spread to seventeen states. About half a year after Marx wrote the above letter, in January, 1878, the Knights of Labor was organized as a national union.

2. Rutherford B. Hayes.

3. "The Moor," a favorite nickname.

Karl Marx. Engraving by Oscar L. Geyer. CULVER PICTURES.

H B Hall Jr

James Buchanan, fifteenth President of the United States. He was the last President before the "whirlwind" of the Civil War. PICTURE COLLECTION NYPL

Abraham Lincoln. Photographed by Alexander Gardner at Washington, D.C., on Sunday, Nov. 8, 1863, eleven days before the Gettysburg Address.

(Top, left) Napoleon III, Emperor of France. (Top, right) Lord John Russell, British Foreign Minister during the Civil War. (Bottom, left) Lord Palmerston, British Prime Minister. (Bottom, right) Benjamin Disraeli, Opposition leader in the House of Commons during the Civil War. THE GRANGER COLLECTION

(Top, left) Preston Smith Brooks, Congressman from South Carolina, who assaulted Senator Sumner. (Top, right) John Bright, British Liberal. (Bottom, left) Carl Schurz, German-born General of Volunteers, USA. (Bottom, right) Charles Sumner, Senator from Massachusetts. THE GRANGER COLLECTION

Allan Pinkerton, President Abraham Lincoln, and Major General John A. McClernand. Photographed at Antietam, Maryland, on Oct. 3, 1862, by Alexander Gardner. THE GRANGER COLLECTION

Gettysburg, July 1-3, 1863. Some of the dead of the 24th Michigan Infantry Regiment, which lost 80 percent of its men. Photographed by Timothy O'Sullivan. THE GRANGER COLLECTION

Ulysses S. Grant, appointed General-in-Chief of the Union Armies in 1863. Steel engraving by William E. Marshall.

Robert E. Lee, General-in-Chief of the Confederate Armies.

Horace Greeley. American journalist and political leader. Photographed in 1872 by Napoleon Sarony. THE GRANGER COLLECTION

Stephen Arnold Douglas, presidential candidate against Lincoln. Photocopy of a daguerreotype by Mathew Brady. THE GRANGER COLLECTION

(Above) Harpers Ferry, looking south. (Below) A scene from the Battle of Fredericksburg, December, 1862. A Confederate force of 75,000 shattered a Union army of 113,000 under the command of General Burnside.

(Above) Libby Prison, Richmond. (Below) Andersonville Prison, Georgia.
THE GRANGER COLLECTION

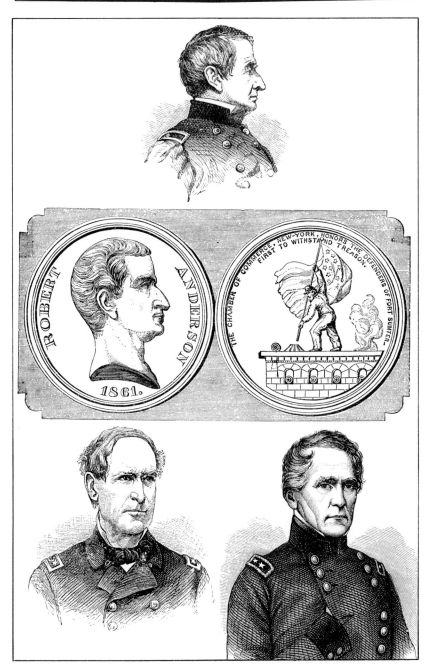

(Above) Robert Anderson, Major General, USA, in command of Fort Sumter.
(Center) Fort Sumter Medal. (Bottom, left) David Glasgow Farragut, Vice-Admiral, USN. (Bottom, right) John Ellis Wool, Major General, USA.

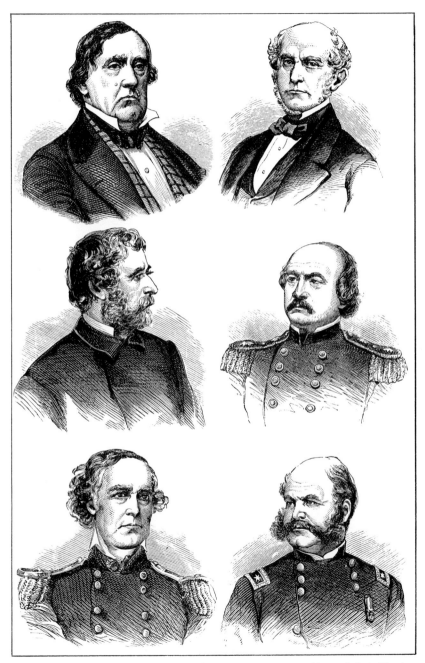

(Top, left) Lewis Cass, Secretary of State, 1857-1860. (Top, right) Charles Francis Adams, U.S. Minister to England, 1861-1868. (Center, left) John Charles Frémont, Major General, USA. (Center, right) Benjamin Franklin Butler, Major General, USA. (Bottom, left) Samuel Ryan Curtis, Major General, USA. (Bottom, right) Ambrose Everett Burnside, Major General, USA.

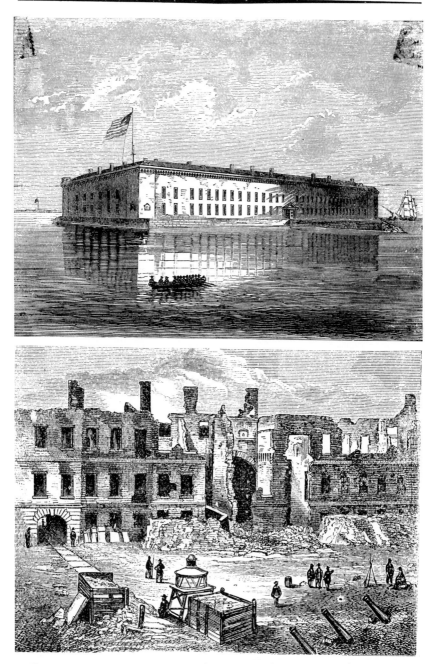

(Above) Fort Sumter in 1860. (Below) Internal appearance of Fort Sumter after the bombardment. PICTURE COLLECTION NYPL

From letter to Friedrich Adolph Sorge (*in Hoboken*)
LONDON, OCTOBER 19, 1877

. . . Apropos. A few years (not many) ago there appeared a sort of Blue Book (I don't know whether official or not) on the conditions of the miners in Pennsylvania,[1] who, as is well known, live in the most feudal dependence upon their moneylords (I believe the thing was published after a bloody conflict[2]). It is of the highest importance for me to have this publication, and if you can get it for me I shall send you the cost; if not, perhaps you can get me the title, and I will then turn to Harney (in Boston).

From letter written in English to Nicolai Frantzevich Danielson (*in Petersburg*)
LONDON, APRIL 10, 1879

Dear Sir:

. . . In regard to your most remarkable letter[1] I shall confine myself to a few observations. The railways sprang up first as the *couronnement de l'œuvre* [crowning work] in those countries where modern industry was most developed, England, United States, Belgium, France, etc. I call them "*couronnement de l'œuvre*" not only in the sense that they were at last (together with steamships for oceanic intercourse and the telegraphs) the means of communication adequate to the modern means of production, but also in so far as they were the basis of the immense joint stock companies, forming at the same time a new starting point for all other sorts of joint stock companies, to commence with banking companies. They gave in one word an impetus never before suspected to the *concentration of capital* and also to the accelerated and immensely enlarged *cosmopolitan activity of loanable capital*, thus embracing the whole world in a network of financial swindling and mutual indebtedness, the capitalistic form of "international" brotherhood.

On the other hand, the appearance of the railroad system in the

---

1. In August, 1878, after a long search, Sorge sent Marx the publication he requested: "Annual Report of the Secretary of Internal Affairs of the Commonwealth of Pennsylvania, for 1876–1877."

2. The Pennsylvania coal miners' strike, which lasted from the end of 1874 to mid-1875.

---

1. Of March 5, 1879. A month earlier, on February 5, Danielson had sent Marx a number of rare books on Russian finances and economics.

leading countries of capitalism allowed, and even forced, states where
capitalism was confined to a few summits of society suddenly to create
and enlarge their capitalistic superstructure in dimensions altogether
disproportionate to the bulk of the social body carrying on the great
work of production in the traditional modes. There is therefore not
the least doubt that in those states the railway's creation has accelerated
the social and political disintegration, as in the more advanced states
it hastened the final development and therefore the final change, of
capitalistic production. In all states except England the governments
enriched and fostered the railway companies at the expense of the
public exchequer. In the United States, to their profit, they received
a great part of the public land as a present, not only the land necessary
for the construction of the lines but many miles of land along both
sides of the lines, covered with forests, etc. So they become the greatest
landlords, the small immigrating farmers preferring of course land so
situated as to ensure their produce ready means of transport.

The system inaugurated in France by Louis Philippe, of handing
over the railways to a small band of financial aristocrats, endowing
them with long terms of possession, guaranteeing the interest out of the
public pocket, etc., etc., was pushed to the utmost limit by Louis
Bonaparte, whose regime, in fact, was essentially based upon the traf-
fick in railway concessions. . . .

It is, to conclude my letter with this (since the time for putting
it in the post draws nearer and nearer), impossible to find real analo-
gies between the United States and Russia. In the former the expenses
of the government diminish daily and its public debt is quickly and
yearly reduced; in the latter public bankruptcy is a goal more and
more appearing to become unavoidable. The former has freed itself
(although in a most infamous way, for the advantage of the creditors
and at the expense of the *menu peuple* [small people]) of its paper
money, the latter has no more flourishing fabric than that of paper
money. In the former the concentration of capital and the gradual
expropriation of the masses is not only the vehicle, but also the natural
offspring (though artificially accelerated by the Civil War), of an
unprecedented rapid industrial development, agricultural progress, etc.;
the latter reminds you rather of the time of Louis XIV and Louis
XV, where the financial, commercial, industrial superstructure, or
rather the *façades* of the social edifices, looked (although they had a
much more solid foundation than in Russia) like a satyr upon the stagnant state of the bulk of production (the agricultural one) and the
famine of the producers. The United States has at present overtaken
England in the rapidity of economic progress, though it still lags behind in the extent of acquired wealth; but at the same time the masses
are quicker, and have great political means in their hands, to resent the

form of a progress accomplished at their expense. I need not prolong antithesis.

Apropos. Which do you consider the best Russian work on credit and banking? . . .

Your devoted

A. WILLIAMS[2]

From postscript to letter to Engels (in Eastbourne)
RAMSGATE, AUGUST 25, 1879

The chief of the Massachusetts Labor Statistics Bureau, Wright, sent me all the Reports from 1874–1879 (thus not knowing about Harney's previous shipments), together with a compendium of the Massachusetts census, informing me at the same time that he "shall be pleased in future to send you our publications as soon as issued."[1]

Such "decent items" are arriving only from Russia and the United States.

My old patron Dana called last Friday at Maitland Park.[2] Tussy[3] sent me his card.

From letter to Friedrich Adolph Sorge (in Hoboken)
LONDON, SEPTEMBER 19, 1879

Dear Friend:

. . . Of American journals, I receive only the by no means weighty *Paterson Labor Standard*. I received, with thanks, your last shipments, the Labor Bureau statistics of Pennsylvania, Ohio, and Massachusetts (also [Ira] Steward's speech). I am pleased that the chief of the Massachusetts bureau informed me by letter that henceforth he will be sending me the publications (also the census) directly upon their appearance. . . .

Your devoted

KARL MARX

---

2. A cover name that Marx often used, especially in correspondence likely to be opened by European secret police.

1. Marx wrote the quoted words in English.
2. Marx's London address.
3. Marx's daughter Eleanor.

From letter written in English to Nicolai Frantzevich Danielson
(in St. Petersburg)
LONDON, FEBRUARY 19, 1881

Dear Sir:

 . . . In the United States the railway kings have become the butt of attacks, not only, as before this, on the part of the farmers and other industrial *"entrepreneurs"* of the West, but also on the part of the grand representatives of commerce—the New York Chamber of Commerce. The Octopodus railway king and financial swindler Gould has, on his side, told the New York commercial magnates: You now attack the railways because you think them most vulnerable considering their present unpopularity; but take heed: after the railways *every sort of corporation* (it means in the Yankee dialect, joint stock company) will have its turn; then, later on, all forms of associated capital; finally *all forms of capital;* you are thus paving the way to—*communism*, whose tendencies are already more and more spreading among the people. M. Gould *"a le flair bon"* ["has a good scent"]. . . .

Your devoted
KARL MARX

From first draft of letter written in French to Vera Ivanovna Sassulitch
LONDON, MARCH, 1881

 . . . Another favorable circumstance for the preservation of the Russian commune (in its development) is that it is not only contemporary with capitalist production and has outlasted the period when that system of society still showed itself to be intact, but also that today that system, in Western Europe as well as in the United States, finds itself in conflict with science, with the masses of the people, and with the forces of production it engenders. In a word, it [the Russian commune] finds capitalism in a crisis, which will end only with its abolition, with the return of modern societies to the "archaic" type of communal ownership, or, as an American author,[1] who is in no way suspect as harboring revolutionary tendencies but who is supported in his researches by the government in Washington, says—the new system toward which modern society is tending "will be a revival of the

---

1. Lewis Henry Morgan.

archaic societal type in a superior form." One should not be frightened overmuch by the word "archaic."

Letter written in English to John Swinton (in New York)
LONDON, JUNE 2, 1881

Dear Mr. Swinton:

I need hardly recommend you the bearer of these lines, my excellent friend Mr. Hartmann. I send you through him a photogram of mine; it is rather bad, but the only one left to me.

As to the book of Mr. Henry George,[1] I consider it as a last attempt to save the capitalistic regime. Of course this is not the meaning of the author, but the older disciples of Ricardo—the radical ones— fancied already that by the public appropriation of the rent of land everything would be righted. I have referred to this doctrine in the *Misère de la Philosophie* [*Poverty of Philosophy*] (published in 1847, against Proudhon).

Mrs. Marx sends you her best compliments. Unfortunately her illness assumes more and more a fatal character.

> *Believe me, dear sir,*
> *Yours most sincerely,*
>
> KARL MARX

From letter to Friedrich Adolph Sorge (in Hoboken)*
LONDON, JUNE 20, 1881

Dear Sorge:

. . . Before I received your copy of Henry George I had received two others, one from Swinton and one from Willard Brown; I therefore gave one to Engels and one to Lafargue. Today I must confine myself to a very brief formulation of my opinion of the book. In theory, the man is totally *arrière* [backward]. He understands nothing about the nature of surplus value, and so he wanders about in speculations that follow the English pattern, but are even behind the English in the portions on surplus value that have attained independent existence, that is, the relationship of profit, rent, interest, etc. His

---

1. *Progress and Poverty* (New York, 1880).
* The original is in the New York Public Library, Manuscript Division.

fundamental dogma is that everything would be all right if land rent
were paid to the state. (You will also find payment of this kind among
the transitional measures included in the *Communist Manifesto*.) This
idea originally belonged to the bourgeois economists; it was first put
forward (apart from a similar demand at the end of the eighteenth
century) by the earliest radical disciples of Ricardo, just after his
death. I said of it in 1847, in my book against Proudhon:[1] "We understand such economists as Mill (the elder, not his son John Stuart, who
also repeats this in a somewhat modified form), Cherbuliez, Hilditch,
and others demanding that rent should be handed over to the state to
serve in place of taxes. That is a frank expression of the hate the *industrial capitalist* bears toward the *landed proprietor*, who seems to him
a useless thing, an excrescence on the total body of bourgeois production."[2]

We ourselves, as I have already indicated, adopted this appropriation of land rent by the state among numerous other transitional
measures, which, as is likewise stated in the *Manifesto*, are and must
be self-contradictory.

But the first one to turn this desideratum of the radical English
bourgeois economists into the socialist panacea, to explain this procedure as the solution of the antagonisms inherent in the present mode
of production, was Colins, a Belgian-born ex-officer of Napoleon's
Hussars, who in the latter days of Guizot and the early days of
Napoleon the Little [Napoleon III] favored the world with fat tomes
from Paris about this "discovery" of his, which is like his other discovery,
namely, that even if there is no God, there is an "immortal" human
soul and that animals have "no feelings." For if they had feelings, that
is, souls, we would be cannibals and a kingdom of righteousness could
never be established on earth. His "antilandownership theory," together with his theory of the soul, etc., has been preached monthly for
years in the Paris *Philosophie de l'Avenir*[3] by his few remaining
followers, mostly Belgians. They call themselves "*collectivistes ra-
tionnels*" ["rational collectivists"], and have praised Henry George.

After them, and along with them, among others, the Prussian
banker and former lottery collector Samter from East Prussia, a block-
head, spun out this "socialism" in a fat tome.[4]

All these "socialists" since Colins have this in common, that they
leave *wage labor*, and thus *capitalist production*, untouched, and de-

---

1. *The Poverty of Philosophy*.
2. The quoted sentences were written in French.
3. *La Philosophie de l'Avenir. Revue du socialisme rationnel*, appeared monthly
from 1875 to 1900.
4. Adolph Samter, *Social-Lehre. Ueber die Befriedigung der Bedürfnisse in der
menschlichen Gesellschaft* [Social Doctrine. Concerning the Satisfaction of Needs
in Human Society] (Leipzig, 1875).

ceive themselves or the world into believing that through the transformation of land rents into a state tax, all the evils of capitalist production would disappear by themselves. The whole thing is thus merely a socialistically embellished attempt to save the capitalist rule, and, indeed, to establish it anew on an even wider basis than the present one.

This cloven hoof which is at the same time an ass's hoof, also unmistakably peeps out of the declarations of Henry George. It is the more unforgivable in him, since he, on the contrary, should have asked the question: How did it happen that in the United States, where relatively—that is, compared to civilized Europe—land was accessible to the great masses of the people and to a certain degree (again relatively) still is, the capitalist economy and the corresponding enslavement of the working class have developed more *rapidly* and more *shamelessly* than in any other country?

On the other hand, George's book, like the sensation it has made among you, has importance in that it is a first, even though disappointing, attempt at emancipation from orthodox political economy.

Moreover, H. George does not seem to know about the earlier *American* Anti-Renters,[5] who were more practical than theoretical. He is otherwise a writer of talent (with a Yankee talent for advertising too), as, for example, is shown by his article on California in the *Atlantic*.[6] He also has the repulsive presumption and arrogance that invariably characterize all such panacea-hatchers. . . .

Salut fraternel.

Yours,

K. MARX

---

5. A tenant-farmer movement of the 1840s.
6. The reference is probably to George's article, "The Kearney Agitation in California," in the *Popular Science Monthly*, August, 1880.

THE CIVIL WAR

The American Question in England*

September 18, 1861

M RS. BEECHER STOWE's letter to Lord Shaftesbury, whatever its intrinsic merit may be, has done a great deal of good by forcing the anti-Northern organs of the London press to speak out and lay before the general public the ostensible reasons for their hostile tone against the North and their ill-concealed sympathies with the South, which looks rather strange on the part of people affecting an utter horror of slavery. Their first main grievance is that the present American war is "not one for the abolition of slavery," and that therefore the high-minded Britisher, used to undertake wars of his own and interest himself in other people's wars only on the basis of "broad humanitarian principles," cannot be expected to feel any sympathy with his Northern cousins. "In the first place," says the *Economist*, "the assumption that the quarrel between the North and South is a quarrel between Negro freedom on the one side and Negro slavery on the other is as impudent as it is untrue." "The North," says the *Saturday Review*, "does not proclaim Abolition, and never pretended to fight for antislavery. The North has not hoisted for its oriflamme the sacred symbol of justice to the Negro; its *cri de guerre* is not unconditional abolition." "If," says the *Examiner*, "we have been deceived about the real significance of the sublime movement, who but the Federalists themselves have to answer for the deception?"

Now in the first instance, the premise must be conceded. The war has not been undertaken with a view to put down slavery, and the United States authorities themselves have taken the greatest pains to protest against any such idea. But then, it ought to be remembered that it was not the North, but the South, which undertook this war; the former acting only on the defense. If it be true that the North, after

* Published in the *New-York Daily Tribune* October 11, 1861.

[53]

long hesitations and an exhibition of forbearance unknown in the annals of European history, drew at last the sword, not for crushing slavery, but for saving the Union, the South, on its part, inaugurated the war by loudly proclaiming "the peculiar institution" as the only and main end of the rebellion. It confessed to fight for the liberty of enslaving other people, a liberty which, despite the Northern protests, it asserted to be put in danger by the victory of the Republican party and the election of Mr. Lincoln to the presidential chair. The Confederate Congress boasted that its newfangled Constitution, as distinguished from the Constitution of the Washingtons, Jeffersons, and Adamses, had recognized for the first time slavery as a thing good in itself, a bulwark of civilization, and a divine institution. If the North professed to fight but for the Union, the South gloried in rebellion for the supremacy of slavery. If antislavery and idealistic England felt not attracted by the profession of the North, how came it to pass that it was not violently repulsed by the cynical confessions of the South?

The *Saturday Review* helps itself out of this ugly dilemma by disbelieving the declarations of the seceders themselves. It sees deeper than this, and discovers "that slavery had very little to do with secession," the declarations of Jeff Davis and company to the contrary being mere "conventionalisms" with "about as much meaning as the conventionalisms about violated altars and desecrated hearths, which always occur in such proclamations."

The staple of argument on the part of the anti-Northern papers is very scanty, and throughout all of them we find almost the same sentences recurring, like the formulas of a mathematical series, at certain intervals, with very little art of variation or combination. "Why," exclaims the *Economist*, "it is only yesterday, when the secession movement first gained serious head, on the first announcement of Mr. Lincoln's election, that the Northerners offered to the South, if they would remain in the Union, every conceivable security for the performance and inviolability of the obnoxious institution—that they disavowed in the most solemn manner all intention of interfering with it— that their leaders proposed compromise after compromise in Congress, all based upon the concession that slavery should not be meddled with." "How happens it," says the *Examiner*, "that the North was ready to compromise matters by the largest concessions to the South as to slavery? How was it that a certain geographical line was proposed in Congress within which slavery was to be recognized as an essential institution? The Southern states were not content with this."

What the *Economist* and the *Examiner* had to ask was not only why the Crittenden and other compromise measures were *proposed* in Congress, but why they were not *passed*. They affect to consider those compromise proposals as accepted by the North and rejected by the

South, while, in point of fact, they were baffled by the Northern party that had carried the Lincoln election. Proposals never matured into resolutions, but always remaining in the embryo of *pia desideria*, the South had, of course, never any occasion either of rejecting or acquiescing. We come nearer to the pith of the question by the following remark of the *Examiner:* "Mrs. Stowe says, 'The slave party, finding they could no longer use the Union for their purposes, resolved to destroy it.' There is here an admission that up to that time the slave party had used the Union for their purposes, and it would have been well if Mrs. Stowe could have distinctly shown where it was that the North began to make its stand against slavery."

One might suppose that the *Examiner* and the other oracles of public opinion in England had made themselves sufficiently familiar with contemporaneous history to not need Mrs. Stowe's information on such all-important points. The progressive abuse of the Union by the slave power, working through its alliance with the Northern Democratic party, is, so to say, the general formula of United States history since the beginning of this century. The successive compromise measures mark the successive degrees of the encroachment by which the Union became more and more transformed into the slave of the slaveowner. Each of these compromises denotes a new encroachment of the South, a new concession of the North. At the same time none of the successive victories of the South was carried but after a hot contest with an antagonistic force in the North, appearing under different party names with different watchwords and under different colors. If the positive and final result of each single contest told in favor of the South, the attentive observer of history could not but see that every new advance of the slave power was a step forward to its ultimate defeat. Even at the time of the Missouri Compromise the contending forces were so evenly balanced that Jefferson, as we see from his memoirs, apprehended the Union to be in danger of splitting on that deadly antagonism. The encroachments of the slaveholding power reached their maximum point when, by the Kansas-Nebraska Bill, for the first time in the history of the United States, as Mr. Douglas himself confessed, every legal barrier to the diffusion of slavery within the United States territories was broken down; when afterward a Northern candidate [James Buchanan] bought his presidential nomination by pledging the Union to conquer or purchase in Cuba a new field of dominion for the slaveholder; when later on, by the Dred Scott decision, diffusion of slavery by the federal power was proclaimed as the law of the American Constitution, and lastly, when the African slave trade was *de facto* reopened on a larger scale than during the times of its legal existence. But concurrently with this climax of Southern encroachments, carried by the connivance of the Northern Democratic party, there were unmistakable signs of Northern antagonistic agencies having gathered such strength as must soon turn the balance of power. The Kansas war, the formation of the Republican party, and the large vote cast for Mr. Frémont during the presidential election of 1856, were so many palpable proofs that the North had accumulated sufficient energies to rectify the aberrations which United States history, under the slaveowners' pressure, had undergone for half a century, and to make it return to the true principles of its development. Apart from those political phenomena, there was one broad statistical and economical fact indicating that the abuse of the Federal Union by the slave interest had approached the point from which it would have to recede forcibly or *de bonne grâce* [with good grace]. That fact was the growth of the Northwest, the immense strides its population had made from 1850 to 1860, and the new and reinvigorating influence it could not but bear on the destinies of the United States.

Now was all this a secret chapter of history? Was "the admission" of Mrs. Beecher Stowe wanted to reveal to the *Examiner* and the other political *illuminati* of the London press the carefully hidden truth that "up to that time the slave party had used the Union for their purposes"? Is it the fault of the American North that the English pressmen were taken quite unawares by the violent clash of the antagonistic forces, the friction of which was the moving power of its history for half a century? Is it the fault of the Americans that the English press mistake for the fanciful crotchet hatched in a single day what was in the reality the matured result of long years of struggle? The very fact that the formation and the progress of the Republican party in America have hardly been noticed by the London press speaks volumes as to the hollowness of its antislavery tirades. Take, for instance, the two antipodes of the London press, the London *Times* and *Reynolds' Weekly Newspaper,* the one the great organ of the respectable classes, and the other the only remaining organ of the working class. The former, not long before Mr. Buchanan's career drew to an end, published an elaborate apology for his administration and a defamatory libel against the Republican movement. Reynolds, on his part, was, during Mr. Buchanan's stay at London, one of his minions, and since that time never missed an occasion to write him up and to write his adversaries down. How did it come to pass that the Republican party, whose platform was drawn up on the avowed antagonism to the encroachments of the slavocracy and the abuse of the Union by the slave interest, carried the day in the North? How, in the second instance, did it come to pass that the great bulk of the Northern Democratic party, flinging aside its old connections with the leaders of slavocracy, setting at naught its traditions of half a century, sacrificing great commercial interests and greater political prejudices, rushed to the support of the present Republican administration and offered it men and money with an unsparing hand?

Instead of answering these questions the *Economist* exclaims: "Can we forget that Abolitionists have habitually been as ferociously persecuted and maltreated in the North and West as in the South? Can it be denied that the testiness and halfheartedness, not to say insincerity, of the government at Washington have for years supplied the chief impediment which has thwarted our efforts for the effectual suppression of the slave trade on the coast of Africa; while a vast proportion of the clippers actually engaged in that trade have been built with Northern capital, owned by Northern merchants and manned by Northern seamen?"

This is, in fact, a masterly piece of logic. Antislavery England cannot sympathize with the North breaking down the withering influence of slavocracy, because she cannot forget that the North, while bound by that influence, supported the slave trade, mobbed the Abolitionists, and had its democratic institutions tainted by the slavedriver's prejudices. She cannot sympathize with Mr. Lincoln's administration because she had to find fault with Mr. Buchanan's administration. She must needs sullenly cavil at the present movement of the Northern resurrection, cheer up the Northern sympathizers with the slave trade, branded in the Republican platform, and coquet with the Southern slavocracy, setting up an empire of its own, because she cannot forget that the North of yesterday was not the North of today. The necessity of justifying its attitude by such pettifogging Old Bailey pleas proves more than anything else that the anti-Northern part of the English press is instigated by hidden motives, too mean and dastardly to be openly avowed.

As it is one of its pet maneuvers to taunt the present Republican administration with the doings of its proslavery predecessors, so it tries hard to persuade the English people that the *New York Herald* ought to be considered the only authentic expositor of Northern opinion. The London *Times* having given out the cue in this direction the *servum pecus* [slavish multitude] of the other anti-Northern organs, great and small, persist in beating the same bush.

So says the *Economist:* "In the light of the strife, New York papers and New York politicians were not wanting who exhorted the combatants, now that they had large armies in the field, to employ them, not against each other, but against Great Britain—to compromise the internal quarrel, the slave question included, and invade the British territory without notice and with overwhelming force." The *Economist* knows perfectly well that the *New York Herald*'s efforts, which were eagerly supported by the London *Times*, at embroiling the United States into a war with England, only intended securing the success of secession and thwarting the movement of Northern regeneration.

Still there is one concession made by the anti-Northern English press. The *Saturday* [*Review*] snob tells us: "What was at issue in Lincoln's election, and what has precipitated the convulsion, was merely the limitation of the institution of slavery to states where that institution already exists." And the *Economist* remarks: "It is true enough that it was the aim of the Republican party which elected Mr. Lincoln to prevent slavery from spreading into the unsettled Territories. . . . It may be true that the success of the North, if complete and unconditional, would enable them to confine slavery within the fifteen states which have already adopted it, and might thus lead to its eventual extinction—though this is rather probable than certain."

In 1859, on the occasion of John Brown's Harpers Ferry expedition, the very same *Economist* published a series of elaborate articles with a view to prove that, by dint of an *economical law*, American slavery was doomed to gradual extinction from the moment it should be deprived of its power of expansion. That "economical law" was perfectly understood by the slavocracy. "In fifteen years more," said Toombs, "without a great increase in slave territory, either the slaves must be permitted to flee from the whites, or the whites must flee from the slaves." The limitation of slavery to its constitutional area, as proclaimed by the Republicans, was the distinct ground upon which the menace of secession was first uttered in the House of Representatives on December 19, 1859. Mr. Singleton (Mississippi) having asked Mr. Curtis (Iowa) if the Republican party would never let the South have another foot of slave territory while it remained in the Union, and Mr. Curtis having responded in the affirmative, Mr. Singleton said *this would dissolve the Union.* His advice to Mississippi was the sooner it got out of the Union the better—"gentlemen should recollect that Jefferson Davis led our forces in Mexico, and still he lives, perhaps to lead the Southern army." Quite apart from the *economical law* which makes the diffusion of slavery a vital condition for its maintenance within its constitutional areas, the leaders of the South had never deceived themselves as to the necessity for keeping up their *political* sway over the United States. John Calhoun, in the defense of his propositions to the Senate, stated distinctly on February 19, 1847, that the Senate was "the only balance of power left to the South in the government," and that the creation of new slave states had become necessary "for the retention of the equipoise of power in the Senate." Moreover, the oligarchy of the 300,000 slaveowners could not even maintain their sway at home save by constantly throwing out to their white plebeians the bait of prospective conquests within and without the frontiers of the United States. If, then, according to the oracles of the English press, the North had arrived at the fixed resolution of circumscribing slavery within its present limits, and of thus extinguishing it in a constitutional way, was this not sufficient to enlist the sympathies of antislavery England?

But the English Puritans seem indeed not to be contented save by an explicit Abolitionist war. "This," says the *Economist*, "therefore, not being a war for the emancipation of the Negro race, on what other ground can we be fairly called upon to sympathize so warmly with the Federal cause?" "There was a time," says the *Examiner*, "when our sympathies were with the North, thinking that it was really in earnest in making a stand against the encroachments of the slave states, and in adopting emancipation as a measure of justice to the black race."

However, in the very same number in which these papers tell us that they cannot sympathize with the North because its war is no Abolitionist war, we are informed that "the desperate expedient of proclaiming Negro emancipation and summoning the slaves to a general insurrection" is a thing "the mere conception of which is repulsive and dreadful," and that "a compromise" would be "far preferable to success purchased at such a cost and stained by such a crime."

Thus the English eagerness for the Abolitionist war is all cant. The cloven foot peeps out in the following sentences: "Lastly," says the *Economist*, "is the Morrill tariff a title to our gratitude and to our sympathy, or is the certainty that, in case of Northern triumph, that tariff should be extended over the whole republic a reason why we ought to be clamorously anxious for their success?" "The North Americans," says the *Examiner*, "are in earnest about nothing but a selfish protective tariff. . . . The Southern states were tired of being robbed of the fruits of their slave labor by the protective tariff of the North."

The *Examiner* and the *Economist* complement each other. The latter is honest enough to confess at last that with it and its followers sympathy is a mere question of tariff, while the former reduces the war between North and South to a tariff war, to a war between protection and free trade. The *Examiner* is perhaps not aware that even the South Carolina Nullifiers of 1832, as General Jackson testified, used protection only as a pretext for secession; but even the *Examiner* ought to know that the present rebellion did not wait upon the passing of the Morrill tariff for breaking out. In point of fact, the Southerners could not have been tired of being robbed of the fruits of their slave labor by the protective tariff of the North, considering that from 1846–61 a free trade tariff had obtained.

The *Spectator* characterizes in its last number the secret thought of some of the anti-Northern organs in the following striking manner:

What, then, do the anti-Northern organs really profess to think desirable, under the justification of this plea of deferring to the inexorable logic of facts? They argue that disunion is desirable, just because, as we have said, it is the only possible step to a conclusion of this "causeless and fratricidal strife"; and next, of course, only as an afterthought, and as a humble apology for Providence and "justification of the ways of God to man," now that the inevitable necessity stands revealed—for further reasons discovered as beautiful adaptations to the moral exigencies of the country, when once the issue is discerned. It is discovered that it will be very much for the advantage of the states to be dissolved into rival groups. They will mutually check each other's ambition; they will neutralize each other's power, and if ever England should get into a dispute with one or more of them, mere jealousy will bring the antagonistic groups to our aid. This will be, it is urged, a very wholesome state of things, for it will relieve us from anxiety and it will encourage political "competition," that great safeguard of honesty and purity, among the states themselves.

Such is the case—very gravely urged—of the numerous class of Southern sympathizers now springing up among us. Translated into English—and we grieve that an English argument on such a subject should be of a nature that requires translating—it means that we deplore the present great scale of this "fratricidal" war, because it may concentrate in one fearful spasm a series of chronic petty wars and passions and jealousies among groups of rival states in times to come. The real truth is, and this very un-English feeling distinctly discerns this truth, though it cloaks it in decent phrases, that rival groups of American states could not live together in peace or harmony. The chronic condition would be one of malignant hostility rising out of the very causes which have produced the present contest. It is asserted that the different groups of states have different tariff interests. These different tariff interests would be sources of constant petty wars if the states were once dissolved, and slavery, the root of all the strife, would be the spring of innumerable animosities, discords, and campaigns. No stable equilibrium could ever again be established among the rival states. And yet it is maintained that this long future of incessant strife is the providential solution of the great question now at issue, the only real reason why it is looked upon favorably being this, that whereas the present great-scale conflict may issue in a restored and stronger political unity, the alternative of infinitely multiplied small-scale quarrels will issue in a weak and divided continent, that England cannot fear.

Now we do not deny that the Americans themselves sowed the seeds of this petty and contemptible state of feeling by the unfriendly and bullying attitude they have so often manifested to England, but we do say that the state of feeling on our part is petty and contemptible. We see that in a deferred issue there is no hope of a deep and enduring tranquillity for America, that it means a decline and fall of the American nation into quarrelsome clans and tribes, and yet hold up our hands in horror at the present "fratricidal" strife because it holds out hopes of finality. We exhort them to look favorably on the indefinite future of small strifes, equally fratricidal and probably far more demoralizing, because the latter would draw out of our side the thorn of American rivalry.

The British Cotton Trade*

September 21, 1861

THE CONTINUAL RISE in the prices of raw cotton begins at last to seriously react upon the cotton factories, their consumption of cotton being now 25 percent less than the full consumption. This result has been brought about by a daily lessening rate of production, many mills working only four or three days per week, part of the machinery being stopped, both in those establishments where short time has been commenced and in those which are still running full time, and some mills being temporarily altogether closed. In some places, as at Blackburn, for instance, short time has been coupled with a reduction of wages. However, the short-time movement is only in its incipient state and we may predict with perfect security that some weeks later the trade will have generally resorted to three days' working per week, concurrently with a large stoppage of machinery in most establishments. On the whole, English manufacturers and merchants were extremely slow and reluctant in acknowledging the awkward position of their cotton supplies. "The whole of the last American crop," they said, "has long since been forwarded to Europe. The picking of the new crop has barely commenced. Not a bale of cotton could have reached us more than has reached us, even if the war and the blockade had never been heard of. The shipping season does not commence till far in November, and it is usually the end of December before any large exportations take place. Till then, it is of little consequence whether the cotton is retained on the plantations or is forwarded to the ports as fast as it is bagged. If the blockade ceases any time before the end of this year, the probability is that by March or April we shall have received just as full a supply of cotton as if the blockade had never been declared." In the innermost recesses of the mercantile mind

* Published in the *New-York Daily Tribune* October 14, 1861.

the notion was cherished that the whole American crisis, and consequently the blockade, would have ceased before the end of the year, or that Lord Palmerston would forcibly break through the blockade. The latter idea has been altogether abandoned, since, beside all other circumstances, Manchester became aware that two vast interests, the monetary interest, having sunk an immense capital in the industrial enterprises of Northern America, and the corn trade, relying on Northern America as its principal source of supply, would combine to check any unprovoked aggression on the part of the British Government. The hopes of the blockade being raised in due time for the requirements of Liverpool or Manchester, or the American war being wound up by a compromise with the secessionists, have given way before a feature hitherto unknown in the English cotton market, viz., American operations in cotton at Liverpool, partly on speculation, partly for reshipment to America. Consequently for the last two weeks the Liverpool cotton market has been feverishly excited, the speculative investments in cotton on the part of the Liverpool merchants being backed by speculative investments on the part of the Manchester and other manufacturers eager to provide themselves with stocks of raw material for the winter. The extent of the latter transactions is sufficiently shown by the fact that a considerable portion of the spare warehouse room in Manchester is already occupied by such stocks, and that throughout the week beginning with September 15 and ending with September 22, middling Americans[1] had increased ⅜ d. per pound and fair ones ⅝ d.

From the outbreak of the American war the prices of cotton were steadily rising, but the ruinous disproportion between the prices of the raw material and the prices of yarns and cloth was not declared until the last weeks of August. Till then, any serious decline in the prices of cotton manufactures which might have been anticipated from the considerable decrease of the American demand had been balanced by an accumulation of stocks in first hands, and by speculative consignments to China and India. Those Asiatic markets, however, were soon overdone. "Stocks," says the *Calcutta Price Current* of August 7, 1861, "are accumulating, the arrivals since our last being no less than 24,000,000 yards of plain cottons. Home advices show a continuation of shipments in excess of our requirements, and so long as this is the case, improvement cannot be looked for. . . . The Bombay market, also, has been greatly oversupplied." Some other circumstances contributed to contract the Indian market. The late famine in the northwestern provinces has been succeeded by the ravages of the cholera, while throughout lower Bengal an excessive fall of rain, laying the country under water, seriously damaged the rice crops. In letters from Calcutta which

---

1. Medium-quality cotton.

reached England last week, sales were reported giving a net return of
9¼ d. per pound for 40s twist, which cannot be bought at Manchester
for less than 11⅜ d., while sales of 4C-inch shirtings, compared with
present rates at Manchester, yield losses at 7½ d., 9d., and 12d. per
piece. In the China market, prices were also forced down by the accumulation of the stocks imported. Under these circumstances, the
demand for the British cotton manufactures decreasing, their prices
can, of course, not keep pace with the progressive rise in the price of
the raw material; but on the contrary the spinning, weaving, and printing of cotton must, in many instances, cease to pay the costs of production. Take, as an example, the following case, stated by one of the
greatest Manchester manufacturers, in reference to coarse spinning:

Sept. 17, 1860	Per lb.	Margin	Cost of Spinning per lb.
Cost of cotton	6¼ d.	4d.	3d.
16s warp sold for	10¼ d.	—	—
Profit, 1d. per lb.			
Sept. 17, 1861			
Cost of cotton	9d.	2d.	3½ d.
16s warp sold for	11d.	—	—
Loss, 1½ d. per lb.			

The consumption of Indian cotton is rapidly growing, and with a
further rise in prices the Indian supply will come forward at increasing
ratios; but still it remains impossible to change, at a few months' notice,
all the conditions of production and turn the current of commerce.
England pays now, in fact, the penalty for her protracted misrule of
that vast Indian empire. The two main obstacles she has now to grapple
with in her attempts at supplanting American cotton by Indian cotton
are the want of means of communication and transport throughout
India, and the miserable state of the Indian peasant, disabling him from
improving favorable circumstances. Both these difficulties the English
have themselves to thank for. English modern industry, in general, relied upon two pivots equally monstrous. The one was the potato as the
only means of feeding Ireland and a great part of the English working
class. This pivot was swept away by the potato disease and the subsequent Irish catastrophe. A larger basis for the reproduction and maintenance of the toiling millions had then to be adopted. The second
pivot of English industry was the slave-grown cotton of the United
States. The present American crisis forces them to enlarge their field
of supply and emancipate cotton from slave-breeding and slave-con-

suming oligarchies. As long as the English cotton manufacturers depended on slave-grown cotton, it could be truthfully asserted that they rested on a twofold slavery, the indirect slavery of the white man in England and the direct slavery of the black man on the other side of the Atlantic.

The London *Times* and Lord Palmerston*

October 5, 1861

. . . IF, THEN, the *Times* is able by misstatement and suppression thus to falsify public opinion in regard to events that happened but yesterday in the British House of Commons, its power of misstatements and suppression in regard to events occurring on a distant soil, as in the case of the American War, must, of course, be unbounded. If in treating of American affairs it has strained all its forces to exasperate the mutual feelings of the British and Americans, it did not do so from any sympathy with the British Cotton Lords nor out of regard for any real or supposed English interest. It simply executed the orders of its master [Palmerston]. From the altered tone of the London *Times* during the past week, we may, therefore, infer that Lord Palmerston is about to recede from the extremely hostile attitude he had assumed till now against the United States. In one of its today leaders, the *Times*, which for months had exalted the aggressive powers of the Secessionists, and expatiated upon the inability of the United States to cope with them, feels quite sure of the military superiority of the North. That this change of tone is dictated by the master becomes quite evident from the circumstances that other influential papers, known to be connected with Palmerston, have simultaneously veered round. One of them, the *Economist*, gives rather a broad hint to the public-opinion-mongers that the time has come for "carefully watching" their pretended "feelings toward the United States." The passage in the *Economist*[1] which I allude to, and which I think worth quoting as a proof of the new orders received by Palmerston's pressmen, runs thus:

> On one point we frankly avow that the Northerners have a right to complain, and on one point also we are bound to be more upon

* Published in the *New-York Daily Tribune* October 21, 1861.
1. The *Economist*, September 28, 1861.

our guard than perhaps we have uniformly been. Our leading journals have been too ready to quote and repeat as embodying the
sentiments and representing the politics of the United States, newspapers notorious at all times for their disreputable character and
little influence, and now more than suspected of being Secessionists,
at least, of sailing under false colors, and professing extreme Northern opinions, while writing in the interests and probably the pay of
the South. Few Englishmen can, for example, with any decent fair-
ness, pretend to regard the *New York Herald* as representing either
the character or views of the Northern section of the Republic.
Again: we ought to be very careful lest our just criticism of the
Unionists should degenerate by insensible gradation into approval
and defenses of the Secessionists. The tendency in all ordinary minds
to *partisanship* is very strong. Now, however warmly we may
resent much of the conduct and the language of the North, we
must never forget that the Secession of the South was forced on
with designs and inaugurated with proceedings which have our
heartiest and most rooted disapprobation. We, of course, must con-
demn the protective tariff of the Union as an oppressive and be-
nighted folly. Of course, we reciprocate the wish of the South for
low duties and unfettered trade. Of course, we are anxious that the
prosperity of States which produce so much raw material and want
so many manufactured goods should suffer no interruption or re-
verse. But, at the same time, it is impossible for us to lose sight of
the indisputable fact that the real aim and ultimate motive of secession was *not* to defend their right to hold slaves in their own
territory (which the Northerners were just as ready to concede as
they do claim), but to extend slavery over a vast, undefined district,
hitherto free from that curse, but into which the planters fancied
they might hereafter wish to spread. This object we have always
regarded as unwise, unrighteous and abhorrent. The state of society
introduced in the Southern States by the institution of domestic
servitude appears to English minds more and more detestable and
deplorable the more they know of it. And the Southerners should
be made aware that no pecuniary or commercial advantage which
this country might be supposed to derive from the extended cultivation of the virgin soils of the planting States, and the new Territories which they claim, will ever in the slightest degree modify our
views on these points, or interfere with the expression of those
views, or warp or hamper our action whenever action shall become
obligatory or fitting. It is believed that they (the Secessionists) still
entertain the extraordinary notion that by *starving* France and
England—by the loss and suffering anticipated as the consequences
of an entire privation of the American supply—they will compel
those Governments to interfere on their behalf, and force the
United States to abandon the blockade . . . There is not the remotest
chance that either Power would feel justified for a moment in pro-
jecting such an act of decided and unwarrantable hostility against

the United States . . . We are less dependent on the South than the South is upon us, as they will ere long begin to discover. We, therefore, pray them to believe that slavery, so long as it exists, must create more or less of a moral barrier between us, and that even tacit approval is as far from our thoughts as the impertinence of an open interference; that Lancashire is not England; and, for the honor and spirit of our manufacturing population be it said also, that even if it were, *Cotton would not be King*.

All I intended to show for the present was that Palmerston, and consequently the London press, working to his orders, is abandoning the hostile attitude against the United States. The causes that have led to this *revirement* [sudden change], as the French call it, I shall try to explain in a subsequent letter. Before concluding, I may still add that Mr. Forster, M.P. for Bradford, delivered last Tuesday [October 1], in the theatre of Bradford Mechanics' Institute, a lecture "On the Civil War in America," in which he traced the true origin and character of that war, and victoriously refuted the misstatements of the Palmerstonian press.

The North American Civil War*

October 20, 1861

FOR MONTHS the London press, weeklies and dailies, has repeated the same litany on the American Civil War. While it insults the free states of the North, it anxiously defends itself against the suspicion of sympathizing with the slave states of the South. In fact, it continually writes two articles: one in which it attacks the North, and another in which it excuses attacks on the North. *Qui s'excuse s'accuse.*

In essence, the extenuating arguments read: The war between the North and South is a tariff war. The war, furthermore, is not for any principle, does not touch the question of slavery, and in fact turns on the Northern desire for sovereignty. Finally, even if justice is on the side of the North, does it not remain a vain endeavor to try to subjugate eight million Anglo-Saxons by force! Would not the separation of the South release the North from all connection with Negro slavery and assure to it, with its twenty million inhabitants and its vast territory, a higher, hitherto scarcely dreamed of development? Hence must not the North welcome secession as a fortunate event, instead of wanting to put it down by a bloody and futile civil war?

We will examine the *plaidoyer* [speech for the defense] of the English press point by point.

The war between North and South—so runs the first excuse—is a mere tariff war, a war between a protection system and a free-trade system, and England naturally stands on the side of free trade. Should the slaveowner enjoy the fruits of slave labor in their entirety or should he be cheated of a portion of these by the protectionists of the North? That is the question which is at issue in this war. It was reserved for the *Times* to make this brilliant discovery. The *Economist*, the *Examiner*, the *Saturday Review*, and *tutti quanti* [all such] have expounded

---

* Published in *Die Presse*, Vienna, October 25, 1861.

[69]

the theme further. It is characteristic of this discovery that it was made, not in Charleston, but in London. In America, of course, everyone knew that from 1846 to 1861 a free-trade system prevailed, and that Representative Morrill put through his protectionist tariff in Congress only in 1861, after the rebellion had already broken out. Secession, therefore, did not take place because Congress passed the Morrill Tariff Act; at most, Congress passed the Morrill protective tariff because secession had taken place. When South Carolina committed her first act of secession in 1832, the protectionist tariff of 1828 served her, to be sure, as a pretext, but only as a pretext, as is known from a statement by General Jackson. This time, however, the old pretext has not been used again. In the Secession Congress at Montgomery all reference to the tariff question was avoided, because the cultivation of sugar in Louisiana, one of the most influential Southern states, depends entirely on the protective tariff.

But, the London press pleads further, the war in the United States is nothing but a war for the preservation of the Union by force. The Yankees cannot make up their minds to strike fifteen stars from their flag. They want to cut a colossal figure on the world stage. Yes, it would be different if the war were waged for the abolition of slavery! The question of slavery, however, as the *Saturday Review,* among others, categorically declares, has absolutely nothing to do with this war.

Above all, it is to be remembered that the war did not emanate from the North, but from the South. The North finds itself on the defensive. For months it had quietly looked on while the Secessionists appropriated to themselves the Union's forts, arsenals, shipyards, customs houses, pay offices, ships, and supplies of arms, insulted its flag, and took prisoner bodies of its troops. Finally the Secessionists resolved to force the Union government out of its passive attitude by a sensational act of war, and *solely for this reason* proceeded to the bombardment of Fort Sumter near Charleston. On April 11 [1861] their General Beauregard, in a parley with Major Anderson, the commander of Fort Sumter, had learned that the fort had supplies for only three days more and accordingly must be peacefully surrendered after this period. In order to forestall this peaceful surrender, the Secessionists opened the bombardment early on the following morning (April 12), which brought about the fall of the place in a few hours. Hardly had this news been telegraphed to Montgomery, the seat of the Secession Congress, when War Minister Walker publicly declared in the name of the new Confederacy: "No man can say where the war that opened today will end." At the same time he prophesied that "before the first of May the flag of the Southern Confederacy will wave from the dome of the old Capitol in Washington and within a short time perhaps also from Faneuil Hall in Boston." Only then ensued the Proclamation in which Lincoln summoned 75,000 men to protect the Union. The bombardment of Fort Sumter cut off the only possible constitutional way out, namely, the summoning of a general convention of the American people, as Lincoln had proposed in his Inaugural Address.[1] For Lincoln there remained only the choice of fleeing from Washington, evacuating Maryland and Delaware, and surrendering Kentucky, Missouri, and Virginia, or of answering war with war.

The question of the principle of the American Civil War is answered by the battle slogan with which the South broke the peace. Stephens, the Vice-President of the Southern Confederacy, declared in the Secession Congress that what essentially distinguished the Constitution newly hatched at Montgomery from the Constitution of Washington and Jefferson was that now for the first time slavery was recognized as an institution good in itself, and as the foundation of the whole state edifice, whereas the Revolutionary Fathers, men steeped in the prejudices of the eighteenth century, had treated slavery as an evil imported from England and to be eliminated in the course of time. Another matador of the South, Mr. Spratt, cried out: "For us it is a question of establishing a great slave republic." If, therefore, the North drew the sword only in defense of the Union, had not the South already declared that the continuation of slavery was no longer compatible with the continuation of the Union?

Just as the bombardment of Fort Sumter gave the signal for the opening of the war, so the election victory of the Republican party of the North, the election of Lincoln as President, gave the signal for secession. On November 6, 1860, Lincoln was elected. On November 8, 1860, it was telegraphed from South Carolina: "Secession is regarded here as an accomplished fact"; on November 10 the legislature of Georgia occupied itself with secession plans; and on November 15 a special session of the Mississippi legislature was called to take secession into consideration. But Lincoln's victory was itself only the result of a split in the *Democratic* camp. During the election struggle the Democrats of the North united their votes on Douglas, and the Democrats of the South on Breckinridge, and to this splitting of the Democratic votes the Republican party owed its victory. Whence came the preponderance of the Republican party in the North on the one hand?

---

1. First Inaugural Address, March 4, 1861: ". . . While I make no recommendation of amendments, I fully recognize the rightful authority of the people over the whole subject, to be exercised in either of the modes prescribed in the instrument [the Constitution] itself, and I should, under existing circumstances, favor rather than oppose a fair opportunity being afforded the people to act upon it. I will venture to add that to me the convention mode seems preferable. . . ."

Whence came, on the other hand, the split within the Democratic party, whose members, North and South, had operated unitedly for more than half a century?

Under the presidency of Buchanan, the sway that the South had gradually usurped over the Union through its alliance with the Northern Democrats attained its zenith. The last Continental Congress of 1787 and the first Constitutional Congress of 1789–90 had legally excluded slavery from all territories of the Republic northwest of the Ohio. (Territory, as is known, is the name given to the colonies lying within the United States itself that have not yet attained the population level constitutionally prescribed for becoming autonomous states.) The so-called Missouri Compromise (1820), in consequence of which Missouri entered the ranks of the United States as a slave state, excluded slavery from the rest of the area north of 36° 30′ latitude and west of Missouri. By this compromise the slavery area was increased by several degrees of longitude, while on the other hand a definite geographical line setting bounds to future propaganda for it seemed to be drawn. This geographical barrier, in its turn, was overthrown in 1854 by the so-called Kansas-Nebraska Bill, whose originator was Stephen A. Douglas, then leader of the Northern Democrats. The bill, which passed both houses of Congress, repealed the Missouri Compromise, placed slavery and freedom on the same footing, bade the Union government to treat them both with equal indifference, and left it to the sovereignty of the people, that is, the majority of the settlers, to decide whether or not slavery was to be introduced in a territory. Thus for the first time in the history of the United States every geographical and legal limit to the extension of slavery in the territories was removed. Under this new legislation the hitherto free Territory of New Mexico, a territory five times larger than the state of New York, was transformed into a slave territory, and the area of slavery was extended from the border of the Mexican Republic to 38° north latitude. In 1859 New Mexico received a slave code that vies with the statute books of Texas and Alabama in barbarism. Nevertheless, as the census of 1860 proves, among some 100,000 inhabitants New Mexico does not yet number half a hundred slaves. It had, therefore, sufficed for the South to send some adventurers with a few slaves across the border, and then, with the help of the central government, its officials and suppliers, to drum up in New Mexico a sham popular representation which imposed slavery on the territory, and with it the rule of the slaveholders.

However, this convenient method did not prove applicable in other territories. The South accordingly went one step further and appealed from Congress to the Supreme Court of the United States. This Supreme Court, which numbers nine judges, five of whom belong to the South,[2] had long been the most willing tool of the slaveholders. It decided in 1857, in the notorious Dred Scott case, that every American citizen possesses the right to take with him into any territory any property recognized by the Constitution. The Constitution recognizes slaves as property and obliges the Union government to protect this property. Hence, on the basis of the Constitution, slaves could be forced by their owners to labor in the territories, and so every individual slaveholder is entitled to introduce slavery into hitherto free territories against the will of the majority of the settlers. The right to exclude slavery was taken from the territorial legislatures, and the duty to protect the pioneers of the slave system was imposed on Congress, as well as on the Union government.

If the Missouri Compromise of 1820 had further extended the geographical boundary line of slavery in the territories, if the Kansas-Nebraska Bill of 1854 had wiped out every geographical boundary line and replaced it with a political barrier—the will of the majority of the settlers, and also the Supreme Court of the United States by its decision of 1857, tore down even this political barrier and transformed all the territories of the Republic, present and future, from places for the cultivation of free states into places for the cultivation of slavery.

At the same time, the more severe law on the surrendering of fugitive slaves enacted under Buchanan's administration in 1850 was ruthlessly carried out in the states of the North. To play the part of slave catchers for the southern slaveholders, appeared to be the constitutional vocation of the North. On the other hand, in order to hinder the colonization of the territories by free settlers as much as possible, the slaveholders' party frustrated all the so-called Free-Soil measures, that is, measures which were to secure to the settlers a definite amount of uncultivated public land free of charge.

As in domestic affairs, so also in the foreign policy of the United States, the interest of the slaveholders served as the lodestar. Buchanan had in fact won the office of President with the issue of the Ostend Manifesto,[3] in which the acquisition of Cuba, whether by purchase or by force of arms, is proclaimed as the great aim of national policy. Under his administration Northern Mexico was divided up among American land speculators, who impatiently awaited the signal to

2. The five southern Justices were John A. Campbell, from Alabama; John Catron, from Tennessee; Peter V. Daniel, from Virginia; Roger B. Taney (Chief Justice), from Maryland; and James M. Wayne, from Georgia.

3. The Ostend Manifesto, drawn up at Ostend, Belgium, by James Buchanan, then U. S. Minister to Great Britain, on October 18, 1854, declared that the value of Cuba to the United States was such that the island might be taken by force, if necessary: ". . . Cuba is as necessary to the North American republic as any of its present members . . . We shall be justified in wresting it from Spain if we possess the power. . . ." The manifesto being widely denounced, it was repudiated by U. S. Secretary of State (1853–57) William L. Marcy.

attack Chihuahua, Coahuila, and Sonora. The restless, piratical expeditions of the filibusters against the states of Central America were no less directed from the White House in Washington. In the closest connection with this foreign policy, whose manifest purpose was conquest of new territory for the extension of slavery and the rule of the slaveholders, stood the *reopening of the slave trade*, secretly supported by the Union Government. Stephen A. Douglas himself declared in the American Senate on August 20, 1859, that during the last year more Negroes had been brought in from Africa than ever before in any single year, even at the time when the slave trade was still legal. The number of slaves imported in the last year amounted to 15,000.

Abroad, armed propaganda for slavery was the avowed aim of national policy; the Union had in fact become the slave of the 300,000 slaveholders who dominate the South. A series of compromises, which the South owed to its alliance with the Northern Democrats, had led to this result. On this alliance all the attempts, periodically repeated since 1817, to resist the ever increasing encroachments of the slaveholders had hitherto been frustrated. Finally there came a turning point.

The Kansas-Nebraska Bill, which wiped out the geographical boundary line of slavery and made its introduction into the new territories subject to the will of the majority of the settlers, had hardly gone through when armed emissaries of the slaveholders, border rabble from Missouri and Arkansas, with bowie knife in one hand and revolver in the other, fell upon Kansas and by the most unheard-of atrocities sought to drive the settlers from the territory they had colonized. These raids were supported by the central government in Washington. Hence a tremendous reaction. Throughout the North, but particularly in the Northwest, a relief organization was formed to support Kansas with men, arms, and money. Out of this relief organization arose the Republican party, which therefore owes its origin to the struggle for Kansas. After the attempt to transform Kansas into a slave territory by force of arms, the South sought to achieve the same result by way of political intrigues. Buchanan's administration in particular did its utmost to bring Kansas into the ranks of the United States as a *slave state*, with a slavery constitution imposed on it. Hence renewed struggle, this time conducted mainly in Congress at Washington. Even Stephen A. Douglas, the chief of the Northern Democrats, now (1857–58) entered the lists against the government and its southern allies, because imposition of a slave constitution would have been contrary to the principles of sovereignty of the settlers expressed in the Nebraska Bill of 1854. Douglas, Senator from Illinois, a northwestern state, would naturally have lost all his influence if he had wanted to concede to the South the right to steal by force of arms or acts of

Congress territories colonized by the North. Hence just as the struggle for Kansas called the Republican party into being, so at the same time it also occasioned the first split within the Democratic party itself.

The Republican party put forward its first platform for the presidential election in 1856. Although its candidate, John Frémont, was not victorious, the huge number of votes cast for him at least proved the rapid growth of the Party, especially in the Northwest.[4] In their second national presidential convention (May 17, 1860) the Republicans repeated their platform of 1856, enriched with a few additions. Its principal contents were the following: Not another foot of new territory is conceded to slavery. The filibustering policy abroad must cease. The reopening of the slave trade is stigmatized. Finally, Free-Soil laws are to be enacted for the furtherance of free colonization.

The decisively important point in this platform was that not a foot of new terrain was conceded to slavery; rather, the latter was to remain once and for all confined to the limits of the states where it already existed legally. Slavery was thus to be formally interned; but continuous expansion of territory and continuous extension of slavery beyond their old limits is a law of life for the slave states of the Union.

The cultivation of the southern export articles—cotton, tobacco, sugar, etc.—carried on by slaves, is remunerative only as long as it is conducted with large gangs of slaves, on a mass scale, and on wide expanses of a naturally fertile soil that requires only simple labor. Intensive cultivation, which depends less on fertility of the soil than on investment of capital, intelligence, and labor energy, is contrary to the nature of slavery. Hence the rapid transformation of states like Maryland and Virginia, which formerly employed slaves for the production of export articles, into states that bred slaves for export to the Deep South. Even in South Carolina, where the slaves form four-sevenths of the population, the cultivation of cotton has for years been almost completely stationary as a result of the exhaustion of the soil. Indeed, by force of circumstances South Carolina is already in part transformed into a slave-producing state, since it now sells slaves to the states of the extreme South and Southwest for four million dollars annually. As soon as this point is reached, the acquisition of new territories becomes necessary, so that one section of the slaveholders may provide new, fertile lands with slaves, and by this means a new market for slave breeding, and hence for slave selling, may be created for the section left behind. There is, for example, no doubt that without the acquisition of Louisiana, Missouri, and Arkansas by the United

---

4. In the presidential election of 1856, John C. Frémont received 1,341,028 popular votes, or 33 percent of the total. Of this number 559,864 votes were cast in Illinois, Indiana, Iowa, Michigan, Ohio, and Wisconsin—or 41.7 percent of the total in those six states.

States, slavery in Virginia and Maryland would long ago have been extinguished. In the Secessionist Congress at Montgomery, Senator Toombs, one of the spokesmen of the South, has strikingly formulated the economic law that demands the constant expansion of the territory of slavery.

"If," said he, "in fifteen years there is no great increase in slave territory, either the slaves will have to be allowed to flee from the whites, or the whites must flee from the slaves."

The representation of the individual states in the House of Representatives of the Congress depends, as is known, on the number of people constituting their respective populations. As the populations of the free states grow far more rapidly than those of the slave states, the number of northern representatives was bound to overtake that of the southern very rapidly. Accordingly, the real seat of the political power of the South is transferred more and more to the American Senate, where every state, be its population great or small, is represented by two senators. To maintain its influence in the Senate, and through the Senate its hegemony over the United States, the South, therefore, required a continual formation of new slave states. This, however, was possible only through conquest of foreign lands, as in the case of Texas, or through the transformation of the territories belonging to the United States first into slave territories and later into slave states, as in the case of Missouri, Arkansas, etc. John Calhoun, whom the slaveholders admire as their statesman par excellence, declared in the Senate as early as February 19, 1847, that the Senate alone placed a balance of power in the South's hands, that extension of the slave territory was necessary to preserve this equilibrium between South and North in the Senate, that the attempts of the South to create new slave States by force were therefore justified.

Finally, the number of actual slaveowners in the southern part of the Union amounts to no more than 300,000, a narrow oligarchy confronted by many millions of so-called "poor whites," whose numbers constantly grew through concentration of landed property and whose condition can best be compared to that of the Roman plebeians in the period of Rome's extreme decline. Only by the acquisition, and the prospect of acquisition, of new territories, as well as by filibustering expeditions, is it possible to square the interests of these "poor whites" with those of the slaveholders, to give their turbulent impulses for action an innocuous direction and, to tame them with the prospect of themselves one day becoming slaveholders.

A tight restriction of slavery within the old terrain was bound, therefore, according to economic law, to lead to its gradual extinction, to the annihilation, in the political sphere, of the hegemony that the slave states exercised through the Senate, and finally to expose the slaveholding oligarchy within its own states to threatening dangers from the "poor whites." With the principle that any further extension of slave territories was to be prohibited by law, the Republicans therefore attacked the rule of the slaveholders at its root. The Republican election victory was accordingly bound to lead to an open struggle between North and South. However, this election victory, as already mentioned, was itself determined by the split in the Democratic camp.

The Kansas struggle had already brought forth a split between the slave party and the Democrats of the North allied to it. With the presidential election of 1860, the same conflict now broke out again in a more general form. The Democrats of the North, with Douglas as their candidate, made the introduction of slavery into the territories dependent on the will of the majority of the settlers. The slaveholders' party, with Breckinridge as its candidate, maintained that the Constitution of the United States brings slavery legally in its train, which is what the Supreme Court had also declared: slavery, in and of itself, was already legal in all territories and required no special naturalization. Hence while the Republicans prohibited any increase of slave territories, the Southern party laid claim to all territories of the Republic as legally guaranteed domains. What, by way of example, they had attempted with regard to Kansas—to force slavery on a territory through the central government against the will of the settlers themselves—they now set up as law for all the territories of the Union. Such a concession lay outside the power of the Democratic leaders and would only have occasioned the desertion of their army to the Republican camp. On the other hand, Douglas' "squatters' sovereignty" could not satisfy the slaveholders' party. What it wanted to effect had to be effected within the next four years under the new President, could be effected only by means of the central government, and brooked no further delay. It did not escape the slaveholders that a new power had come into existence, the Northwest, whose population, having almost doubled between 1850 and 1860, was already quite equal to the white population of the slave states[5]—a power that was not inclined by tradition, temperament, or mode of life to let itself be dragged from compromise to compromise in the manner of the old northern states. The Union still had value to the South only insofar as it handed over federal power to it as a means of carrying out the slave policy. If not, then it was better to make the break now than to look on at the development of the Republican party and the upsurge of the Northwest for another four

---

5. The census of 1860 gave the twelve "East North Central" (Ohio, Indiana, Illinois, Michigan, Wisconsin) and "West North Central" (Minnesota, Iowa, Missouri, North Dakota, South Dakota, Nebraska, Kansas) states a combined population of 9,096,716. The seventeen "southern" states, including the border states and Texas, had a total population of 11,133,361.

years, and begin the struggle under more unfavorable conditions. The slaveholders' party, therefore, played *va banque* [on a single card]! When the Democrats of the North declined to continue playing the part of the "poor whites" of the South, the South procured Lincoln the victory by splitting the vote, and then used this victory as a pretext for drawing the sword from the scabbard.

The whole movement rested, and rests, as one sees, on the *slavery question*. Not in the sense of whether the slaves within the existing slave states should be directly emancipated or not, but whether the twenty million free men of the North should subordinate themselves any longer to an oligarchy of 300,000 slaveholders; whether the vast territories of the Republic should become planting grounds for free states or for slavery; finally, whether the national policy of the Union should take armed propaganda for slavery in Mexico and Central and South America as its motto.

In another article we will examine the assertion of the London press that the North must approve secession as the most favorable and only possible solution of the conflict.

The Crisis in England*

(*Ca.*) *November 1, 1861*

TODAY, as fifteen years ago, England faces a catastrophe that threatens
to strike at the root of her entire economic system. As is known, the
potato formed the exclusive food of Ireland and of a not inconsiderable
part of the English working people when the potato blight of 1845 and
1846 struck the root of Irish life with decay. The results of that great
catastrophe are also known. The Irish population declined by some
two million, of which one part starved to death and the other fled
across the Atlantic Ocean. At the same time this enormous misfortune
helped the English free-trade party to triumph; the English landed
aristocracy was compelled to sacrifice one of its most lucrative monopolies, and the abolition of the Corn Laws assured a broader and sounder
basis for the reproduction and maintenance of the working millions.

What the potato was to Irish agriculture, cotton is to the dominant
industrial branch of Great Britain. On its manufacture depends the
subsistence of a mass of people greater than the total number of inhabitants of Scotland and than two-thirds of the present number of
inhabitants of Ireland. For according to the census of 1861, the population of Scotland consisted of 3,061,117 persons and of Ireland still only
5,764,543, while more than four million in England and Scotland live
directly or indirectly by the cotton industry. Now the cotton plant is
not, indeed, sick. Just as little is its production the monopoly of a few
regions of the earth. On the contrary, no other plant that supplies
material for clothing thrives in equally extensive areas in America,
Asia, and Africa. The cotton monopoly of the slave states of the
American Union is not a natural, but a historical monopoly. It grew
and developed simultaneously with the monopoly of the English cotton
industry in the world market. In the year 1793, shortly after the

* Published in *Die Presse*, Vienna, November 6, 1861.

period of the great mechanical inventions in England, a Quaker in Connecticut, Eli Whitney, invented the cotton gin, a machine for cleaning cotton, separating the cotton fiber from the cotton seed. Before that invention, one day of a Negro's most strenuous labor hardly sufficed to separate a pound of cotton fiber from the cotton seed. After the invention of the cotton gin, an old Negro woman could comfortably supply fifty pounds of fiber daily, and gradual improvements have since doubled the efficiency of the machine. Now the fetters on cotton cultivation in the United States were splintered. Hand in hand with the English cotton industry, it grew swiftly into a great commercial power. In the course of development, England now and then seemed to take fright at the monopoly of American cotton, as at a specter that threatened danger. Such a moment occurred, for example, at the time when the emancipation of Negroes in the English colonies was purchased for £20,000,000. It was a matter of misgiving that the industry in Lancashire and Yorkshire should rest on the sovereignty of the slave whip in Georgia and Alabama, while the English nation imposed on itself such great sacrifices to abolish slavery in its own colonies. Philanthropy, however, does not make history, at least not commercial history. Similar misgivings arose whenever a cotton crop failure occurred in the United States, and when, moreover, such a natural phenomenon was exploited by the slaveholders, who combined to raise the price of cotton artificially. The English cotton spinners and weavers threatened rebellion against "King Cotton." Manifold projects for procuring cotton from Asian and African sources came to light. Thus, for example, 1850. However, the subsequent good crop in the United States triumphantly defeated such yearnings for emancipation. Indeed, during the past few years the American cotton monopoly has reached dimensions scarcely dreamed of before, partly in consequence of the free-trade legislation which repealed the hitherto existing differential tariff on the cotton grown by slaves; partly in consequence of the giant strides made simultaneously by the English cotton industry and American cotton cultivation during the last decade. In the year 1857 the consumption of cotton in England already amounted to nearly one and a half billion pounds.

Now, suddenly, the American Civil War threatens this great pillar of English industry. While the Union blockades the harbors of the southern states, in order to cut off the secessionists' chief source of income by preventing the export of their cotton crop this year, the Confederacy lends compelling force to this blockade with its decision not to export a bale of cotton of its own accord, but rather to force England to come and fetch her cotton from the southern harbors herself. England is to be driven to the point of forcibly breaking the blockade, of then declaring war on the Union, and thus of throwing her sword into the scale on the side of the slave states.

From the beginning of the American Civil War the price of cotton rose continuously, but for a considerable time to a smaller degree than was to be expected. On the whole, the English commercial world appeared to look on the American crisis very phlegmatically. The reason for this cold-blooded way of viewing things was unmistakable. The whole of the last American crop had gone to Europe long ago. The yield of a new crop is never shipped before the end of November, and this shipment rarely attains major dimensions before the end of December. Until then, therefore, it remained a matter of complete indifference whether the cotton bales were held back on the plantations or transported to the harbors of the South immediately after their baling. Should the blockade cease at any time before the end of the year, England could safely count on receiving her customary cotton imports in April or March, quite as if the blockade had never taken place. The English commercial world, largely misled by the English press, succumbed, however, to the delusion that a war spectacle of perhaps six months would end with recognition of the Confederacy by the United States. But at the end of August North Americans appeared in the Liverpool market to buy cotton, partly for speculation in Europe, partly for reshipment to North America. This unheard-of event opened the eyes of the English. They began to understand the seriousness of the situation. Since then the Liverpool cotton market has been in a state of feverish excitement. Cotton prices were soon driven 100 percent above their average level; the speculation in cotton assumed the same wild features that characterized the speculation in railways in 1845. The spinning and weaving mills in Lancashire and other seats of the British cotton industry cut their labor time to three days a week; parts of the mills stopped their machines altogether; the harmful reaction in other branches of industry was not wanting, and at this moment all of England trembles at the approach of the greatest economic catastrophe that has yet threatened her.

The consumption of Indian cotton is naturally increasing, and the rising prices will insure further increase of importation from the ancient home of cotton. Nevertheless, it remains impossible to revolutionize the conditions of production and the course of trade at a few months' notice, so to speak. England is, in fact, now expiating her long misrule of India. Her present spasmodic attempts to replace American cotton with Indian encounter two great obstacles: the lack of means of communication and transport in India, and the wretched condition of the Indian peasant, which prevents him from taking advantage of the momentarily favorable circumstances. But apart from this, apart from the process of refinement that Indian cotton still has to go through to take the place of American cotton, even under the most favorable circumstances it would require *years* before India could produce the requisite quantity of cotton for export. It is statistically established, however, that the stock of cotton in Liverpool will be exhausted in *four months*. It will last that long only if the limitation of labor time to three days a week continues, and if the complete stoppage of some of the machinery is carried out by the British cotton spinners and weavers to a still greater extent than hitherto. Such a procedure is already subjecting the factory districts to the greatest social sufferings. But if the American blockade continues beyond January! What then?

The London *Times* on the Orléans
Princes in America*

October 12, 1861

ON THE OCCASION of the King of Prussia's visit at Compiègne,[1] the London *Times* published some racy articles, giving great offense on the other side of the Channel. The *Pays, Journal de l'Empire,* in its turn characterized the *Times* writers as people whose heads were poisoned by gin, and whose pens were dipped into mud. Such occasional exchanges of invective are only intended to mislead public opinion as to the intimate relations connecting Printing House Square to the Tuileries. There exists beyond the French frontiers no greater sycophant of the Man of December [Napoleon III] than the London *Times,* and its services are the more invaluable the more that paper now and then assumes the tone and the air of a Cato censor toward its Caesar. The *Times* had for months heaped insult upon Prussia. Improving the miserable MacDonald affair, it had told Prussia that England would feel glad to see a transfer of the Rhenish provinces from the barbarous sway of the Hohenzollern to the enlightened despotism of a Bonaparte. It had not only exasperated the Prussian dynasty but the Prussian people. It had written down the idea of an Anglo-Prussian alliance in case of a Prussian conflict with France. It had strained all its powers to convince Prussia that she had nothing to hope from England, and that the next best thing she could do would be to come to some understanding with France. When at last the weak and trimming monarch of Prussia resolved upon the visit at Compiègne, the *Times* could proudly exclaim: *Quorum magna pars fui* [in which I had a large share], but now the time had also arrived for obliterating from the memory of the British the fact that the *Times* had been the pathfinder of the Prussian

---

* Published in the *New-York Daily Tribune* November 7, 1861.
1. October 6, 1861.

monarch. Hence the roar of its theatrical thunders. Hence the counter roars of the *Pays, Journal de l'Empire.*

The *Times* had now recovered its position of the deadly antagonist of Bonapartism, and therefore the power of lending its aid to the Man of December. An occasion soon offered. Louis Bonaparte is, of course, most touchy whenever the renown of rival pretenders to the French crown is concerned. He had covered himself with ridicule in the affair of the Duc d'Aumale's pamphlet against Plon-Plon,[2] and, by his proceedings, had done more in furtherance of the Orléanist case than all the Orléanist partisans combined. Again, in these latter days, the French people were called upon to draw a parallel between Plon-Plon and the Orléans princes. When Plon-Plon set out for America there were caricatures circulated in the Faubourg St. Antoine representing him as a fat man in search of a crown, but professing at the same time to be a most inoffensive traveler, with a peculiar aversion to the smell of powder. While Plon-Plon is returning to France with no more laurels than he gathered in the Crimea and in Italy, the Princes of Orléans cross the Atlantic to take service in the ranks of the national army.[3] Hence a great stir in the Bonapartist camp. It would not do to give vent to Bonapartist anger through the venal press of Paris. The imperialist fears would thus only be betrayed, the pamphlet scandal renewed, and odious comparisons provoked between exiled princes who fight under the republican banner against the enslavers of working millions, with another exiled prince, who had himself sworn in as an English special constable to share in the glory of putting down an English workingmen's movement.[4]

Who should extricate the Man of December out of his dilemma? Who but the London *Times?* If the same London *Times* which on the 6th, 8th, and 9th of October, 1861, had roused the furies of the *Pays, Journal de l'Empire,* by its rather cynical strictures on the visit at Compiègne—if that very same paper should come out on the 12th of October with a merciless onslaught on the Orléans princes because of their enlistment in the ranks of the national army of the United States, would Louis Bonaparte not have proved his case against the Orléans princes? Would the *Times* article not be done into French, commented upon by the Paris papers, sent by the *Préfet de Police* to all the journals of all the departments, and circulated throughout the whole of France, as the impartial sentence passed by the London *Times,* the personal foe of Louis Bonaparte, upon the last proceedings of the

2. The Duc d'Aumale was the son of King Louis Philippe. Plon-Plon was a nickname for Louis Bonaparte, Napoleon III.
3. Prince Joinville, the Duke of Penthièvre, the Count of Paris, and the Duke of Chartres all participated in the Civil War on the Northern side.
4. Louis Bonaparte helped put down the Chartists when he lived in London.

Orléans princes? Consequently the *Times* of today has come out with a most scurrilous onslaught on these princes.

Louis Bonaparte is, of course, too much of a businessman to share the judicial blindness in regard to the American war of the official public-opinion mongers. He knows that the true people of England, of France, of Germany, of Europe, consider the cause of the United States as their own cause, as the cause of liberty, and that, despite all paid sophistry they consider the soil of the United States as the free soil of the landless millions of Europe, as their land of promise, now to be defended sword in hand, from the sordid grasp of the slaveholder. Louis Napoleon knows, moreover, that in France the masses connect the fight for the maintenance of the Union with the fight of their forefathers for the foundation of American independence, and that with them every Frenchman drawing his sword for the national government appears only to execute the bequest of Lafayette. Bonaparte, therefore, knows that if anything is able to win the Orléans princes good opinions from the French people it will be their enlistment in the ranks of the national army of the United States. He shudders at this very notion, and consequently the London *Times*, his censorious sycophant, today tells the Orléans princes that "they will derive no increase of popularity with the French nation from stooping to serve on this ignoble field of action." Louis Napoleon knows that all the wars waged in Europe between hostile nations since his *coup d'état* [1851] have been mock wars, groundless, wanton, and carried on on false pretenses. The Russian [Crimean] war, and the Italian war [1859], not to speak of the piratical expeditions against China, Cochin China, and so forth, never enlisted the sympathies of the French people, instinctively aware that both wars were carried on only with the view to strengthening the chains forged by the *coup d'état*. The first grand war of contemporaneous history is the American war.

The people of Europe know that the Southern slavocracy commenced that war with the declaration that the continuance of slavocracy was no longer compatible with the continuance of the Union. Consequently the people of Europe know that a fight for the continuance of the Union is a fight against the continuance of the slavocracy —that in this contest the highest form of popular self-government till now realized is giving battle to the meanest and most shameless form of man's enslaving recorded in the annals of history.

Louis Bonaparte feels, of course, extremely sorry that the Orléans princes should embark in just such a war, so distinguished, by the vastness of its dimensions and the grandeur of its ends, from the groundless, wanton, and diminutive wars Europe has passed through since 1849. Consequently, the London *Times* must needs declare: "To overlook the difference between a war waged by hostile nations, and this most groundless and wanton civil conflict of which history gives us any account, is a species of offense against public morals."

The *Times* is, of course, bound to wind up its onslaught on the Orléans princes because of their "stooping to serve on such an ignoble field of action," with a deep bow before the victor of Sebastopol and Solferino. "It is unwise," says the London *Times*, "to challenge a comparison between such actions as Springfield and Manassas, and the exploits of Sebastopol and Solferino." The next mail will testify to the premeditated use made of the *Times* article by the imperialist organs. A friend in times of need is proverbially worth a thousand friends in times of prosperity, and the secret ally of the London *Times* is just now very badly off.

A dearth of cotton, backed by a dearth of grain; a commercial crisis coupled with an agricultural distress, and both of them combined with a reduction of customs revenues and a monetary embarrassment compelling the Bank of France to screw its rate of discount to 6 percent, to enter into transactions with Rothschilds and Baring for a loan of two millions sterling on the London market, to pawn abroad French government stock, and with all that to show but a reserve of 12,000,-000 against liabilities amounting to more than 40,000,000. Such a state of economical affairs prepares just the situation for rival pretenders to stake double. Already there have been bread riots in the Faubourg St. Antoine, and this of all times is therefore the most inappropriate time for allowing Orléans princes to catch popularity. Hence the fierce forward rush of the London *Times*.

The Civil War in the United States*

October, 1861

"LET HIM GO, he is not worth thy anger!" This advice of Leporello to Don Juan's deserted love, English statesmanship cries out again and again to the North of the United States—recently through the mouth of Lord John Russell. If the North lets the South go, it frees itself from all admixture with slavery, from its historical original sin, and creates the foundation for a new and higher development.

In reality, if North and South constituted two separate countries, like perhaps England and Hanover, their separation would then be no more difficult than was the separation of England and Hanover. But "the South" is neither a territory completely detached from the North geographically nor a moral unity. It is not a country at all, but a battle slogan.

The advice of an amicable separation presupposes that the Southern Confederacy, although it assumed the offensive in the Civil War, at least wages it for defensive purposes. It is believed that for the slave-holder's party the issue is merely one of uniting the territories it has hitherto dominated into an independent group of states and with-drawing from the sovereignty of the Union. Nothing could be more false. "*The South needs its whole territory*. It will and must have it." With this battle cry the Secessionists invaded Kentucky. By their "whole territory" they mean in the first place all the so-called border states—Delaware, Maryland, Virginia, North Carolina, Kentucky, Tennessee, Missouri, and Arkansas. In addition, they lay claim to all the territory south of the line that runs from the northwest corner of Missouri to the Pacific Ocean. Hence, what the slaveholders call the South embraces more than three-quarters of the territory hitherto

---

* Written in late October and published in *Die Presse*, Vienna, November 7, 1861.

[87]

comprised in the Union. A large part of the territory thus claimed is still in the possession of the Union and would first have to be conquered from it. None of the so-called border states, however, even those in the possession of the Confederacy now, has ever been an *actual slave state*. Rather, these states constitute that area of the United States in which the system of slavery and the system of free labor exist side by side and contend for mastery, the actual field of battle between South and North, between slavery and freedom. The war of the Southern Confederacy is thus not a war of defense, but a war of conquest, a war of conquest for the extension and perpetuation of slavery.

The mountain chain that begins in Alabama and stretches northward to the Hudson River—to some extent, the spinal column of the United States—cuts the so-called South into three parts. The mountainous country formed by the Allegheny Mountains with their two parallel ranges, the Cumberland Range to the west and the Blue [Ridge] Mountains to the east, is a wedgelike divide between the lowlands along the western shores of the Atlantic Ocean and the lowlands in the southern valleys of the Mississippi. The two lowland areas cut by the mountainous country, with their vast rice swamps and far-flung cotton plantations, are the actual area of slavery. The long wedge of mountainous country driven into the heart of slavery, with its correspondingly clear atmosphere, invigorating climate, and soil rich in coal, salt, limestone, iron ore, gold—in short, every raw material necessary for many-sided industrial development—is already for the most part free country. In accordance with its physical nature, the soil here can be cultivated successfully only by free small farmers. Here the slave system vegetates only sporadically, and has never struck roots. In the largest part of the so-called border states, the inhabitants of these highlands comprise the core of the free population, which in the interests of self-preservation already sides with the Northern party.

Let us consider the contested area in detail.

Delaware, the northeasternmost of the border states, is factually and morally in the possession of the Union. All attempts of the Secessionists to form even one party faction favorable to them have from the beginning of the war been frustrated by the unanimity of the population. The slave element of this state has long been in the process of expiring. From 1850 to 1860 alone the number of slaves diminished by half, so that with a total population of 112,218, Delaware now numbers merely 1,700 slaves. Nevertheless, Delaware is demanded by the Southern Confederacy and would, in fact, be militarily untenable for the North as soon as the South possessed itself of Maryland.

In Maryland itself the above-mentioned conflict between highland and lowland takes place. In a total population of 687,034, there are here 87,188 slaves. That the overwhelming majority of the population sides with the Union the recent general elections to the Congress in Washington have again strikingly proved. The army of 30,000 Union troops which occupies Maryland at the moment is not only to serve the Army of the Potomac as a reserve, but, in particular, is also to hold in check the rebellious slaveowners in the interior of the state. For here is manifested a phenomenon similar to what we see in other border states, where the great mass of the people stands for the North and a numerically insignificant slaveholders' party for the South. What it lacks in numbers the slaveholders' party makes up in the means of power that many years of possessing all State offices, hereditary pre-occupation with political intrigue, and concentration of great wealth in the hands of a few have secured for it.

Virginia now constitutes the great cantonment where the main army of Secession and the main army of the Union confront one another. In the northwest highlands of Virginia the mass of slaves amounts to 15,000, while the free population, which is twenty times larger, consists in its majority of independent farmers. The eastern lowlands of Virginia, on the other hand, have nearly half a million slaves. The principal source of income comes from breeding slaves for sale in the southern states. As soon as the ringleaders of the low-lands had put through the secession ordinance by intrigues in the state legislature at Richmond, and had in all haste opened the gates of Virginia to the Southern army, northwest Virginia seceded from the Secession, formed a new state, and under the banner of the Union now defends its territory, arms in hand, against the Southern invaders.

Tennessee, with 1,109,847 inhabitants, of whom 275,784 are slaves, finds itself in the hands of the Southern Confederacy, which has sub-jected the whole state to martial law and to a system of proscription that recalls the days of the Roman Triumvirate. In the winter of 1861, when the slaveholders proposed a general convention of the people to vote for or against secession, the majority of the people refused any convention, in order to cut off any pretext for the secession movement. Later, when Tennessee was already overrun militarily and subjected to a system of terror by the Southern Confederacy, more than a third of the voters at the elections still declared themselves for the Union. Here, as in most of the border states, the mountainous country, East Tennessee, forms the actual center of resistance to the slaveowners' party. On June 17, 1861, a general convention of the people of East Tennessee met in Greenville, declared itself for the Union, deputed the former governor of the state, Andrew Johnson, one of the most ardent Unionists, to the Senate in Washington, and published a "dec-laration of grievances," which exposed all the means of deception, in-trigue, and terror by which Tennessee had been "voted out" of the

Union. Since then the Secessionists have held East Tennessee in check by force of arms.

Relationships similar to those in West Virginia and East Tennessee are found in northern Alabama, northwestern Georgia, and northern North Carolina.

Farther west, in the border state of Missouri, with 1,173,317 inhabitants and 114,985 slaves—the latter mostly concentrated in the northwestern part of the state—the people's convention of August, 1861, decided for the Union. [Claiborne Fox] Jackson, the governor of the state and tool of the slaveholders' party, rebelled against the legislature of Missouri, was outlawed, and now heads the armed hordes that invaded Missouri from Texas, Arkansas, and Tennessee to bring her to her knees before the Confederacy and sever her bond with the Union by the sword. Next to Virginia, Missouri at present constitutes the main theater of the Civil War.

New Mexico, not a state, but merely a territory, into which twenty-five slaves were imported during Buchanan's presidency in order to send a slave constitution after them from Washington, has not craved the South, as even the latter concedes. But the South craves New Mexico, and accordingly has spewed an armed band of adventurers from Texas over the border. New Mexico has implored the protection of the Union government against these liberators.

It will have been observed that we put particular emphasis on the numerical proportion of slaves to free men in the individual border states. This proportion is in reality decisive. It is the thermometer with which the vital temperature of the slave system must be measured. The soul of the whole secessionist movement is South Carolina. It numbers 402,541 slaves and 301,271 free men. In second place is Mississippi, which gave the Southern Confederacy its dictator, Jefferson Davis. It numbers 436,696 slaves and 354,699 free men. In third place is Alabama, with 435,132 slaves and 529,164 free men.

The last of the contested border states which we still have to mention is Kentucky. Its most recent history is particularly characteristic of the policy of the Southern Confederacy. Kentucky numbers 1,135,-712 inhabitants and 225,490 slaves. In three successive general elections by the people—in the winter of 1861, when elections to a congress of the border states were held; in June, 1861, when the elections to the Congress in Washington took place; finally, in August, 1861, in the elections for the Kentucky legislature—an ever increasing majority decided for the Union. On the other hand, Magoffin, the governor of Kentucky, and sundry high officials of the state are fanatical partisans of the slaveholders' party, as is Breckinridge, representative of Kentucky to the Senate in Washington, Vice-President of the United States under Buchanan, and candidate of the slaveholders' party in the presidential election of 1860. Too weak to win Kentucky for Secession, the slaveholders' influence was strong enough to make it tractable to a declaration of neutrality at the outbreak of the war. The Confederacy recognized the neutrality policy so long as it served Confederate purposes and so long as the South was preoccupied with defeating the resistance in East Tennessee. Hardly was this end attained when it knocked at the gates of Kentucky with the butt of a musket and the cry: "*The South needs its whole territory. It will and must have it!*"

Simultaneously from the Southwest and West its corps of freebooters broke into the "neutral" state. Kentucky awoke from its dream of neutrality, its legislature openly took sides with the Union, surrounded the traitorous governor with a committee of public safety, called the people to arms, declared Breckinridge an outlaw, and ordered the Secessionists to evacuate the invaded territory immediately. This was the signal for war. An army of the Southern Confederacy is moving on Louisville, while volunteers from Illinois, Indiana, and Ohio are pouring in to save Kentucky from the armed missionaries of slavery.

The attempts of the Confederacy to incorporate Missouri and Kentucky, for example, against the will of those states, prove the hollowness of the pretext that it is fighting for the rights of the individual states against the encroachments of the Union. On the individual states that it counts as part of the "South" it confers, to be sure, the right to separate from the Union, but by no means the right to remain in the Union.

Even the real slave states, no matter how much external war, internal military dictatorship, and slavery give them momentarily the appearance of harmony, are nevertheless not without resisting elements. A striking example is Texas, with 180,388 slaves out of 601,039 inhabitants. The law of 1845, by virtue of which Texas entered the ranks of the United States as a slave state, entitled it to form not simply one, but five states out of its territory. Thereby the South would have gained ten new votes, instead of two, in the American Senate, and increasing the number of its votes in the Senate was a main objective of southern policy at that time. From 1845 to 1860, however, the slaveowners found it unfeasible to cut up Texas, where the German population plays a great role, even into two states, without giving the party of free labor the upper hand over the party of slavery in the second state. This is the best proof of the power of the opposition to the slaveholding oligarchy in Texas itself.

Georgia is the largest and most populous of the slave states. Out of 1,057,327 inhabitants it numbers 462,230 slaves, thus nearly half of the population. Despite this, the slaveholders' party has not yet succeeded in getting the constitution imposed on the South at Montgomery sanctioned in Georgia by a general vote of the people.

In the state convention of Louisiana, which met on March 21, 1861, at New Orleans, Roselius, the political veteran of the state, declared: "The Montgomery constitution is not a constitution but a conspiracy. It does not inaugurate a people's government but *an odious and unlimited oligarchy*. The people were not permitted to participate in this matter. The Montgomery Convention has dug the grave of political freedom, and now we are called upon to attend its funeral."

For the oligarchy of the 300,000 slaveholders utilized the Congress of Montgomery not only to proclaim the separation of the South from the North. At the same time the oligarchy used it to overthrow the internal constitutions of the slave states, to subjugate completely the part of the white population that had still maintained some independence under the democratic Constitution and protection of the Union. Between 1856 and 1860 the political spokesmen, jurists, moralists, and theologians of the slaveholders' party already sought to prove, not so much that Negro slavery is justified, but rather that color is a matter of indifference and the working class is everywhere born for slavery.

Thus one sees that the war of the Southern Confederacy is, in the true sense of the word, a war of conquest for the extension and perpetuation of slavery. The majority of the border states and territories are still in possession of the Union, whose side they have taken first through the ballot box and then with arms. But the Confederacy counts them for the "South" and seeks to conquer them from the Union. In the border states, which the Confederacy has temporarily occupied, it holds the highlands in check through martial law. Inside the slave states proper, it supplants the hitherto existing democracy with an unrestricted oligarchy of 300,000 slaveholders.

By abandoning its plans of conquest the Southern Confederacy would give up its viability and the objective of the secession. Indeed, secession took place only because the transformation of the border states and territories into slave states seemed no longer attainable within the Union. On the other hand, with a peaceful cession of the contested territory to the Southern Confederacy, the North would surrender to the slave republic more than three-quarters of the entire territory of the United States. The North would lose the Gulf of Mexico altogether, the Atlantic Ocean with the exception of the small strip from Penobscot Bay to the Bay of Delaware, and would even cut itself off from the Pacific Ocean. Missouri, Kansas, New Mexico, Arkansas, and Texas would draw California after them. The great agricultural states in the basin between the Rocky Mountains and the Alleghenies, in the valleys of the Mississippi, the Missouri, and the Ohio rivers, unable to wrest the mouth of the Mississippi from the strong and hostile hands of the slave republic, would be compelled by their economic interests to secede from the North and enter the

Southern Confederacy. These northwestern states, in their turn, would draw all the northern states lying farther east, perhaps with the exception of the New England states, after them into the same vortex of Secession.

Thus in fact there would take place, not a dissolution of the Union, but a *reorganization* of it, a *reorganization on the basis* of slavery, under the recognized control of the slaveholding oligarchy. The plan of such a reorganization has been openly proclaimed by the principal speakers of the South at the Montgomery Congress and explains the paragraph of the new constitution which leaves it open to every state of the old Union to join the new Confederacy. The slave system would infect the whole Union. In the northern states, where Negro slavery is unworkable in practice, the white working class would be gradually depressed to the level of helotry. This would be in accord with the loudly proclaimed principle that only certain races are capable of freedom, and that as in the South real labor is the lot of the Negro, so in the North it is the lot of the German and the Irishman, or their direct descendants.

The present struggle between the South and the North is therefore nothing but a conflict between two social systems, the system of slavery and the system of free labor. The struggle broke out because the two systems can no longer live peacefully side by side on the North American continent. It can end only with the victory of one system or the other.

If the border states, the disputed areas wherein both systems have hitherto contended for control, are a thorn in the flesh of the South, so, on the other hand, it cannot be ignored that in the course of the war up to now they have constituted the main weakness of the North. One part of the slaveholders in these districts pretended loyalty to the North at the bidding of the conspirators of the South; another part found that in fact it was in accord with their real interests and traditional ideas to go with the Union. Both have equally crippled the North. Anxiety about keeping the "loyal" slaveholders in the border states in good humor, fear of throwing them into the arms of Secession —in a word, tender regard for the interests, prejudices, and sensibilities of these dubious allies—has smitten the Union government with incurable weakness since the beginning of the war, driven it to half-measures, forced it to dissemble away the principle of the war and to spare the enemy's most vulnerable spot, the root of the evil—*slavery itself*.

When, only recently, Lincoln faintheartedly revoked Frémont's Missouri Proclamation on the emancipation of Negroes belonging to the rebels, this was done only out of concern at the loud protest from the "loyal" slaveholders of Kentucky. Nevertheless, a turning point has already been reached. With Kentucky, the last border state has been forced into the series of battlefields between South and North. With the actual war for the border states in the border states themselves, the question of winning or losing them is withdrawn from the sphere of diplomatic and parliamentary negotiations. One part of the slave-holders will throw off the mask of loyalty; the other part will content itself with the prospect of monetary compensation, such as Great Britain gave the West Indian planters. Events themselves push toward the promulgation of the decisive slogan—*emancipation of the slaves.*

The extent to which even the most hardened Democrats and diplomats of the North feel themselves drawn to this point is shown by some very recent publications. General Cass, Secretary of War under Buchanan and until now one of the most ardent allies of the South, declares in an open communication that the emancipation of the slaves is a *conditio sine qua non* [indispensable condition] for saving the Union. Dr. Brownson, the spokesman of the Catholic party of the North, by his own admission the most energetic opponent of the emancipation movement from 1836 to 1860, publishes in his latest *Review*, for October, an article *for* Abolition.

"If we," he says among other things, "have opposed Abolition hereto-fore because we would preserve the Union, we must *a fortiori* now op-pose slavery whenever, in our judgment, its continuance becomes in-compatible with the maintenance of the Union, or of the nation as a free republican state."[1]

Finally, the *World,* a New York organ of the diplomats of the Washington cabinet, concludes one of its latest noisy articles against the Abolitionists with these words: "On the day when it is decided that either slavery or the Union must go down, on that day the death sentence will be passed on slavery. If the North cannot triumph *with-out* emancipation, it will triumph *with* emancipation."

---

1. *Brownson's Quarterly Review,* II, New York, 1861.

Economic Notes*

November 3, 1861

AT THE PRESENT MOMENT, general politics does not exist in England. The country's attention is occupied with the French financial, commercial, and agricultural crisis, the shortage of cotton, and the American question.

In competent circles here, there is no doubt for a moment that the Bank of France's note-jobbing with a few big houses on both sides of the Channel is a palliative of the weakest sort. All that could be achieved, and has been achieved, by this was a *momentary* lessening of the outflow of money to England. The repeated attempts of the Bank of France to recruit metal auxiliary troops in Petersburg, Hamburg, and Berlin merely damage its credit without filling its coffers. Raising the interest rate on treasury bills to keep them in circulation, and the necessity to effect a remission of the payments on the new Italian loan of Victor Emmanuel—both are viewed here as serious symptoms of the French financial sickness. It is known, moreover, that at the present moment two projects are contending for precedence in the Tuileries. The full-blooded Bonapartists, headed by Persigny and Péreire (of the Crédit Mobilier), want to make the Bank of France entirely subject to governmental authority, reduce it to a mere office of the Finance Ministry, and use the institution, thus transformed, as a paper-money factory.

It is known that this principle was originally the basis of the organization of the Crédit Mobilier. The less adventurous party, represented by Fould and other renegades of Louis Philippe's time, is proposing a new national loan which, according to some, is to amount to 400,000,000 francs, and according to others, 700,000,000. The *Times*, in a leading article today, probably reflects the views of the City

---

* Published in *Die Presse*, Vienna, November 9, 1861.

[London's financial community] when it says that France is completely paralyzed by her economic crisis and is robbed of her European influence. Nevertheless, the *Times* and the City are mistaken. If the December power [Louis Napoleon's France] should succeed in surviving the winter without great internal storms, it will blow the war trumpet in the spring. The internal distress will not be cured thereby, but only drowned out.

In an earlier letter I pointed out that the cotton swindle in Liverpool during the past few weeks fully reminds one of the maddest days of the railroad mania of 1845. Dentists, surgeons, lawyers, cooks, widows, workers, scribes and lords, comedians and clergymen, soldiers and tailors, newspapermen and landlords, man and wife, all speculated in cotton. Quite small quantities, one to four bales, were bought, sold, and resold. Larger quantities remained for months in the same warehouse although they changed owners twenty times. He who bought cotton at ten o'clock sold it again at eleven o'clock with an addition of half a penny per pound. Thus the same cotton often circulated through various hands half a dozen times in ten hours. This week, however, there came a lull, and for no more rational reason than that a pound of cotton (namely, middling [New] Orleans cotton) had risen to a shilling, that twelve pence make a shilling and are thus a round figure. So everyone undertook to sell out as soon as this maximum was reached. Hence a sudden increase in supply, and consequent reaction. As soon as the Englishman makes himself conversant with the possibility that a pound of cotton can rise *above* a shilling, the St. Vitus dance will return more madly than ever.

The latest official monthly report of the Board of Trade on British exports and imports has by no means dispelled the gloomy mood. The export tables cover the nine-month period from January to September, 1861. Compared with the same period in 1860, they show a decline of about £8,000,000. Of this, £5,671,730 fall to exports to the United States alone, while the rest is distributed over British North America, the East Indies, Australia, Turkey, and Germany. An increase is shown only in Italy. Thus, for example, the export of British cotton commodities to Sardinia, Tuscany, Naples, and Sicily has risen from £656,802 for the year 1860 to £1,294,287 for 1861; the export of British cotton yarn from £348,158 to £583,373; the export of iron from £120,867 to £160,912, etc. These figures are not without weight in the scale of British sympathy for Italian freedom.

While the export trade of Great Britain has thus declined by almost £8,000,000, her import trade has risen in still greater proportion, a circumstance that by no means facilitates adjustment of the balance. This growth of imports is due particularly to the increase in wheat imports. During the first eight months of 1860, the value of imported wheat amounted to only £6,796,139, whereas for the same period this year it amounts to £13,431,387.

The most remarkable phenomenon revealed by the import tables is the rapid increase of French imports, which have now reached a volume (annual) of nearly £18,000,000, while English exports to France are not much greater than those of Holland. Continental politicians have hitherto overlooked this entirely new phenomenon of modern commercial history. It proves that the economic dependence of France on England is perhaps six times as great as the economic dependence of England on France—if, that is to say, one not only considers the English export and import tables, but also compares them with the French export and import tables. It then follows that England has now become the main export market for France, while France has remained a quite secondary export market for England. Hence, despite all chauvinism and all Waterloo rodomontades, the nervous fear of a conflict with "perfidious Albion."

Finally, one other important fact emerges from the latest English export and import tables. While English exports to the United States fell by more than 25 percent in the first nine months of this year, in comparison with the same period of 1860, the Port of New York alone has increased its exports to England by £6,000,000 during the first eight months of the present year. During this period the export of American gold to England has practically ceased, while for weeks now, on the contrary, gold has been flowing from England to New York. It is, in fact, England and France whose harvest deficiencies cover the North American deficit, while the Morrill Tariff and the economy inseparable from a civil war have simultaneously decimated the consumption of English and French manufactures in North America. And now compare these statistical facts with the jeremiads of the *Times* on the financial ruin of North America!

The Intervention in Mexico (I)*

TODAY's *Times* has a leading article in its well-known jocular-kaleido-scopic, would-be humorous manner, on the French Government's in-vasion of the Dappental and on Switzerland's protest against this violation of territory.[1] The oracle of Printing House Square[2] recalls how, at the time of the most acute struggle between English manufacturers and land-owners, little children employed in the factories were instructed to throw needles into the most delicate parts of the machinery and thus derange the motion of the whole powerful automaton. The machinery is Europe, the little child is Switzerland, and the needle she throws into the smoothly running automaton is—Louis Bonaparte's invasion of her territory, or rather, her outcry at his invasion. Thus the needle is suddenly transformed into the outcry at the needle's puncture, and the simile into dupery of the reader who expects a simile. The *Times* is further cheered by its discovery that the Dappental consists of a single village called Cressonières. It ends its short article with a complete contradiction of its beginning. Why, it exclaims, make such an ado about this infinitely small Swiss bagatelle, when every quarter of Europe will be in flames next spring? One should not forget that until recently Europe has been an orderly automaton. The whole article appears to be sheer nonsense, yet it makes its own sense. It is a declaration that in the Swiss affair, Palmerston has given carte blanche to his allies on the other side of the Channel. The explanation of the declaration is found in the dry notice in the *Moniteur* that on October

---

* Published in *Die Presse*, Vienna, November 12, 1861.
1. On October 28, 1861, French troops invaded the Dappental, in Canton Vaud, a part of which was finally ceded to France in exchange for some French territory turned over to Switzerland.
2. The address of the London *Times*.

31 England, France, and Spain had concluded an agreement for a joint *intervention in Mexico*. The *Times*'s article on the Dappental and the *Moniteur's* notice on Mexico stand as close together as the Canton of Vaud and Veracruz are far apart.

It is credible that Louis Bonaparte counted intervention in Mexico among the many possibilities that he constantly keeps in preparation for the diversion of the French people. It is certain that Spain, whose cheap successes in Morocco and Santo Domingo have gone to her head, dreams of a restoration in Mexico. But it is sure that France's project had not yet matured and that both France and Spain were opposed to a crusade against Mexico under *English* command.

On September 24 Palmerston's private *Moniteur*, the *Morning Post*, reported the details of an agreement that England, France, and Spain had reached for a joint intervention in Mexico. One day later *La Patrie* denied the existence of such an agreement. On September 27 the *Times* refuted *La Patrie* without naming it. According to the article in the *Times*, Lord Russell had *communicated* to the French Government the English decision to intervene, whereupon M. de Thouvenel replied that the Emperor of the French had arrived at a similar decision. Now it was Spain's turn. The Spanish Government declared in a semiofficial organ that it proposed to intervene in Mexico, but in no way alongside England. It rained *dementis* [denials]. The *Times* announced categorically that "the President of the American Union had given his full assent to the proposed expedition." Hardly had this news reached the other side of the Atlantic Ocean when all the American government organs branded it a lie, since President Lincoln was siding with, and not against, Mexico. From all this it follows that the intervention plan in its present form originated in the Cabinet of St. James's.

No less puzzling and contradictory than the statements concerning the origin of the agreement were the statements about its objectives. One Palmerston organ, the *Morning Post*, announced that Mexico is not an organized state with an existing government, but a mere robbers' nest. It was to be treated as such. The expedition had only one object— the satisfaction of the Mexican state's creditors in England, France, and Spain. To this end, the combined military forces would occupy the main ports of Mexico, collect the import and export duties on her coast, and hold this "material guarantee" until all debt claims were satisfied.

The other Palmerston organ, the *Times*, declared, on the contrary, that from long experience England was "steeled against plunderings on the part of bankrupt Mexico." It was not a question of the private interests of creditors, but "they hope that the mere presence of a combined squadron in the Gulf of Mexico, and the occupation of certain ports, would be sufficient to stimulate the Mexican Government to new exertions for the maintenance of internal peace and to force the malcontents to a more constitutional opposition than brigandage."

According to this, therefore, the expedition would take place for the purpose of supporting the official government of Mexico. At the same time, however, the *Times* indicates that "Mexico City is sufficiently healthful, should it be necessary to penetrate that far."

The most original means of strengthening a government indisputably consists of the sequestration of its income and its territories by force. On the other hand, mere occupation of the ports and collection of duties in them can only move the Mexican Government to set up customs houses farther inland. Import duties on foreign commodities and export duties on American ones would in this way be doubled; the intervention would in fact satisfy the claims of European creditors by levying an extortion on European-Mexican trade. The Mexican Government can become solvent only by internal consolidation, and it can consolidate itself at home only so long as its independence is respected abroad.

If the alleged objectives of the expeditions are contradictory, the alleged means for achieving these alleged objectives are even more so. The English government organs themselves admit that if one thing or another is attainable by unilateral intervention of France or England or Spain, everything becomes unattainable by *joint* intervention of these states.

One recalls that the Liberal party in Mexico under Juárez, the official President of the Republic, now has the upper hand at almost all points; that the Catholic party under General Marquez has suffered defeat after defeat, and that the robber gang it organized has been driven back to the Sierras of Querétaro and become dependent on an alliance with Mejía, the Indian chief there. The last hope of the Catholic party was *Spanish* intervention.

"The only point," says the *Times*, "on which there may be a possible split between ourselves and our allies concerns the government of the Republic. England wishes to see it left in the hands of the Liberal party, while France and Spain are suspected of a partiality for the ecclesiastical rule that has been recently overthrown. It would be strange if France were to make herself the protector of priests and bandits in both the Old and the New World. Just as in Italy the partisans of Francis II at Rome were equipped for their work of making Naples ungovernable, so in Mexico the highways, indeed, the streets of the capital city, are infested with robbers, whom the Church party openly declares to be its friends."

And precisely for this reason England strengthens the Liberal Government by undertaking a crusade against it in alliance with France and

Spain; she seeks to suppress anarchy by supplying the prostrated clerical party in its last gasps with fresh allied troops from Europe!

Except during the short winter months, the coasts of Mexico, pestilential as they are, can be held only by conquest of the country itself. But a third English organ, the *Economist*, declares the conquest of Mexico to be impossible.

"If it is desired," says this paper, "to thrust upon her a British prince with an English army, then the fiercest wrath of the United States would be aroused. France's jealousy would make such a conquest impossible, and a motion to this effect would be almost unanimously rejected by an English Parliament the moment it was submitted. For her part, England cannot entrust the government of Mexico to France. Of Spain, there can be no question at all."

The whole expedition, therefore, is a mystification whose key *La Patrie* gives in these words: "The agreement recognizes the necessity of installing in Mexico a strong government that can maintain peace and order there."

It is simply a question of replacing the Holy Alliance, with its principle of intervention by European countries in the domestic governmental affairs of the states of America, with a new Holy Alliance. The first plan of this sort was drafted by Chateaubriand for the Bourbons of Spain and France at the time of the Restoration. It was frustrated by Canning and by Monroe, the President of the United States, who declared any European interference in the internal affairs of American states to be outlawed. Since then the American Union has constantly asserted the Monroe Doctrine as international law. The present Civil War, however, has created the right situation for securing to the European monarchies an intervention precedent which they can expand later. This is the real object of the English-French-Spanish intervention. Its immediate result can be, and is intended to be, only the restoration of the anarchy just dying out in Mexico.

Apart from all general standpoints of international law, the occurrence has the great importance for Europe that, by concessions in the realm of Continental politics, England has purchased the support of Louis Bonaparte for the Mexican expedition.

The Intervention in Mexico (II)*

November 8, 1861

THE CONTEMPLATED intervention in Mexico by England, France, and Spain is in my opinion one of the most monstrous enterprises ever chronicled in the annals of international history. It is a contrivance of the true Palmerston make, astounding the uninitiated by an insanity of purpose and an imbecility of the means employed which appear quite incompatible with the known capacity of the old schemer.

It is probable that among the many irons which, to amuse the French public, Louis Bonaparte is compelled to always keep in the fire, a Mexican expedition may have figured. It is sure that Spain, whose never overstrong head has been quite turned by her recent cheap successes in Morocco and Santo Domingo, dreams of a restoration in Mexico, but nevertheless, it is certain that the French plan was far from being matured, and that both France and Spain strove hard against a joint expedition to Mexico under English leadership.

On September 24, Palmerston's private *Moniteur*, the London *Morning Post*, first announced in detail the scheme for the joint intervention, according to the terms of a treaty just concluded, as it said, between England, France, and Spain. This statement had hardly crossed the Channel when the French Government, through the columns of the Paris *Patrie* gave it the direct lie. On September 27 the London *Times*, Palmerston's national organ, first broke its silence on the scheme in a leader contradicting, but not quoting, the *Patrie*. The *Times* even stated that Earl Russell had communicated to the French government the resolution arrived at on the part of England of interfering in Mexico, and that M. de Thouvenel replied that the Emperor

* Published in the *New-York Daily Tribune* November 23, 1861. In addition to the preceding article on the same subject and with the same title, see also "The Mexican Imbroglio," page 175, for other comment on the Mexican situation.

of the French had come to a similar conclusion. Now it was the turn of Spain. A semiofficial paper of Madrid, while affirming Spain's intention to meddle with Mexico, repudiated at the same time the idea of a joint intervention with England. The *dementis* were not yet exhausted. The *Times* had categorically asserted that "the full assent of the American President had been given to the expedition." All the American papers taking notice of the *Times* article have long since contradicted its assertion.

It is therefore certain, and has even been expressly admitted by the *Times*, that the joint intervention in its present form is of English— i.e., Palmerstonian—make. Spain was cowed into adherence by the pressure of France; and France was brought round by concessions made to her in the field of European policy. In this respect, it is a significant coincidence that the *Times* of November 6, in the very number in which it announces the conclusion at Paris of a convention for the joint interference in Mexico, simultaneously published a leader pooh-poohing and treating with exquisite contumely the protest of Switzerland against the recent invasion of her territory—viz., the Dappental—by a French military force. In return for his fellowship in the Mexican expedition, Louis Bonaparte had obtained carte blanche for his contemplated encroachment on Switzerland, and, perhaps, on other parts of the European continent. The transactions on these points between England and France have lasted throughout the whole of the months of September and October.

There exist in England no people desirous of an intervention in Mexico save the Mexican bondholders, who, however, had never to boast the least sway over the national mind. Hence the difficulty of breaking to the public the Palmerstonian scheme. The next best means was to bewilder the British elephant by contradictory statements, proceeding from the same laboratory, compounded of the same materials, but varying in the doses administered to the animal.

The *Morning Post*, in its print of September 24, announced there would be "no territorial war in Mexico," that the only point at issue was the monetary claims on the Mexican exchequer; that "it would be impossible to deal with Mexico as an organized and established government," and that consequently "the principal Mexican ports would be temporarily occupied and their customs revenues sequestered."

The *Times* of September 27 declared, on the contrary, that "to dishonesty, to repudiation, to the legal and irremediable plunder of our countrymen by the default of a bankrupt community, we were steeled by long endurance," and that, consequently, "the private robbery of the English bondholders" lay not, as the *Post* had it, at the bottom of the intervention. While remarking, *en passant*, that "the city of Mexico was sufficiently healthy, should it be necessary to penetrate so far," the *Times* hoped, however, that "the mere presence of a combined squadron in the Gulf, and the seizure of certain ports, will urge the Mexican Government to *new* exertions in keeping the peace, and will convince the malcontents that they must confine themselves to some form of opposition more constitutional than brigandage." If, then, according to the *Post*, the expedition was to start because there "exists no government in Mexico," it was, according to the *Times*, only intended as encouraging and supporting the *existing* Mexican government. To be sure! The oddest means ever hit upon for the consolidation of a government consists in the seizure of its territory and the sequestration of its revenue.

The *Times* and the *Morning Post* having once given out the cue, John Bull was then handed over to the minor ministerial oracles, systematically belaboring him in the same contradictory style for four weeks, until public opinion had at last become sufficiently trained to the idea of a joint intervention in Mexico, although kept in deliberate ignorance of the aim and purpose of that intervention. At last, the transactions with France had drawn to an end; the *Moniteur* announced that the convention between the three interfering powers had been concluded on October 31, and the *Journal des Débats*, one of whose co-proprietors is appointed to the command of one of the vessels of the French squadron, informed the world that no permanent territorial conquest was intended; that Vera Cruz and other points on the coast were to be seized, an advance to the capital being agreed upon in case of noncompliance by the constituted authorities in Mexico with the demands of the intervention; that, moreover, a strong government was to be imported into the republic.

The *Times*, which ever since its first announcement on September 27 seemed to have forgotten the very existence of Mexico, had now again to step forward. Everybody ignorant of its connection with Palmerston, and the original introduction in its columns of his scheme, would be induced to consider the today's leader of the *Times* as the most cutting and merciless satire on the whole adventure. It sets out by stating that "the expedition is a *very remarkable* one" (later on it says a curious one). "Three states are combining to coerce a fourth into good behavior, *not so much by way of war as by authoritative interference in behalf of order.*"

Authoritative interference in behalf of order! This is literally the Holy Alliance slang, and sounds very *remarkable* indeed on the part of England, glorying in the nonintervention principle! And why is "the way of war, and of declaration of war, and all other behests of international law," supplanted by "an authoritative interference in behalf of order"? Because, says the *Times*, there "exists no government in

Mexico." And what is the professed aim of the expedition? "To address demands to the constituted authorities at Mexico."

The only grievances complained of by the intervening powers, the only causes which might give to their hostile procedure the slightest shade of justification, are easily to be summed up. They are the monetary claims of the bondholders and a series of personal outrages said to have been committed upon subjects of England, France, and Spain. These were also the reasons of the intervention as originally put forth by the *Morning Post*, and as some time ago officially endorsed by Lord John Russell in an interview with some representatives of the Mexican bondholders in England. Today's *Times* states: "England, France, and Spain have concerted an expedition to bring Mexico to the performance of her specific engagements, and to give protection to the subjects of the respective crowns." However, in the progress of its article, the *Times* veers round and exclaims: "We shall, no doubt, succeed in obtaining at least a recognition of our pecuniary claims, in fact, a single British frigate could have obtained that amount of satisfaction at any moment. We may trust, too, that the more scandalous of the outrages committed will be expiated by more immediate and substantial atonements; but it is clear that, if only this much was to be brought about we need not have resorted to such extremities as are now proposed."

The *Times*, then, confesses in so many words that the reasons originally given out for the expedition are shallow pretexts; that for the attainment of redress nothing like the present procedure was needed; and that, in point of fact, the "recognition of monetary claims, and the protection of European subjects" have nothing at all to do with the present joint intervention in Mexico. What, then, is its real aim and purpose?

Before following the *Times* in its further explanations, we will, *en passant*, note some more "curiosities" which it has taken good care not to touch upon. In the first instance, it is a real "curiosity" to see Spain —Spain out of all other countries—turn crusader for the sanctity of foreign debts! Last Monday's *Courrier des Dimanches* already summons the French Government to improve the opportunity, and compel Spain "into the eternally delayed performance of her old standing engagements to French bondholders."

The second still greater "curiosity" is that the very same Palmerston who, according to Lord John Russell's recent declaration, is about invading Mexico to make its government pay the English bondholders, has himself, voluntarily, and despite the Mexican Government, *sacrificed* the treaty rights of England and the security mortgaged by Mexico to her British creditors.

By the treaty concluded with England in 1826, Mexico became

bound to not allow the establishment of slavery in any of the territories
constituting her then empire. By another clause of the same treaty, she
tendered England, as a security for the loans obtained from British
capitalists, the mortgage of 45,000,000 acres of the public lands in
Texas. It was Palmerston who, ten or twelve years later, interfered as
the mediator for Texas against Mexico. In the treaty then concluded
by him with Texas, he sacrificed not only the *antislavery cause*, but
also the *mortgage on the public lands*, thus robbing the English bondholders of the security. The Mexican Government protested at the
time, but meanwhile, later on Secretary John C. Calhoun could permit
himself the jest of informing the Cabinet of St. James's that its desire
"of seeing slavery abolished in Texas" would be best realized by an-
nexing Texas to the United States. The English bondholders lost, in
fact, any claim upon Mexico, by the voluntary sacrifice on the part of
Palmerston of the mortgage secured to them in the treaty of 1826.

But, since the London *Times* avows that the present intervention
has nothing to do either with monetary claims or with personal outrages, what, then, in all the world, is its real or pretended aim?

"*An authoritative interference in behalf of order.*" England, France,
and Spain, planning a new Holy Alliance, and having formed themselves into an armed areopagus for the restoration of order all over the
world. "Mexico," says the *Times*, "*must be rescued from anarchy*, and
put in the way of self-government and peace. A strong and stable government must be established" there by the invaders, and that government is to be extracted from "some Mexican party."

Now, does any one imagine that Palmerston and his mouthpiece,
the *Times*, really consider the joint intervention as a means to the
professed end, viz.: the extinction of anarchy, and the establishment
in Mexico of a strong and stable government? So far from cherishing
any such chimerical creed, the *Times* states expressly in its first leader
of September 27: "The only point on which there may possibly be a
difference between ourselves and our allies regards the government of
the Republic. England will be content to see it remain in the hands of
the Liberal Party which is now in power, while France and Spain
are suspected of a partiality for the ecclesiastical rule which has recently been overthrown. . . . It would, indeed, be strange if France
were, in both the old and new world, to make herself the protector of
priests and bandits." In today's leader the *Times* goes on reasoning in
the same strain, and resumes its scruples in the sentence: "It is hard to
suppose that the intervening powers could all concur in the absolute
preference of either of the two parties between which Mexico is divided, and equally hard to imagine that a compromise would be found
practicable between enemies so determined."

Palmerston and the *Times*, then, are fully aware that there "exists a government in Mexico"; that the Liberal Party, ostensibly favored by England, "is now in power"; that "the ecclesiastical rule" has been "overthrown"; that Spanish intervention was the last forlorn hope of the priests and bandits; and finally, that Mexican anarchy was dying away. They know, then, that the joint intervention, with no other avowed end save the rescue of Mexico from anarchy, will produce just the opposite effect, weaken the constitutional government, strengthen the priestly party by a supply of French and Spanish bayonets, rekindle the embers of civil war, and, instead of extinguishing, restore anarchy to its bloom.

The inference the *Times* itself draws from those premises is really "remarkable" and "curious." "Although," it says, "the considerations may induce us to look with some anxiety to the results of the expedition, they do not militate against the expediency of the expedition itself."

It does, consequently, not militate against the expediency of the expedition itself, that the expedition militates against the only ostensible purpose. It does not militate against the means that it baffles its own avowed end.

The greatest "curiosity" pointed out by the *Times*, I have, however, still kept *in petto*. "If," says it, "President Lincoln should accept the invitation, which is provided for by the convention, to participate in the approaching operations, the character of the work would become more curious still."

It would, indeed, be the greatest "curiosity" of all if the United States, living in amity with Mexico, should associate with the European order-mongers, and, by participating in their acts, sanction the interference of a European armed areopagus with the internal affairs of American states. The first scheme of such a transplantation of the Holy Alliance to the other side of the Atlantic was, at the time of the Restoration, drawn up for the French and Spanish Bourbons by Chateaubriand. The attempt was baffled by an English Minister, Mr. Canning, and an American President, Mr. Monroe. The present convulsion in the United States appeared to Palmerston an opportune moment for taking up the old project in a modified form. Since the United States, for the present, must allow no foreign complication to interfere with their war for the Union, all they can do is to *protest*. Their best well-wishers in Europe hope that they will protest, and thus, before the eyes of the world, firmly repudiate any complicity in one of the most nefarious schemes.

This military expedition of Palmerston's, carried out by a coalition with two other European powers, is started during the prorogation, without the sanction, and against the will of the British Parliament. The first extraparliamentary war of Palmerston's was the Afghan War, softened and justified by the production of forged papers. Another war of that [kind] was his Persian war of 1857–58. He defended it at the time on the plea that "the principle of the previous sanction of the House did not apply to *Asiatic* wars." It seems that neither does it apply to *American* wars. With the control of the foreign wars, Parliament will lose all control over the national exchequer, and parliamentary government turn to a mere farce.

The Dismissal of Frémont*

November 19, 1861

FRÉMONT'S DISMISSAL from the General Command in Missouri forms a turning point in the developing history of the Civil War. Frémont has two great sins to expiate. He was the first candidate of the Republican party for the presidency (1856), and he is the first Northern general who (August 30, 1861) threatened the slaveholders with the emancipation of the slaves. Hence he remains a rival of candidates for the presidency in the future and an obstacle to the compromisers of the present.

During the last two decades there had developed in the United States the extraordinary practice of not electing to the presidency any man who occupied a decisive position in his own party. The names of such men, to be sure, were used for election demonstrations, but as soon as it came down to real business, they were dropped and replaced by obscure mediocrities of merely local influence. In this manner Polk, Pierce, Buchanan, etc., became Presidents. In this manner also A. Lincoln. General Andrew Jackson was in reality the last President of the United States who owed his office to his personal importance, while all his successors, on the contrary, owed it to their personal insignificance.

In the election year 1860, the most distinguished names of the Republican party were Frémont and Seward. Known for his adventures during the Mexican War, for his intrepid exploration of California, and for his candidacy in 1856, Frémont was too striking a figure even to come into consideration as soon as it was no longer a question of a mere Republican demonstration but of a Republican success. Hence he did not appear as a candidate. It was otherwise with Seward, the Republican senator in the Congress at Washington, governor of the

* Published in *Die Presse*, Vienna, November 26, 1861.

state of New York, and since the formation of the Republican party undoubtedly its foremost orator. It required a series of mortifying defeats to induce Mr. Seward to renounce his own candidacy and to give his oratorical patronage to the then more or less unknown A. Lincoln. But as soon as he saw his attempted candidacy frustrated, he imposed himself as the Republican Richelieu on a man whom he held to be a Republican Louis XIII. He contributed thereby to making Lincoln President, on condition that Lincoln make him Secretary of State, a position that is to some extent comparable to that of a British Prime Minister. In fact, Lincoln was hardly elected President when Seward secured the Secretaryship of State. Thereupon a singular change took place in the attitude of the Demosthenes of the Republican party, whose prediction of an "irrepressible conflict" between the system of free labor and the system of slavery had made him famous.[1] Although elected on November 6, 1860, Lincoln did not assume his presidential office until March 4, 1861. In the interval, during the winter session of Congress, Seward made himself the focus of all attempts at compromise; the Northern organs of the South, such as, for example, the *New York Herald,* whose *bête noire* Seward had been until then, suddenly lauded him as the statesman of reconciliation, and in truth it was not his fault that peace at any price did not come to pass. Seward openly regarded the Secretaryship of State as a mere stepping stone and was less preoccupied with the "irrepressible conflict" of the present than with the presidency of the future. He has provided fresh proof that virtuosos of the tongue are dangerously insufficient statesmen. Read his state dispatches! What a revolting mixture of greatness of phrase and pettiness of mind, of postures of strength and acts of weakness!

For Seward, therefore, Frémont was the dangerous rival, whom it was necessary to destroy; an undertaking that seemed to be so much the easier since Lincoln, in accord with his lawyer's tradition, has an aversion for all originality, clings anxiously to the letters of the Constitution, and fights shy of anything that could mislead the "loyal" slaveholders of the border states. Frémont's character offered a different mold. He is patently a man of pathos, somewhat bombastic and haughty, and not free of all melodramatic flights. First, the government tried to provoke him to voluntary resignation by a succession of petty chicaneries. When this did not succeed, it deprived him of his command at the very moment when the army organized by him confronted the enemy in southwest Missouri and a decisive battle was imminent.

Frémont is the idol of the northwestern states, which celebrate him as the "Pathfinder." They regard his dismissal as a personal insult. If

---

1. Speech by Seward at Rochester, New York, October 25, 1858.

the Union Government should meet with a few more misfortunes like Bull Run and Ball's Bluff, it has itself given the opposition, which will then rise up against it and smash the hitherto prevailing diplomatic system of waging war, its leader in John Frémont. We shall return later to the indictment that the War Department in Washington has published against the dismissed General.

The *Trent* Affair

The Trent affair was a notable episode in the international phase of the American Civil War. It involved relations with Great Britain, a powerful country of potentially crucial importance to the outcome of that war.

The beginning of the conflict found British opinion divided. On the pro-Confederacy side were the aristocracy, which sympathized with the southern plantation owners; and commercial interests, which hoped for cheaper raw materials, particularly cotton, from an independent South. On the pro-Northern side were British liberals, who saw in the Civil War a struggle to preserve democracy; and the working class, which felt that the fate of free labor was at stake. Much of the London press, spearheaded by the influential Times, which Marx read assiduously, was pro-South.

The British, led by Lord Palmerston as Prime Minister and Lord John Russell as Foreign Minister, leaned toward the Confederacy, and had contact with William L. Yancey and Pierre A. Rost, the Southern commissioners (diplomatic representatives who, since their government was not officially recognized in England, lacked diplomatic rank), but cautiously avoided direct intervention.

Some three weeks after President Lincoln proclaimed a blockade of the Confederate coast, Britain (quickly followed by France), on May 13, 1861, issued a proclamation of neutrality which, while not giving the Confederacy official recognition, granted it belligerent status. In protest, U. S. Secretary of State William H. Seward, on May 21, instructed the American Minister to England, Charles Francis Adams, that he "desist from all intercourse whatever . . . with the British Government, so long as it shall continue intercourse . . . with the domestic enemies of this country." Foreign Minister Russell promised Adams that he would not see the Confederate commissioners again. On June 1 Great Britain closed British ports to armed privateers of both sides.

Later that year, in November, the Confederacy, in search of international recognition and military assistance, commissioned James M. Mason and John Slidell to go to Britain and to the Continent as diplomatic agents. The two men ran the blockade to Havana, where they boarded a British mail steamer, the Trent, bound for England. Acting on his own responsibility, Captain Charles Wilkes, in command of the U. S. warship San Jacinto, intercepted the Trent on November 8, searched it, forcibly removed the two Confederate commissioners with their secretaries and dispatches, and placed them in confinement as political prisoners in Fort Warren, Boston Harbor.

News of the Trent seizure provoked a storm of indignation in England, as can be seen from Marx's accounts in the following pages. Lord Russell stated publicly that the forcible boarding of a British vessel "pursuing a lawful and innocent voyage" was "an act of violence which was an affront to the British flag and a violation of international law," and that the proper procedure would have been to take the vessel with all its passengers to some neutral port for adjudication.

While Captain Wilkes was being enthusiastically hailed by the public as a hero, the Lincoln Administration moved quietly to undo the "error." On December 26 Secretary Seward "cheerfully liberated," as he wrote, the two commissioners, who were then placed aboard a British vessel.

The release of the Southern envoys, who, in the words of Commissioner Mason, had been "treated with every possible courtesy by Captain Wilkes and his officers," closed the incident.

The Trent affair, which Marx describes and analyzes here in detail, thus ended without war between Great Britain and the United States. When Mason and Slidell arrived in England at the end of January, 1862, interest in the whole affair had declined to such an extent that their arrival went practically unnoticed.

November 28, 1861*

THE CONFLICT of the English mail steamer *Trent* with the North American warship *San Jacinto* in the narrow passage of the Old Bahama Channel is the lion among the events of the day. On the afternoon of November 27 the mail steamer *La Plata* brought information concerning the incident to Southampton, whence the electric telegraph immediately flashed it to all parts of Great Britain. That same evening the London Stock Exchange was the stage of stormy scenes similar to those at the time of the proclamation of the Italian war. Quotations of government stocks sank three-quarters to one percent. The wildest

---

* Published in *Die Presse*, Vienna, December 2, 1861.

rumors ran through London. The American Ambassador, Adams, had been handed his passport, an embargo was imposed on all American ships in the Thames, etc. At the same time an indignation meeting of merchants took place at the Stock Exchange in Liverpool, to demand measures from the English government for satisfaction of the violated honor of the British flag. Every normal Englishman went to bed with the conviction that he would go to sleep in a state of peace but wake up in a state of war.

Despite all this, it is almost categorically certain that the conflict between the *Trent* and the *San Jacinto* carries *no* war in its train. The semiofficial press—like the *Times* and the *Morning Post*—strikes a peaceful note and pours juridically cool deductions upon the flares of passion. Papers like the *Daily Telegraph*, which at the slightest *mot d'ordre* [word of command] roar for the British lion, are true models of moderation. Only the Tory Opposition press—the *Morning Herald* and the *Standard*—lashes out. These facts force every expert to the conclusion that the ministry has already decided not to make a *casus belli* out of the "untoward event."

It must be added that the event, if not the details of its performance, was anticipated. On October 12, Messrs. Slidell, Ambassador of the Confederacy to France, and Mason, Ambassador of the Confederacy to England, together with their secretaries, Eustis and McFarland, had run the blockade from Charleston on the steamer *Theodora* and sailed for Havana, there to seek the opportunity of a passage to Europe under the English flag. Their arrival was daily awaited in England. North American warships had set out from Liverpool to intercept the gentlemen and their dispatches on this side of the Atlantic Ocean. The English Ministry had already submitted the question, whether the North Americans were entitled to such a step, to its official law counsels for their opinion. The reply of these counsels is said to have been in the affirmative.

The legal question revolves in a narrow circle. Since the foundation of the United States, North America has adopted English maritime law in all its rigor. A main principle of this maritime law is that all neutral merchantmen are subject to search by belligerent parties.

"This right," said Lord Stowell in a decision that has become famous, "offers the sole security that no contraband is carried on neutral ships."

The greatest American authority, Kent,[1] declares in the same sense: "The duty of self-preservation gives to belligerent nations this right . . . The doctrine of the English admiralty on the right of visitation

---

1. James Kent, *Commentaries on American Law* Vol. I, Part I (New York, 1826).

and search . . . has been recognized in its fullest extent by the courts of justice in this country."

It was not, as is sometimes mistakenly assumed, opposition against the right of search that brought about the Anglo-American War of 1812 to 1814. Rather, America declared war because England unlawfully arrogated to herself the search even of American *warships*, under the pretext of seizing deserting English sailors.

The *San Jacinto*, therefore, had a right to search the *Trent* and to confiscate any contraband found on it. That *dispatches* in possession of Mason, Slidell, & Co. come under the category of contraband the *Times*, the *Morning Post*, etc., themselves admit. The question remains whether Messrs. Mason, Slidell, & Co. were themselves contraband and were, therefore, confiscable! The point is a ticklish one, and differences of opinion prevail among the doctors of law. Pratt,[2] the foremost English authority on "contraband," in his chapter, "Quasi-Contraband —Dispatches, Passengers," specifically refers to "communication of information and orders of a belligerent government to its officers abroad, or the transportation of military passengers." Messrs. Mason and Slidell, if not officers, were equally not ambassadors, since their government is recognized by neither England nor France. What are they, then? In justification of the very wide conception of contraband asserted by England during the Anglo-French wars, Jefferson, in the *Memoir*,[3] already remarks that, in the nature of things, contraband excludes any conclusive definition and necessarily leaves great scope for arbitrariness.[4] In any case, however, one sees that from the standpoint of English law the *legal question* shrinks to a Duns Scotus controversy,[5] the explosive force of which will not go beyond an exchange of diplomatic notes.

The *political* side of the North American procedure was evaluated quite correctly by the *Times* in these words: "Even Mr. Seward himself must know that the voices of the Southern commissioners, sounding from their captivity, are a thousand times more eloquent in London

2. Frederic Thomas Pratt, *Law of Contraband of War* (London, 1856).

3. Thomas Jefferson, *Memoir, Correspondence, and Private Papers* (ed. by Thomas Jefferson Randolph; 4 vols., London, 1829).

4. Jefferson to Robert R. Livingston (U. S. Minister to France), September 9, 1801: ". . . We believe the practice of seizing what is called contraband of war is an abusive practice, not founded in natural right. War between two nations cannot diminish the rights of the rest of the world remaining at peace . . . And what is *contraband*, by the law of nature? Either everything which may aid or comfort the enemy, or nothing. Either all commerce which would accommodate him is unlawful, or none is. The difference between articles of one or another description is a difference in degree only. No line between them can be drawn."

5. The method used by Duns Scotus (ca. 1265–1308), the Scholastic philosopher, of positing arguments with "*pro*" and "*contra*."

and in Paris than they would have been if they had been heard in St. James's and the Tuileries."

And is not the Confederacy already represented in London by Messrs. Yancey and Mann?

We regard this latest operation of Mr. Seward's as the characteristic tactlessness of a self-conscious weakness that simulates strength. If the naval adventure hastens Seward's removal from the Washington cabinet, the United States will have no reason to record it as an "untoward event" in the annals of its Civil War.

November 29, 1861 *

YESTERDAY the counsel of the crown had to give their opinion on the naval adventure in the Bahama Channel. Their records of the case consisted of the written reports of the English officers left behind on board the *Trent* and the oral testimony of Commodore Williams, who was on board the *Trent* as Admiralty agent, but who arrived in Southampton November 27 aboard the steamer *La Plata*, when the telegraph summoned him immediately to London. The crown counsel recognized the right of the *San Jacinto* to board and search the *Trent*. As Queen Victoria's proclamation of neutrality at the outbreak of the American Civil War expressly counts *dispatches* among articles of war, there could be no doubt on this point either. There thus remained the question whether Messrs. Mason, Slidell, & Co. were themselves contraband and, therefore, confiscable. The crown counsel seem to be of this opinion, for they dropped the whole *material* question of law. According to the report in the *Times*, their judgment blames the commander of the *San Jacinto* for only a single *procedural error*. Instead of Messrs. Mason, Slidell, & Co., he should have taken the *Trent* itself in tow as a prize, brought it to the nearest American port, and there surrendered it to the judgment of a North American prize court. This is incontestably the procedure corresponding to English and, therefore, to North American maritime law.

It is equally incontestable that the English frequently violated this rule during the anti-Jacobin war and proceeded in the summary fashion of the *San Jacinto*. However that may be, by this opinion of the crown counsel the whole conflict is reduced to a *technical error* and hence deprived of any immediate import. Two circumstances make it easy for the Union Government to accept this view and, therefore, to afford formal satisfaction. First, Captain Wilkes, the commander of the *San Jacinto*, could not have received any direct instructions from Washington. On his return voyage from Africa to New York, he

---

* Published in *Die Presse*, Vienna, December 3, 1861.

landed on November 2 at Havana, which he left again on November 4, while his encounter with the *Trent* on the open seas took place on November 8. Captain Wilkes's stay of only two days in Havana did not permit any exchange of notes between him and his government. The Union consul was the only American authority with whom he could deal. Secondly, however, he had obviously lost his head, as his failure to insist on the surrender of the dispatches proves.

The importance of the incident lies in its moral effect on the English people and the political capital that could easily be made out of it by the English cotton friends of the Secession. Characteristic of the latter is the Liverpool indignation meeting organized by them and previously mentioned by me. The meeting took place on November 27, at three o'clock in the afternoon, in the cotton auction rooms of the Liverpool Exchange, an hour after the arrival of the alarming telegram from Southampton.

After vain attempts to force the chairmanship on Mr. Cunard, owner of the steamers plying between Liverpool and New York, and other high dignitaries of commerce, a young merchant named Spence, notorious for a partisan pamphlet in favor of the slave republic, took the chair. Contrary to the rule of English meetings, he, as chairman, proposed the motion: "To urge the government to assert the dignity of the British flag by demanding prompt satisfaction for the insult inflicted on it."

Tremendous applause, hand clapping and cheers upon cheers! The main argument of the opening speaker on the slave republic's behalf consisted in stating that slave ships had hitherto been protected by the American flag from the right to search claimed by England. And then this philanthropist launched furious attacks on the slave trade! He admitted that England had brought about the War of 1812 to 1814 with the United States by its insistence upon searching the Union's warships for deserting English sailors.

"But," he continued with wonderful dialectic, "but there is a difference between asserting the right to search to take back deserters from the English Navy, and the right to seize by force men of the highest respectability, such as Messrs. Mason and Slidell, despite the protection of the English flag!"

But he played his highest trump at the end of his diatribe.

"The other day," he roared, "while I was on the European continent, I heard an observation made as to the course of our conduct in regard to the United States, and I was unable to reply to the allusion without a blush—that the feeling of every intelligent man upon the Continent was that we would submit to any outrage and suffer every indignity offered to us by the government of the United States. Our patience has been exercised long enough—as long as it was possible to control it. At last we have arrived at facts"(!): "this is a very hard and startling fact" (!) "and it is the duty of every Englishman to apprise the government of how strong and unanimous is the feeling of this great community on the outrage offered to our flag."

This senseless bombast was greeted with a cannonade of applause. Opposing voices were howled down, hissed down, and stamped down. To the remark of a Mr. Campbell that the whole meeting was "irregular," the inexorable Spence replied: "I perfectly agree with you that it is a little irregular but at the same time the fact that we have met to consider is rather an irregular fact." To the proposal of a Mr. Turner to adjourn the meeting to the following day, so that "the city of Liverpool could have its say and a clique of cotton brokers could not usurp its name," cries of "Collar him, throw him out!" resounded from all sides. Mr. Turner, unperturbed, repeated his motion, which, however, again contrary to all the rules of English meetings, was not put to the vote. Spence triumphed. In fact, however, nothing has cooled the mood of London as much as the report of Mr. Spence's victory.

December 4, 1861*

IT IS of interest at present to become acquainted to some extent with the leading figures in the *Trent* drama. On one side stands the active hero, Captain Wilkes, the commander of the *San Jacinto*, on the other side the passive heroes, J. M. Mason and John Slidell. Captain Charles Wilkes is a direct descendant of the brother of the famous English demagogue Wilkes, who for a moment threatened to shake the throne of George III. At that time the struggle with the North American colonies saved the Hanoverian dynasty from the outbreak of an English revolution whose symptoms were perceptible both in the outcry of a Wilkes and the letters of a Junius. Captain Wilkes, born in New York in 1798, and in the service of the American Navy for forty-three years, commanded the squadron that explored the North and South Pacific Ocean, from 1838 to 1842, at the order of the federal government. He has published a report of this expedition in five volumes. He is also the author of a work on *Western America*, which contains some valuable information on California and the Oregon Territory. It is now certain that Wilkes improvised his surprise attack independently and without instructions from Washington.

The two captured commissioners of the Southern Confederacy—Messrs. Mason and Slidell—form a contrast in every respect. Mason, born in 1798, is descended from one of those old aristocratic Virginia

* Published in *Die Presse*, Vienna, December 8, 1861.

families that fled England after the Royalists had been defeated in the battle of Worcester.[1] The grandfather of our hero belonged to the circle of men who, together with Washington, Jefferson, etc., are designated by the Americans as "the revolutionary fathers." Unlike his colleague, John Slidell is neither of aristocratic descent nor a slaveholder by birth. His native city is New York, where his grandfather and father lived as honest chandlers. Mason, after occupying himself in the study of law for some years, entered upon the political stage. From 1826 he figured repeatedly as a member of the Virginia House of Burgesses; in 1837 he made his appearance in the House of Representatives of the American Congress for one session; but his importance dates only from 1847. In that year Virginia chose him for the American Senate, in which he held his seat until the spring of 1861. Slidell, now sixty-eight years old, had to leave New York hurriedly as a consequence of adultery and a duel—in short, because of a scandal. He betook himself to New Orleans, where he lived first by gambling, later by practicing law. Having become a member of the Louisiana legislature, he soon made his way to the House of Representatives and finally to the Senate. As a director of election swindles during the presidential election of 1844, and later as a participant in a swindle in public lands, he had somewhat shocked even the sort of morality that prevailed, and still prevails, in Louisiana.

Mason inherited influence; Slidell acquired it. The two men found and complemented each other in the American Senate, the bulwark of the slave oligarchy. In accordance with the American Constitution, the Senate elects a special Committee on Foreign Relations, which plays about the same role as the Privy Council played in England before the so-called cabinet, theoretically an unknown quantity in the English Constitution, usurped the functions of the Privy Council. Mason was for a long time chairman of that committee, Slidell a prominent member of it.

Mason, firmly convinced that every Virginian is a demigod and every Yankee a plebeian scamp, never tried to hide his contempt for his northern colleagues. Haughty, overbearing, insolent, he knew how to knit his brow in a somber, Zeus-like frown, and, in fact, brought to the Senate the manners indigenous to the plantation. A fanatical eulogizer of slavery, a shameless slanderer of the North and particularly of the northern working classes, a blusterer against England, Mason wearied the Senate with the prolix importunity of a viscous flow of speech that vainly sought to hide its complete vacuity under a hollow pomposity. In recent years, as a sort of demonstration, he wore gray linen homespun in Virginia, but—and this is characteristic

1. On September 3, 1651, Cromwell routed Charles II's army at Worcester.

of the man—the gray coat was adorned with loud buttons, all of which came from a New England state, Connecticut.

While Mason played the *Jupiter tonans* [Jupiter thundering] of the slave oligarchy at center stage, Slidell worked behind the scenes. With a rare talent for intrigue, tireless perseverance, and unconscionable ruthlessness, but at the same time wary, covert, never strutting but always insinuating himself, Slidell was the soul of the southern conspiratorial conclave. One can judge the man's reputation from the fact that when in 1845, shortly before the outbreak of the war with Mexico, he was sent there as envoy, Mexico refused to negotiate with such an individual. Slidell's intrigues made Polk President. Slidell was one of the most pernicious advisers of President Pierce and the evil genius of Buchanan's administration. The two, Mason and Slidell, were the principal sponsors of the Fugitive Slave Act; both of them brought about the bloodbath in Kansas; and both were the secret wirepullers of the measures whereby Buchanan's administration smuggled all the means of secession into the hands of the South, while it left the North defenseless.

As early as 1855 Mason declared on a public occasion in South Carolina that "for the South there is only one way open—immediate, absolute, and eternal separation." In March, 1861, he declared in the Senate that he owed "no allegiance to the Union Government," but retained his seat in the Senate and continued to draw his senatorial salary as long as the safety of his person allowed—a spy in the supreme council of the nation and a fraudulent preyer upon the public exchequer.

Mason's great-grandmother was a daughter of the famous Sir William Temple. He is therefore a distant relative of Palmerston. Mason and Slidell appeared to the people of the North not merely as their political opponents, but as their *personal enemies*. Hence the universal jubilation over their capture, which in its first days has even drowned out concern about the danger threatened from England.

December 7, 1861 *

THE PALMERSTON PRESS—on another occasion I will show that in foreign affairs Palmerston controls nine-tenths of the press as *absolutely* as Louis Bonaparte controls nine-tenths of the French press—feels that it works under "favorable obstacles." On the one hand, it admits that the crown lawyers have reduced the charge against the United States

---

* Published in *Die Presse*, Vienna, December 11, 1861.

to a *mere procedural error*, to a *technical mistake*. On the other hand, it boasts that on the basis of such mere legal chicanery a *categorical ultimatum* has been presented to the United States which can be justified only by a gross violation of law, not by a formal error made in the exercise of a recognized right. The Palmerston press, therefore, now again pleads the *material* question of law. The great importance of the case seems to demand a short examination of the material question of law.

As a preliminary, it may be observed that not a single English newspaper ventures to reproach the *San Jacinto* for boarding and searching the *Trent*. This point, therefore, falls outside the controversy.

Next, we again call to mind the relevant passage of Queen Victoria's neutrality proclamation of May 13, 1861. The passage reads:

"*Victoria R.*

"Whereas we are happily at peace with the Government of the United States . . . we do hereby strictly charge and command all our loving subjects . . . to abstain from violating or contravening . . . our Royal Proclamation . . . by breaking or endeavoring to break any blockade lawfully and actually established . . . or by carrying officers . . . dispatches . . . or any article or articles considered contraband of war . . . All persons so offending will incur and be liable to the several penalties and penal consequences by the said Statute or by the law of nations in that behalf imposed or denounced. And we do hereby declare, that all our subjects, and persons entitled to our protection, who may misconduct themselves . . . will do so at their peril . . . and . . . will . . . incur our high displeasure by such misconduct."

This proclamation of Queen Victoria, therefore, to begin with, declared dispatches to be contraband and subjects the ship that carries such contraband to the penalties of the law of nations. What are these penalties?

Wheaton, an American writer on international law, whose authority is equally recognized on both sides of the Atlantic Ocean, writes in his *Elements of International Law*, page 565: "The fraudulent carrying of despatches of the enemy will also subject the neutral vessel in which they are transported to capture and confiscation. The consequences of such a service are indefinite, infinitely beyond the effect of any contraband that can be conveyed. 'The carrying of two or three cargoes of military stores,' says Sir W. Scott, 'is necessarily an assistance of limited nature; but in the transmission of despatches may be conveyed the entire plan of a campaign, that may defeat all the plans of the other belligerent . . . The confiscation of the noxious article, which constitutes the penalty for contraband . . . would be ridiculous when applied to despatches. There would be no freight dependent on their transportation and therefore this penalty could not, in the nature, of things, be applied. The vehicle in which they are carried must, therefore, be confiscated.' "[1]

Walker, in his *Introduction to American Law*, says: ". . . neutrals may not be concerned in bearing hostile despatches, under the penalty of confiscation of the vehicle, and of the cargo also."[2]

Kent, who is regarded as the final authority in English courts, states in his *Commentaries:* "If, on search of a ship, it is found that she carries enemy despatches, she incurs the penalty of capture and of confiscation by judgment of a prize court."[3]

Dr. Robert Phillimore, "Advocate of Her Majesty in her office of Admiralty," says in his most recent work on international law, page 370: "Official communications from an official person on the public affairs of a belligerent government are such despatches as impress an hostile character upon the carriers of them. The mischievous consequences of such a service cannot be estimated, and extend far beyond the effect of any contraband that can be conveyed, for it is manifest that by the carriage of such despatches the most important operation of a belligerent may be forwarded or obstructed . . . The penalty is confiscation of the ship which conveys the despatches and . . . of the cargo, if both belong to the same master."[4]

Two points, therefore, are established. Queen Victoria's proclamation of May 13, 1861, subjects *English* ships that forward dispatches of the Confederacy to the penalties of international law. According to its English and American commentators, international law inflicts the penalty of capture and confiscation on such ships.

Hence Palmerston's organs *lied* on higher command—and we were naïve enough to believe their lie that the captain of the *San Jacinto* had neglected to search for dispatches on the *Trent* and had therefore found none. The *Trent* had consequently become bullet-proof through this oversight. The American journals of November 17 to 20, which could not yet know about the English lie, *unanimously* declare, on the contrary, that the dispatches were seized and are already being printed for the purpose of submitting them to Congress in Washington. This alters the whole case. Because of these dispatches the *San Jacinto* had the right to take the *Trent* in tow and every American prize court had the duty to confiscate her and her cargo. With the *Trent*, her passengers necessarily also came within the purview of American jurisdiction.

Messrs. Mason, Slidell, & Co., as soon as the *Trent* had touched at

---

1. Henry Wheaton, *Elements of International Law* (Boston, 1857).
2. Timothy Walker, *Introduction to American Law* (Boston, 1855).
3. James Kent, *Commentaries on American Law*, Vol. I (New York, 1826).
4. Robert Phillimore, *Commentaries upon International Law*, Vol. III (Philadelphia, 1857).

[Fort] Monroe, [Virginia], came under American jurisdiction as rebels. If, therefore, instead of towing the *Trent* herself to an American port, the captain of the *San Jacinto* had contented himself with seizing the dispatches and their bearers, he would in no way have worsened the position of Mason, Slidell, & Co., while on the other hand, his procedural error benefited the *Trent*, her cargo and her passengers. And, in fact, it would have been unprecedented for England to wish to declare war on the United States because Captain Wilkes committed a procedural error harmful to the United States but useful to England.

The question whether Mason, Slidell, & Co. were themselves contraband was only raised and could only be raised because Palmerston journals had spread the *lie* that Captain Wilkes had neither searched for nor carried off any dispatches. For in this case Mason, Slidell, & Co. in fact constituted the only object on the ship *Trent* that could possibly fall under the category of contraband. Still, let us disregard this for a moment. Queen Victoria's proclamation designates "officers" of a belligerent party as contraband. Are "officers" merely military officers? Were Mason, Slidell, & Co. "officers" of the Confederacy? "Officers," says Samuel Johnson in his dictionary of the English language, are "men employed by the public," that is, in German: *öffentliche Beamte* [public officials]. Walker gives the same definition. (See his dictionary, edition of 1861.[5])

According to the usage of the English language, therefore, Mason, Slidell, & Co., these emissaries, *id est* [that is] officials of the Confederacy, come under the category of "officers," whom the royal proclamation declares to be contraband. The captain of the *Trent* knew them in this capacity, and hence made himself, his ship, and his passengers confiscable. If, according to Phillimore and all other authorities, a ship is confiscable as the carrier of an enemy dispatch, because it violates neutrality, so it is true in still higher degree of the *person* carrying the dispatches. According to Wheaton, even an enemy *ambassador*, so long as he finds himself in transit, may be seized. But in general, the basis of all international law is that every member of the belligerent group may be regarded and treated as a "belligerent" by the opposing group.

"So long as a man continues to be a citizen of his own country," says Vattel, "he is the enemy of all those with whom his nation is at war."[6]

One sees, therefore, that the English Crown lawyers reduced the point of contention to a mere *procedural error*, not an error *in re* [in substance], but error *in forma* [in form], because in fact *no material violation of law* is in question. The Palmerston journals again babble

---

5. John Walker, *A Critical Pronouncing Dictionary of the English Language* (new ed., Dublin, 1856).

6. Emmerich von Vattel, *Le droit des gens*.

about the material question of law, because a mere procedural error, and one in the interest of the *Trent* at that, offers no tenable pretext for a high-flown ultimatum.

In the meantime, weighty voices have been raised in this matter from two diametrically opposite sides: on the one side Messrs. Bright and Cobden, and on the other side David Urquhart. These men are enemies in principle and in person: the two peacemaking cosmopolites, the other the *"last Englishman"*; the former always ready to sacrifice every international right to international trade, the other hesitating not a moment: *"Fiat justitia, pereat mundus"* ["Let justice be done, though the world perish"], and by "justice" he means "English" justice. The voices of Bright and Cobden are important because they represent a powerful fraction of middle-class interests and are represented in the ministry by Gladstone, Milner-Gibson, and also, more or less, by Sir Cornwall Lewis. The voice of Urquhart is important because international law is his life study and everyone recognizes him as an incorruptible interpreter of it.

The usual newspaper sources will communicate Bright's speech on behalf of the United States and also Cobden's letter, which is conceived in the same sense. Hence I will not linger over them.

Urquhart's organ, the *Free Press*, states in its last number, published on December 4: "We must bombard New York! One could hear this frantic cry eight days ago in the streets of London, on the evening of the arrival of news of a quite insignificant war incident. The act was one which England has committed as a matter of course in every war—namely, the seizure of enemy persons and property on board a neutral ship."

The *Free Press* further develops the point that in 1856, at the Congress in Paris, Palmerston, without authority from the Crown or Parliament, sacrificed English maritime rights *in the interest of Russia,* and then goes on to say: "At that time, in order to justify this sacrifice, Palmerston's organs declared: If we maintained the rights of boarding and search, we would unavoidably be involved in a war with the United States at the moment of the first war in Europe. And now he calls upon us through the same organs to bombard New York because the United States acts according to the same laws that they have in common with us."

In regard to the utterances of the "organs of public opinion," the *Free Press* remarks: "The jackass bray of Baron Münchhausen's vibrating post horn was nothing compared to the clangor of the British press over the capture of Mason and Slidell."

Then it humorously puts together, in "strophe" and "antistrophe," the contradictions by which the English press seeks to convict the United States of a "breach of law."

*November 30, 1861**

SINCE THE declaration of war against Russia I never witnessed an excitement throughout all the strata of English society equal to that produced by the news of the *Trent* affair, conveyed to Southampton by the *La Plata* on the 27th inst. At about 2 o'clock P.M., by means of the electric telegraph, the announcement of the "untoward event" was posted in the newsrooms of all the British exchanges. All commercial securities went down, while the price of saltpeter went up. Consols declined three-quarters of one percent, while at Lloyd's war risks of five guineas were demanded on vessels from New York. Late in the evening the wildest rumors circulated in London, to the effect that the American Minister had forthwith been sent his passports, that orders had been issued for the immediate seizure of all American ships in the ports of the United Kingdom, and so forth. The cotton friends of Secession at Liverpool improved the opportunity for holding, at ten minutes' notice, in the cotton salesroom of the Stock Exchange, an indignation meeting, under the presidency of Mr. Spence, the author of some obscure pamphlet in the interest of the Southern Confederacy. Commodore Williams, the Admiralty agent on board the *Trent*, who had arrived with the *La Plata*, was at once summoned to London.

On the following day, the 28th of November, the London press exhibited, on the whole, a tone of moderation strangely contrasting with the tremendous political and mercantile excitement of the previous evening. The Palmerston papers, the *Times, Morning Post, Daily Telegraph, Morning Advertiser*, and *Sun*, had received orders to calm down rather than to exasperate. The *Daily News*, by its strictures on the conduct of the *San Jacinto*, evidently aimed less at hitting the Federal government than clearing itself of the suspicion of "Yankee prejudices," while the *Morning Star*, John Bright's organ, without passing any judgment on the policy and wisdom of the "act," pleaded its lawfulness. There were only two exceptions to the general tenor of the London press. The Tory scribblers of the *Morning Herald* and the *Standard*, forming in fact one paper under different names, gave full vent to their savage satisfaction of having at last caught the "republicans" in a trap, and finding a *casus belli* ready cut out. They were supported by one other journal, the *Morning Chronicle*, which for years had tried to prolong its checkered existence by alternately selling itself to the poisoner Palmer and the Tuileries. The excitement of the Exchange greatly subsided in consequence of the pacific tone of the leading London papers. On the same 28th of November, Commander Williams

---

* Published in the *New-York Daily Tribune* December 19, 1861.

attended at the Admiralty and reported the circumstances of the occurrence in the Old Bahama Channel. His report, together with the written
depositions of the officers on board the *Trent*, was at once submitted
to the law officers of the crown, whose opinion, late in the evening,
was officially brought to the notice of Lord Palmerston, Earl Russell,
and other members of the government.

On the 29th of November there was to be remarked some slight
change in the tone of the ministerial press. It became known that the
law officers of the crown, on a technical ground, had declared the
proceedings of the frigate *San Jacinto* illegal, and that later in the day
the Cabinet, summoned to a general council, had decided to send by
next steamer to Lord Lyons instructions to conform to the opinion of
the English law officers. Hence the excitement in the principal places
of business, such as the Stock Exchange, Lloyd's, the Jerusalem, the
Baltic, etc., set in with redoubled force, and was further stimulated
by the news that the projected shipments to America of saltpeter had
been stopped on the previous day, and that on the 29th a general order
was received at the Customs House prohibiting the exportation of this
article to any country except under certain stringent conditions. The
English funds further fell three-quarters and at one time a real panic
prevailed in all the stock markets, it having become impossible to trans-
act any business in some securities, while in all descriptions a severe
depression of prices occurred. In the afternoon a recovery in the stock
market was due to several rumors, but principally to the report that
Mr. Adams had expressed his opinion that the act of the *San Jacinto*
would be disavowed by the Washington Cabinet.

On the 30th of November (today) all the London papers, with the
single exception of the *Morning Star*, put the alternative of reparation
by the Washington Cabinet or—war.

Having summed up the history of the events from the arrival of the
La Plata to the present day, I shall now proceed to recording opinions.
There were, of course, two points to be considered—on the one hand
the law, on the other hand the policy, of the seizure of the Southern
commissioners on board an English mail steamer.

As to the legal aspect of the affair, the first difficulty mooted by
the Tory press and the *Morning Chronicle* was that the United States
had never recognized the Southern secessionists as belligerents, and,
consequently, could not claim belligerent rights in regard to them.

This quibble was at once disposed of by the ministerial press itself.
"We," said the *Times*, "have already recognized these Confederate
States as a belligerent power, and we shall, when the time comes, recognize their government. Therefore we have imposed on ourselves all
the duties and inconveniences of a power neutral between two belligerents." Hence, whether or not the United States recognize the Con-

federates as belligerents they have the right to insist upon England submitting to all the duties and inconveniences of a neutral in maritime warfare.

Consequently, with the exceptions mentioned, the whole London press acknowledges the right of the *San Jacinto* to overhaul, visit, and search the *Trent*, in order to ascertain whether she carried goods or persons belonging to the category of "contraband of war." The *Times* insinuation that the English law of decision "was given under circumstances very different from those which now occur"; that "steamers did not then exist, and mail vessels, carrying letters wherein all the nations of the world have immediate interest, were unknown"; that "we" (the English) "were fighting for existence, and did in those days what we should not allow others to do," was not seriously thrown out. Palmerston's private *Moniteur*, the *Morning Post*, declared on the same day that mail steamers were simple merchantmen, not sharing the exemption from the right of search of men-of-war and transports. The right of search on the part of the *San Jacinto* was in point of fact conceded by the London press as well as the law officers of the crown. The objection that the *Trent*, instead of sailing from a belligerent to a belligerent port, was, on the contrary, bound from a neutral to a neutral port, fell to the ground by Lord Stowell's decision that the right of search is intended to ascertain the destination of a ship.

In the second instance, the question arose whether by firing a round shot across the bows of the *Trent*, and subsequently throwing a shell, bursting close to her, the *San Jacinto* had not violated the usage and courtesies appurtenant to the exercise of the right of visitation and search. It was generally conceded by the London press that, since the details of the event have till now been only ascertained by the depositions of one of the parties concerned, no such minor question could influence the decision to be arrived at by the British government.

The right of search exercised by the *San Jacinto* thus being conceded, what had she to look for? For *contraband of war*, presumed to be conveyed by the *Trent*. What is contraband of war? Are the dispatches of the belligerent government contraband of war? Are the persons carrying those dispatches contraband of war? And, both questions being answered in the affirmative, do those dispatches and the bearers of them continue to be contraband of war if found on a merchant ship bound from a neutral port to a neutral port? The London press admits that the decisions of the highest legal authorities on both sides of the Atlantic are so contradictory, and may be claimed with such appearance of justice for both the affirmative and the negative, that, at all events, a *prima facie* case is made out for the *San Jacinto*.

Concurrently with this prevalent opinion of the English press, the English crown lawyers have altogether dropped the material question, and only taken up the formal question. They assert that the law of nations was not violated in *substance* but in *form* only. They have arrived at the conclusion that the *San Jacinto* failed in seizing, on her own responsibility, the Southern commissioners, instead of taking the *Trent* to a Federal port and submitting the question to a Federal prize court, no armed cruiser having a right to make itself a judge at sea. A violation in the *procedure* of the *San Jacinto* is, therefore, all that is imputed to her by the English crown lawyers, who, in my opinion, are right in their conclusion. It might be easy to unearth precedents showing England to have similarly trespassed on the formalities of maritime law, but violations of law can never be allowed to supplant the law itself.

The question may now be mooted whether the reparation demanded by the English Government—that is, the restitution of the Southern commissioners—be warranted by an injury which the English themselves avow to be of form rather than of substance? A lawyer of the Temple, in today's *Times*, remarks in respect to this point: "If the case is not so clearly in our favor as that a decision in the American Court condemning the vessel would have been liable to be questioned by us as manifestly contrary to the laws of nations, then the irregularity of the American captain in allowing the *Trent* to proceed to Southampton clearly redounded to the advantage of the British owners and the British passengers. Could we in such case find a ground of international quarrel in an error of procedure which in effect told in our own favor?"

Still, if the American Government must concede, as it seems to me, that Captain Wilkes has committed a violation of maritime law, whether formal or material, their fair fame and their interest ought alike to prevent them from nibbling at the terms of the satisfaction to be given to the injured party. They ought to remember that they do the work of the secessionists in embroiling the United States in a war with England, that such a war would be a godsend to Louis Bonaparte in his present difficulties, and would consequently be supported by all the official weight of France; and lastly that, what with the actual force under the command of the British on the North American and West Indian stations, what with the forces of the Mexican expedition, the English government would have at its disposal an overwhelming maritime power.

As to the policy of the seizure in the Bahama Channel, the voice not only of the English but of the European press is unanimous in expressions of bewilderment at the strange conduct of the American Government, provoking such tremendous international dangers for gaining the bodies of Messrs. Mason, Slidell, & Co. while Messrs. Yancey and Mann are strutting in London. The *Times* is certainly right in saying: "Even Mr. Seward himself must know that the voices of these Southern commissioners, sounding from their captivity, are a thousand times more eloquent in London and in Paris than they would have been if they had been heard at St. James's and the Tuileries."

The people of the United States, having magnanimously submitted to a curtailment of their own liberties in order to save their country, will certainly be no less ready to turn the tide of popular opinion in England by openly avowing, and carefully making up for, an international blunder the vindication of which might realize the boldest hopes of the rebels.

December 7, 1861*

THE FRIENDS of the United States on this side of the Atlantic anxiously hope that conciliatory steps will be taken by the Federal government. They do so not from a concurrence in the frantic crowing of the British press over a war incident which according to the English crown lawyers themselves resolves itself into a mere error of procedure, and may be summed up in the words that there has been a breach of international law because Captain Wilkes, instead of taking the *Trent*, her cargo, her passengers, and the commissioners, did only take the commissioners. Nor springs the anxiety of the well-wishers of the Great Republic from an apprehension lest, in the long run, it should not prove able to cope with England, although backed by the civil war; and least of all do they expect the United States to abdicate, even for a moment, and in a dark hour of trial, the proud position held by them in the council of nations. The motives that prompt them are of quite a different nature.

In the first instance, the business next in hand for the United States is to crush the rebellion and to restore the Union. The wish uppermost in the minds of the slavocracy and their northern tools was always to plunge the United States into a war with England. The first step of England as soon as hostilities broke out would be to recognize the Southern Confederacy, and the second to terminate the blockade. Secondly, no general, if not forced, will accept battle at the time and under the conditions chosen by his enemy. "A war with America," says the *Economist*, a paper deeply in Palmerston's confidence, "must always be one of the most lamentable incidents in the history of England, but if it is to happen, the present is certainly the period at which it will do us the minimum of harm, and the only moment in our joint annals at which it would confer on us an incidental and partial com-

* Published in the *New-York Daily Tribune* December 25, 1861.

pensation." The very reason accounting for the eagerness of England to seize upon any decent pretext for war at this "only moment" ought to withhold the United States from forwarding such a pretext at this "only moment." You go not to war with the aim to do your enemy "the minimum of harm" and even to confer upon him by the war "an incidental and partial compensation." The opportunity of the moment would all be on one side, on the side of your foe. Is there any great strain of reasoning wanted to prove that an internal war raging in a state is the least opportune time for entering upon a foreign war? At every other moment the mercantile classes of Great Britain would have looked upon the war against the United States with the utmost horror. Now, on the contrary, a large and influential party of the mercantile community has for months been urging on the government to violently break the blockade, and thus provide the main branch of British industry with its raw material. The fear of a curtailment of the English export trade to the United States has lost its sting by the curtailment of that trade having already actually occurred. "They" (the Northern States), says the *Economist,* "are wretched customers, instead of good ones." The vast credit usually given by English commerce to the United States, principally by the acceptance of bills drawn from China and India, has been already reduced to scarcely a fifth of what it was in 1857. Last, not least, Decembrist France, bankrupt, paralyzed at home, beset with difficulty abroad, pounces upon an Anglo-American war as a real godsend, and, in order to buy English support in Europe, will strain all her power to support "Perfidious Albion" on the other side of the Atlantic. Read only the French newspapers. The pitch of indignation to which they have wrought themselves in their tender care for the "honor of England," their fierce diatribes as to the necessity on the part of England to revenge the outrage on the Union Jack, their vile denunciations of everything American, would be truly appalling if they were not ridiculous and disgusting at the same time. Lastly, if the United States give way in this instance, they will not derogate one iota of their dignity. England has reduced her complaint to a mere *error of procedure, a technical blunder* of which she has made herself systematically guilty in all her maritime wars, but against which the United States have never ceased to protest, and which President Madison, in his message inaugurating the War of 1812, expatiated upon as one of the most shocking breaches of international law. If the United States may be defended in paying England with her own coin, will they be accused for magnanimously disavowing, on the part of a single American captain, acting on his own responsibility, what they always denounced as a systematic usurpation on the part of the British Navy! In point of fact, the gain of such a procedure would be all on the American side. England, on the one hand, would have acknowledged the right of the United States to capture and bring to adjudication before an American prize court every English ship employed in the service of the Confederacy. On the other hand, she would, once for all, before the eyes of the whole world, have practically resigned a claim which she was not brought to desist from either in the Peace of Ghent in 1814 or the transactions carried on between Lord Ashburton and Secretary Webster in 1842. The question then comes to this: Do you prefer to turn the "untoward event" to your own account, or, blinded by the passions of the moment, turn it to the account of your foes at home and abroad?

Since this day week, when I sent you my last letter, British consols have again lowered, the decline, compared with last Friday, amounting to 2 percent, the present prices being 89¾ to ⅞ for money and to 90 to ⅛ for the new account on the 9th of January. This quotation corresponds to the quotation of the British consols during the first two years of the Anglo-Russian war. This decline is altogether due to the warlike interpretation put upon the American papers conveyed by the last mail, to the exacerbating tone of the London press, whose moderation of two days' standing was but a feint, ordered by Palmerston, to the dispatch of troops for Canada, to the proclamation forbidding the export of arms and materials for gunpowder, and lastly to the daily ostentatious statements concerning the formidable preparations for war in the docks and maritime arsenals.

Of one thing you may be sure, Palmerston wants a legal pretext for a war with the United States, but meets in the cabinet councils with a most determined opposition on the part of Messrs. Gladstone and Milner-Gibson, and, to a less degree, of Sir Cornwall Lewis. "The noble viscount" is backed by Russell, an abject tool in his hands, and the whole Whig coterie. If the Washington Cabinet should furnish the desired pretext, the present Cabinet will be sprung, to be supplanted by a Tory administration. The preliminary steps for such a change of scenery have been already settled between Palmerston and Disraeli. Hence the furious war cry of the *Morning Herald* and the *Standard*, those hungry wolves howling at the prospect of the long-missed crumbs from the public almoner.

Palmerston's designs may be shown up by calling into memory a few facts. It was he who insisted upon the proclamation acknowledging the secessionists as belligerents, on the morning of the 14th of May, after he had been informed by telegraph from Liverpool that Mr. Adams would arrive at London on the night of the 13th of May. He, after a severe struggle with his colleagues, dispatched 3,000 men to Canada, an army ridiculous if intended to cover a frontier of 1,500 miles, but a clever sleight-of-hand if the Rebellion was to be cheered and the Union to be irritated. He, many weeks ago, urged Bonaparte to propose a joint armed intervention "in the internecine struggle," supported that project in the Cabinet council, and failed only in carrying it by the resistance of his colleagues. He and Bonaparte then resorted to the Mexican intervention as a *pis aller*. That operation served two purposes, by provoking just resentment on the part of the Americans, and by simultaneously furnishing a pretext for the dispatch of a squadron, ready, as the *Morning Post* has it, "to perform whatever duty the hostile conduct of the government of Washington may require us to perform in the waters of the Northern Atlantic." At the time when that expedition was started, the *Morning Post*, together with the *Times* and the smaller fry of Palmerston's press slaves, said that it was a very fine thing, and a philanthropic thing into the bargain, because it would expose the slaveholding Confederacy to two fires—the antislavery North and the antislavery force of England and France. And what says the very same *Morning Post*, this curious compound of Jenkins and Rodomonte, of plush and swash, in its today's issue, on occasion of Jefferson Davis' address? Hearken to the Palmerston oracle:

> We must look to this intervention as one that may be inoperative during a considerable period of time; and while the Northern government is too distant to admit of its attitude entering materially into this question, the Southern Confederacy, on the other hand, stretches for a great distance along the frontier of Mexico, so as to render its friendly disposition to the authors of the insurrection of no slight consequence. The Northern government has invariably railed at our neutrality, but the Southern with statesmanship and moderation has recognized in it all that we could do for either party; and whether with a view to our transactions in Mexico, or to our relations with the cabinet at Washington, the friendly forbearance of the Southern Confederacy is an important point in our favor.

I may remark that the *Nord* of December 3—a Russian paper, and consequently a paper initiated into Palmerston's designs—insinuates that the Mexican expedition was from the first set on foot, not for its ostensible purpose, but for a war against the United States.

General Scott's letter[1] had produced such a beneficent reaction in public opinion, and even on the London Stock Exchange, that the conspirators of Downing Street and the Tuileries found it necessary to let loose the *Patrie*, stating with all the airs of knowledge derived from official sources that the seizure of the Southern commissioners from the *Trent* was directly authorized by the Washington cabinet.[2]

---

1. On December 6, 1861, the London *Times* published a letter from General Winfield Scott in which he expressed the hope of a friendly solution of the *Trent* incident, saying that nobody in the United States wanted a war with England.

2. For further comment on the *Trent* affair, see "The Opinion of the Newspapers and the Opinion of the People," page 138.

A Crisis in the Slavery Question*

December 10, 1861

IN THE UNITED STATES a point of crisis has clearly made its appearance in connection with the issue underlying the whole Civil War—the *slavery question*. General Frémont is dismissed because he has declared the slaves of the *rebels* to be free. Shortly thereafter the government in Washington issues instructions to General Sherman, the commander of the expedition to South Carolina, that go further than Frémont, in that they order that fugitive slaves, even those belonging to *loyal* slaveholders, be received as wage workers and, under certain circumstances, be armed, consoling the "loyal" slaveholders with the prospect of later compensation. Colonel Cochrane goes further than Frémont and demands the general arming of the slaves as a war measure. Secretary of War Cameron publicly approves Cochrane's "opinions." Thereupon the Secretary of the Interior disavows the Secretary of War in the name of the government. The Secretary of War, at a public meeting, repeats his "opinion" with greater vigor, and declares that he will include it in his report to Congress. Like General Dix in eastern Virginia, General Halleck, Frémont's successor in Missouri, drives the refugee Negroes out of the military camp and forbids them to appear in future near his army's positions. At the same time General Wool receives with open arms the black "contrabands" in Fort Monroe; the old leaders of the Democratic party, Senators Dickinson and Croswell (former members of the so-called Regency), declare their agreement with Cochrane and Cameron in an open letter, and Colonel Jennison in Kansas exceeds all his military predecessors with a speech to his troops in which he says, among other things:

"No temporizing with rebels and those who sympathize with them ... I told General Frémont that I would not have taken up the sword

---

* Published in *Die Presse*, Vienna, December 14, 1861.

if I thought that slavery would survive this war. The slaves of the rebels will always find protection in this camp and will be defended to the last man and the last bullet. I want no men who are not Abolitionists among my troops; I have no place for them, and I hope that such people are not found among us, for everybody knows that slavery is the base, the center, and the spearhead of this hellish war . . . If the government should disapprove of the way I am acting, it can have my commission back, but in that case I would act on my own hook, even if I could count on only six men to begin with."

In the border slave states, particularly in Missouri, and to a lesser extent in Kentucky, etc, the slavery question is already solving itself in practice. A tremendous disappearance of slave elements is taking place. Thus 50,000 slaves have vanished from Missouri, some of them having run away and others having been deported by the slaveholders themselves to the more southern states.

One highly important and characteristic event is, peculiarly enough, not mentioned in a single English newspaper. On November 18 delegates from forty-five counties of North Carolina assembled on Hatteras Island, named a provisional government, revoked the Acts of Secession, and proclaimed North Carolina's return to the bosom of the Union. The counties with delegates at this convention were called upon to elect representatives to the Congress in Washington.

The Washington Cabinet and
the Western Powers*

December 20, 1861

ONE OF THE most striking surprises of a war as rich in surprises as the English-French-Turkish-Russian war was incontestably the united declaration on maritime law made in Paris in the spring of 1856. When the war against Russia began, England suspended its most formidable weapons against Russia—the confiscation of enemy-owned commodities on neutral ships, and privateering. At the end of the war England broke these weapons to pieces and sacrificed the fragments on the altar of peace. Russia, the ostensibly defeated party, received a concession that, by means of a series of "armed neutralities," wars, and diplomatic intrigues, she had vainly tried to extort since Catherine II. On the contrary, England, the ostensible victor, renounced the great means of attack and defense that had grown out of her sea power and that she had maintained for a century and a half against a world in arms.

The humanitarian grounds that served as pretext for the declaration of 1856 vanish before the most superficial examination. Privateering is no greater barbarism than the action of volunteer corps or guerrillas in land warfare. The privateers are the guerrillas of the sea. Confiscation of private goods of a belligerent nation also occurs in land warfare. Do military requisitions, for example, hit only the enemy treasury and not the property of private persons also? The nature of land warfare protects enemy property on neutral soil and therefore under the sovereignty of a neutral power. The nature of sea warfare washes away these barriers, since the sea, as the common highway of nations, cannot fall to the sovereignty of any neutral power.

In fact, however, the declaration of 1856 conceals under its philanthropic phrases a great inhumanity. In principle, it transforms war from a war of peoples into a war of governments. It endows property

* Published in *Die Presse*, Vienna, December 25, 1861.

with an inviolability that it denies to persons. It emancipates commerce from the terrors of war and thereby makes the classes engaged in trade and industry indifferent to the terrors of war. For the rest, it is implicit that the humanitarian pretexts of the declaration of 1856 were addressed only to the European gallery, quite like the religious pretexts of the Holy Alliance.

It is a well-known fact that Lord Clarendon, who signed away English maritime rights at the Congress of Paris, acted, as he subsequently confessed in the Upper House, without the prior knowledge of or orders from the crown. His sole authority consisted of a *private letter* from Palmerston. Hitherto Palmerston has not dared demand the sanction of the English Parliament for the declaration of Paris and its signature by Clarendon. Apart from the debates on the contents of the declaration, there was fear of debates on the question whether, independently of crown and Parliament, an English minister may usurp the right to sweep away the old basis of English sea power with a stroke of the pen. That this ministerial *coup d'état* did not lead to stormy interpellations, but, rather, was silently accepted as a *fait accompli*, Palmerston owed to the influence of the Manchester School [of free trade]. The interests represented by it—hence also the philanthropy, civilization and progress—were accordingly found to be an innovation that would allow English commerce to continue pursuing its business with the enemy undisturbed on neutral ships, while sailors and soldiers dueled for the honor of the nation. The Manchester men were jubilant over the fact that by a sudden unconstitutional attack the Minister had bound England to international concessions whose attainment through constitutional parliamentary means was entirely improbable. Hence the indignation of the Manchester party in England at the present moment over the disclosures of the Blue Book submitted by Seward to the Congress in Washington!

As is known, the United States was the only great power that refused to accede to the declaration of Paris of 1856. If it renounced privateering, then it would have to create a great national navy. Any weakening of its means of war at sea threatened it simultaneously with the incubus of a standing army on the European scale. Nonetheless, President Buchanan had stated that he was ready to accept the Declaration of Paris provided the same inviolability was assured to all property, enemy or neutral, found on ships, with the exception of contraband of war. His proposal was rejected. From Seward's Blue Book it now appears that Lincoln, immediately after his assumption of power, offered to England and France the adherence of the United States to the Declaration of Paris, on condition that the prohibition of privateering be extended to the parts of the United States now in revolt, that is, to the Southern Confederacy. The answer he received amounted in practice to a recognition of the belligerent rights of the Southern Confederacy.

"Humanity, progress and civilization" whispered to the cabinets of St. James's and the Tuileries that the prohibition of privateering would extraordinarily reduce the chances of secession and hence of the dissolution of the United States. Hence the Confederacy was hastily recognized as a belligerent party, in order afterwards to reply to the Cabinet in Washington that England and France could naturally not recognize the proposal of one belligerent party as a binding law for the other belligerent party. The same "noble uprightness" has animated all the diplomatic negotiations of England and France with the Union government since the outbreak of the Civil War, and had the *San Jacinto* not held up the *Trent* in the Bahama Straits, any other incident would then have sufficed to provide a pretext for the conflict that Lord Palmerston watched for.

The Opinion of the Newspapers and the
Opinion of the People*

December 25, 1861

CONTINENTAL POLITICIANS who imagine that in the London press they have a thermometer for the temper of the English people are at the present moment drawing inevitably false conclusions. At the first news of the *Trent* affair, English national pride flared up, and the call for war with the United States resounded from practically all sections of society. The London press, on the other hand, affected moderation, and even the *Times* doubted whether a *casus belli* existed at all. Whence this phenomenon? Palmerston was uncertain whether the crown lawyers were in a position to draw up some sort of legal pretext for war. One and a half weeks before the arrival of the *La Plata* in South-ampton, agents of the Southern Confederacy in Liverpool had ad-dressed themselves to the English Cabinet, denounced the intention of American cruisers to put out from English ports and intercept Messrs. Mason, Slidell, etc., on the high seas, and requested the intervention of the English Government. In accordance with the opinion of the Crown lawyers, the latter refused the request. Hence, in the beginning, the pacific and moderate tone of the London Press, in contrast to the belli-cose impatience of the people. Nevertheless, as soon as the Crown lawyers—the Attorney General and the Attorney Solicitor [Solicitor General], both themselves members of the cabinet—had picked out a *technical* pretext for a quarrel with the United States, the relation be-tween people and press turned into the opposite. The war fever in the press rose in proportion as it abated among the people. At this moment a war with America is as unpopular with all strata of the English nation, except the friends of cotton and the country squires, as the howling for war in the press is overwhelming.

* Published in *Die Presse*, Vienna, December 31, 1861.

But now consider the London press! At its head stands the *Times*, whose chief editor, Bob Lowe, was formerly a demagogue in Australia, where he agitated for separation from England. He is a subordinate member of the cabinet, a sort of minister of education and a mere creature of Palmerston. *Punch* is the court jester of the *Times*, which transforms its *sesquipedalia verba* [bombastic words] into flat jokes and inane caricatures. A leading editor of *Punch* was given a post in the Board of Health by Palmerston at an annual salary of £1,000.

The *Morning Post* is in part Palmerston's private property. Another part of this singular institution is sold to the French Embassy. The rest belongs to the *"haute volée"* [high society] and supplies the most precise reports for court parasites and ladies' tailors. The *Morning Post* is therefore notorious among the English people as the *Jenkins*[1] of the press.

The *Morning Advertiser* is the joint property of the "licensed victuallers," that is, the taverns, which, besides beer, may also sell liquor. It is, furthermore, the organ of the English Pietists and ditto of the sporting characters, that is, the people who make a business of horse-racing, betting, boxing, and the like. The editor of this sheet, Mr. Grant, formerly employed by newspapers as a stenographer, and literarily quite an uneducated man, has had the honor of getting invited to Palmerston's private soirées. Since then he has raved about the "truly English minister" whom, at the outbreak of the Russian war, he once denounced as a "Russian agent." It must be added that the pious patrons of this liquor journal stand under the high command of the Earl of Shaftesbury, and that Shaftesbury is Palmerston's son-in-law. Shaftesbury is the pope of the Low Church men, who engraft the *Sanctus Spiritus* [Holy Ghost] on the profane *Spiritus* of the worthy *Advertiser*.

The *Morning Chronicle! Quantum mutatus ab illo!* [How different from what it was!] For nearly half a century the great organ of the Whig Party and the not unfortunate rival of the *Times*, its star paled after the Whig war.[2] It went through all kinds of metamorphoses, turned itself into a penny paper, and sought to live on "sensations," as, for example, by taking the side of the poisoner Palmer. It later sold itself to the French Embassy, which, however, soon regretted throwing away its money. It then threw itself into anti-Bonapartism, but with no better success. Finally it found its long-missed buyer in Messrs. Yancey and Mann—the agents of the Southern Confederacy in London.

The *Daily Telegraph* is the private property of a certain Levy. His

---

1. The English stock figure for lackey.
2. The Crimean War, 1853–1856.

sheet is branded by the English press itself as Palmerston's mob organ. Besides this function, it operates a *chronique scandaleuse*. It is characteristic of this *Telegraph* that when the news about the *Trent* arrived it, on orders from above, declared *war to be impossible*. The dignity and moderation that was dictated to it seemed so strange to itself that since then it has published half a dozen articles on the moderation and dignity it displayed on that occasion. As soon, however, as the order for a turnabout reached it, the *Telegraph*, to compensate itself for the constraint that had been imposed upon it, sought to out-yell all its comrades in noisy clamor for war.

The *Globe* is the ministerial evening paper, receiving official subsidies from all Whig ministries.

The Tory papers, *Morning Herald* and *Evening Standard*, both belonging to the same *boutique*, are governed by a double motive: on the one hand, hereditary hatred of "the *revolted* English colonies," and on the other, a chronic ebb in their finances. They know that a war with America must rupture the present coalition cabinet and pave the way for a Tory cabinet. With the Tory cabinet, official subsidies for the *Herald* and *Standard* would return. Thus hungry wolves cannot howl louder for prey than these Tory sheets do for an American war with its ensuing shower of gold!

Of the London daily press, there remain only the *Daily News* and the *Morning Star* that are worth mentioning; both work against the trumpeters of war. The *Daily News* is impeded in its movement by a connection with Lord John Russell: the influence of the *Morning Star* (organ of Bright and Cobden) is reduced by its character as a "peace-at-any-price" paper.

Most of the London weeklies are mere echoes of the daily press, hence predominantly bellicose. The *Observer* is in the pay of the ministry. The *Saturday Review* strains after *esprit* and believes it has found it by affecting a cynical superiority to "humanitarian" prejudices. To show *"esprit,"* the corrupt lawyers, parsons, and schoolmasters who write for this sheet have, ever since the outbreak of the American Civil War, sneeringly applauded the slaveholders. Naturally, they later blew the war trumpet along with the *Times*. They are already drawing up campaign plans against the United States with a crude ignorance that is hair-raising.

Mention is to be made of the *Spectator*, the *Examiner*, and particularly *MacMillan's Magazine* as more or less respectable exceptions.

We see that on the whole the London press—except for the cotton organs, the provincial papers form a commendable contrast—represents nothing but Palmerston, again and again. Palmerston wants war; the English people do not. The next events will show who will win in this duel, Palmerston or the people. In any case, he is playing a more dangerous game than Louis Bonaparte did at the beginning of 1859.[3]

---

3. In January, 1859, Bonaparte (Napoleon III) was noisily preparing for war in Italy against Austria. The war, in alliance with Sardinia, lasted from April 29 to July 8, 1859.

French News Humbug—Economic
Consequences of War*

December 31, 1861

THE BELIEF in miracles seems to be withdrawn from one sphere only to settle in another. If it is driven out of nature, it rises up in politics. At least that is the view of the Paris newspapers and their allies in the telegraph agencies and the press services. Thus Paris evening papers of yesterday announce: Lord Lyons has stated to Mr. Seward that he will wait until the evening of December 20, and then depart for London, in the event that the cabinet in Washington refuses to surrender the prisoners. The Paris papers, therefore, already knew *yesterday* the steps that Lord Lyons took after receiving the dispatches that were sent him via the *Europa*. Up to *today*, however, news of the arrival of the *Europa* in New York has not yet reached Europe. The *Patrie* and its associates, *before* they are informed of the arrival of the *Europa* in America, publish in Europe news of the events that ensued in the United States on the heels of the *Europa*'s departure. The *Patrie* and its associates obviously believe that conjuring requires no magic. A local journal here remarks in its stock exchange article that these Paris inventions, quite like the incendiary articles in some English papers, serve not only the political speculations of certain persons in power, but equally also the stock exchange speculations of certain private persons.

The *Economist*, hitherto one of the loudest ranters of the war party, publishes in its latest issue a letter from a Liverpool merchant and a leading article in which the English public is warned not in any way to underestimate the dangers of a war with the United States. During the year 1861 England imported grain worth £15,380,901; of this amount nearly £6,000,000 fell to the United States. England would

---

* Published in *Die Presse*, Vienna, January 4, 1862.

suffer more from the inability to buy American grain than the United States from the inability to sell it. The United States would have the advantage of prior information. If it decided for war, then telegrams would immediately fly from Washington to San Francisco, and the American ships in the Pacific Ocean and the China seas would begin war operations many weeks before England could bring the news of the war to India.

Since the outbreak of the Civil War, the American-Chinese trade, like the American-Australian trade, has declined to an enormous extent. But insofar as it is still carried on, it buys its cargoes in most cases with English letters of credit, hence with English capital. On the other hand, English trade from India, China, and Australia, always very considerable, has grown still more since the interruption of the trade with the United States. American privateers would therefore have a great field for privateering, the English a relatively insignificant one. English investments of capital in the United States are greater than the whole of the capital invested in the English cotton industry. American investments in England are nil. The English Navy eclipses the American, but not nearly to the same extent as during the War of 1812 to 1814.

If at that time the American privateers already showed themselves far superior, what about now? An effective blockade of the North American ports, particularly in winter, is entirely out of the question. In the inland waters between Canada and the United States—and superiority here is decisive for land warfare in Canada—the United States would, at the opening of the war, hold absolute sway.

In short, the Liverpool merchant comes to the conclusion: "Nobody in England dares to recommend war merely for the sake of cotton. It would be cheaper for us to feed all the cotton districts for three years at state expense than to wage war with the United States on their behalf for one year."

Ceterum censeo [For the rest I think] that the *Trent* case will not lead to war.

A Pro-America Meeting*

January 1, 1862

THE ANTIWAR MOVEMENT among the English people gains from day to day in energy and scope. Public meetings in various parts of the country insist on settlement by *arbitration* of the dispute between England and America. Memoranda in this sense rain on the chief of the cabinet, and the independent provincial press is virtually unanimous in its opposition to the war cry of the London press.

Below is a detailed report of the meeting held last Monday at Brighton; it emanated from the working class, and the two main speakers, Messrs. Conningham and White, are influential members of Parliament, both sitting on the ministerial side of the House.

Mr. Wood (a worker) proposed the first motion, to the effect "that the dispute between England and America arose out of a misinterpretation of international law, but not out of a deliberate insult to the British flag; that accordingly it is the sense of this meeting that the whole question in dispute be referred to a neutral power for decision by arbitration; that a war with America under existing circumstances is not justifiable, but rather deserves the condemnation of the English people."

In support of this motion, Mr. Wood remarked, among other things: "It is said that this new insult is merely the last link in a chain of insults that America has offered to England. Supposing this to be true, what would it prove in regard to the present cry for war? It would prove that so long as America was undivided and strong, we accepted her insults quietly; but now, in the hour of her peril, we take advantage of a position favorable to us, to revenge the insult. Would not such a procedure brand us as cowards in the eyes of the civilized world?"

---

* Published in *Die Presse*, Vienna, January 5, 1862.

Mr. Conningham: . . . At this moment there is developing in the bosom of the Union an avowed policy of emancipation (Applause), and I express the earnest hope that no intervention on the part of the English government will be allowed (Applause) . . . Will you, freeborn Englishmen, agree to being embroiled in an anti-republican war? For this is the intention of the *Times* and the party that stands behind it . . . I appeal to the workers of England, who have the greatest interest in the preservation of peace, to raise their voices and if necessary their hands to prevent so great a crime (Loud Applause) . . . The *Times* has exerted all means to excite the warlike spirit of the country and with bitter scorn and slanders to engender a hostile mood among Americans . . . I do not belong to the so-called peace party. The *Times* favored Russia's policy and exerted (1853) all its powers to mislead our country into looking on quietly at the military encroachments of Russian barbarism in the East. I was among those who raised their voices against this false policy. At the time of the introduction of the Conspiracy Bill, whose object was to facilitate the extradition of political refugees, no expenditure of effort seemed too great for the *Times* to force this bill through the Lower House. I was one of the ninety-nine members of the House who withstood this encroachment on the liberties of the English people and brought about the Minister's downfall[1] (Applause). This minister is now the head of the cabinet. I prophesy to him that should he try to involve our country in a war with America without good and sufficient reasons, his plan will fail ignominiously. I promise him a new ignominious defeat, a worse defeat than he suffered over the Conspiracy Bill (Loud Applause) . . . I do not know the official communication that was sent to Washington; but the opinion prevails that the crown lawyers have recommended to the government that it take its stand on the quite narrow legal ground that the Southern commissioners could not be seized without the ship that carried them. This is the *conditio sine qua non* [indispensable condition] to the demand for handing over Slidell and Mason.

Suppose the people on the other side of the Atlantic Ocean do not allow their government to hand them over. Will you go to war for the bodies of these two envoys of the slavedrivers? . . . There exists in this country an antirepublican war party. Recall the last Russian war. From the secret dispatches published in Petersburg, it was clear beyond all doubt that the articles published by the *Times* in 1855 were written by a person who had access to the secret Russian state papers and documents. At that time Mr. Layard read the striking passages in the Lower House, and the *Times*, in its consternation, immediately changed its tone and blew the war trumpet next morning . . . The *Times* has repeatedly attacked the Emperor Napoleon and supported our government in its demand

---

1. Lord Palmerston, who was defeated in 1858 over the Conspiracy Bill.

for unlimited credits for land fortifications and floating batteries. After having done this and raised the cry of alarm against France, does the *Times* now wish to leave our coast exposed to the French Emperor by embroiling our country in a transatlantic war. . . ? It is to be feared that the present great war preparations are by no means intended only for the *Trent* case, but for the eventuality of recognition of the government of the slave states. Should England do this, she will cover herself with everlasting shame.

Mr. White: It is due the working class to mention that it is the originator of this meeting and that all the expenses of organizing it are borne by its committee . . . The present government never had the good sense to deal with the people sincerely and honestly . . . I have never for a moment believed that there was the remotest possibility of a war developing out of the *Trent* case. I have told more than one member of the government to his face that not a single member of the government believed in the possibility of a war on account of the *Trent* case. Why, then, these powerful preparations? I believe that England and France have reached an understanding to recognize the independence of the Southern states next spring. By then Great Britain would have a fleet of superior strength in American waters. Canada would be completely equipped for defense. If the Northern states are then inclined to make a *casus belli*, Great Britain will then be prepared. . . .

The speaker then further developed the dangers of a war with the United States, called to mind the sympathy that America showed on the death of General Havelock, the assistance that the American sailors rendered to the English ships in the unlucky engagement at Pei-ho,[2] etc. He concluded with the remark that the Civil War would end with the abolition of slavery and England must therefore stand unconditionally on the side of the North.

The original motion having been unanimously adopted, a memorandum to Palmerston was submitted to the meeting, debated, and adopted.

---

2. In June, 1859, the Chinese repulsed an Anglo-French attempt to penetrate the Pei River; an American commodore helped the British in the struggle.

On the History of Seward's Suppressed Dispatch*

January 14, 1862

THE DEFUNCT TRENT is resurrected; this time, however, as a *casus belli* not between England and the United States, but between the English people and the English Government. The new *casus belli* will be decided in Parliament, which meets next month. Doubtless you have already taken notice of the polemic of the *Daily News* and the *Star* against the *Morning Post* over the suppression and denial of Seward's peace dispatch of November 30, which was read on December 10 to Lord John Russell by the American Ambassador, Mr. Adams. Permit me now to return to this matter. With the assurance of the *Morning Post* that the Seward dispatch had not the remotest bearing on the *Trent* affair, stock exchange securities fell and property worth millions changed hands, lost on the one side, won on the other. In business and industrial circles, therefore, the wholly unjustifiable semiofficial lie of the *Morning Post* disclosed by the publication of Seward's dispatch of November 30 arouses the most tremendous indignation.

The peace news reached London the afternoon of January 9. On the same evening the *Evening Star* (the evening edition of the *Morning Star*) questioned the government about the suppression of Seward's dispatch of November 30.

The following morning, January 10, the *Morning Post* replied as follows: "It will, of course, be asked why it is that we have not heard of this sooner, seeing that Mr. Seward's dispatch must have reached Mr. Adams some time in December. The explanation of this is very simple. It is that the dispatch received by Mr. Adams was *not communicated to the English government.*"

On the evening of the same day, the *Star* completely gave the lie

* Published in *Die Presse*, Vienna, January 18, 1862.

to the *Post* and declared its "rectification" to be a miserable subterfuge. The dispatch had in fact not been "communicated" to Lord Palmerston and Lord Russell by Mr. Adams, but had been "read" to them.

Next morning, Saturday, January 11, the *Daily News* entered the lists and proved from the *Morning Post*'s article of December 21 that the latter and the government had been fully acquainted with Seward's dispatch at that time and had deliberately falsified it. The government now prepared itself for a retreat. On the evening of January 11 the semiofficial *Globe* declared that Mr. Adams had, to be sure, communicated Seward's dispatch to the government on December 19; this, however, "contained no offer on the part of the Washington cabinet," any more than it contained "an immediate apology for the insult to the English flag." This shamefaced confession of a deliberate deception of the English people for three weeks only fanned the flame higher, instead of quenching it. A cry of anger resounded through all the organs of the industrial districts of Great Britain, which yesterday finally found its echo also in the Tory newspapers. The whole question, be it noted, was placed on the order of the day, not by politicians, but by the commercial public. Today's *Morning Star* remarks on the subject:

> Lord John Russell made himself an accomplice in that suppression of the truth which is the virtual suggestion of falsehood—he allowed the *Morning Post* to state, uncontradicted, the very opposite of the truth, but he is incapable of having dictated that mendacious and incalculably pernicious article which appeared on the 21st of December . . . There can be only *one* man high enough in office, and low enough in character, to have inspired the atrocious composition. The Minister who mutilated the Afghan dispatch is alone capable of having suppressed . . . Mr. Seward's message of peace . . . The foolish leniency of the House of Commons condoned the one offense. Will not Parliament and people unite in the infliction of punishment for the other?

A Coup d'État of Lord John Russell*

January 17, 1862

LORD JOHN RUSSELL's position during the recent crisis was a thoroughly vexatious one, even for a man whose whole parliamentary life proves that he has rarely hesitated to sacrifice real power for official position. Nobody has forgotten that Lord John Russell lost the premiership to Palmerston, but no one seems to remember that he acquired the Foreign Office from Palmerston. The whole world has considered it as axiomatic that Palmerston directed the cabinet in his own name and foreign policy under the name of Russell. On the arrival of the first peace news from New York, Whigs and Tories vied with each other in trumpet blasts for the glorification of Palmerston's statesmanship, while the Minister of Foreign Affairs, Lord John Russell, was not even a candidate for the eulogy as his assistant. He was completely ignored. But hardly had the scandal caused by the suppressed American dispatch of November 30 broken out, when Russell's name was resurrected from the dead.

Attack and defense now made the discovery that the *responsible* Minister of Foreign Affairs was called Lord John Russell! But now even Russell's patience gave out. Without waiting for the opening of Parliament, and contrary to all ministerial precedent, he immediately published in the official *Gazette* of January 12 his own correspondence with Lord Lyons. This correspondence proves that Seward's dispatch of November 30 was read by Mr. Adams to Lord John Russell on December 19; that Russell expressly acknowledged this dispatch as an *apology* for the act of Captain Wilkes, and that Mr. Adams, after Russell's disclosures, considered a peaceful outcome of the dispute as certain. After this *official* disclosure, what becomes of the *Morning*

---

* Published in *Die Presse*, Vienna, January 21, 1862.

Post of December 21, which denied the arrival of any dispatch from Seward regarding the *Trent* case; what becomes of the *Morning Post* of January 10, which blamed Mr. Adams for the suppression of the dispatch; what becomes of the entire war noise of the Palmerston press from December 19, 1861, to January 8, 1862? Even more! Lord John Russell's dispatch of December 19, 1861, to Lord Lyons proves that the English Cabinet presented *no war ultimatum;* that Lord Lyons did *not* receive instructions to leave Washington seven days after delivering "this ultimatum"; that Russell ordered the Ambassador to avoid every semblance of a threat; and, finally, that the English Cabinet had decided to make a definitive decision only *after receipt* of the American reply. The whole policy trumpeted by the Palmerston press, which found so many servile echoes on the Continent, is, therefore, a mere chimera. It has never been carried out in real life. It only proves, as a London paper states today, that Palmerston "sought to thwart the declared and binding policy of the responsible advisers of the crown."

That Lord John Russell's *coup de main* struck the Palmerston press like a bolt from the blue is strikingly proved by one fact. The *Times* of yesterday suppressed the Russell correspondence and made no mention of it all. Only today a reprint from the *London Gazette* appears in its columns, introduced and prefaced by a leading article that uneasily avoids the real issue, *the issue between the English people and the English Cabinet,* and touches upon it in the ill-tempered phrase that "Lord Russell has overexerted himself to read an *apology* in Seward's dispatch of November 30." On the other hand, the anger of *Jupiter Tonans* of Printing House Square evaporates in a second leading article, wherein Mr. Gilpin, a member of the ministry, president of the Board of Trade, and a partisan of the Manchester School, is declared to be unworthy of his place in the ministry. For last Tuesday, at a public meeting in Northampton, whose parliamentary representative he is, Gilpin, former book dealer, demagogue, apostle of moderation, whom nobody could take for a hero, criminally urged the English people to prevent, by public demonstrations, an untimely recognition of the Southern Confederacy, which he rudely stigmatized as an offspring of slavery. As if, the *Times* exclaims indignantly, as if Palmerston and Russell—the *Times* now remembers the existence of Lord John Russell once more—had not fought all their lives against slavery! It was surely an indiscretion, a calculated indiscretion on the part of Mr. Gilpin, to call the English people into the lists against the proslavery longings of a ministry to which he himself belongs. But Mr. Gilpin, as already mentioned, is no hero. His whole career evidences little capacity for martyrdom. His indiscretion occurred on the same day as Lord Russell carried out his *coup de main.* Hence we may conclude that the cabinet is no "happy family" and that its individual members have already familiarized themselves with the idea of "separation."

No less noteworthy than the English ministerial sequel to the *Trent* drama is the Russian epilogue. Russia, which during the entire uproar stood silently in the background with folded arms, now springs to the proscenium, claps Mr. Seward on the shoulder—and declares that the moment for the definitive regulation of the maritime rights of neutrals has at last arrived. Russia, as is known, considers herself called upon to put the urgent questions of civilization on the agenda of world history at the right time and in the right place. Russia becomes unassailable by the maritime powers the moment the latter give up, with their belligerent rights against neutrals, their power over Russia's export trade. The Paris Convention of April 16, 1856, which is partly a literal copy of the Russian "Armed" Neutrality Treaty of 1780 against England, is in the meantime not yet law in England. What a trick of fate if the *Anglo-American* dispute ended with the English Parliament and the English crown sanctioning a concession that two British ministers made to Russia on their own authority at the end of the *Anglo-Russian* war.

English Public Opinion*

January 11, 1862

THE NEWS of the pacific solution of the *Trent* conflict was, by the bulk of the English people, saluted with an exultation proving unmistakably the unpopularity of the apprehended war and the dread of its consequences. It ought never to be forgotten in the United States that at least the *working classes* of England, from the commencement to the termination of the difficulty, have never forsaken them. To them it was due that, despite the poisonous stimulants daily administered by a venal and reckless press, not one single public war meeting could be held in the United Kingdom during all the period that peace trembled in the balance. The only war meeting convened on the arrival of the *La Plata*, in the cotton salesroom of the Liverpool Stock Exchange, was a corner meeting where the cotton jobbers had it all to themselves. Even at Manchester, the temper of the working classes was so well understood that an isolated attempt at the convocation of a war meeting was almost as soon abandoned as thought of.

Wherever public meetings took place in England, Scotland, or Ireland, they protested against the rabid war cries of the press, against the sinister designs of the government, and declared for a pacific settlement of the pending question. In this regard, the two last meetings held, the one at Paddington, London, the other at Newcastle-upon-Tyne, are characteristic. The former meeting applauded Mr. Washington Wilkes's argumentation that England was not warranted in finding fault with the seizure of the Southern commissioners; while the Newcastle meeting almost unanimously carried the resolution—first, that the Americans had only made themselves guilty of a *lawful* exercise of the right of search and seizure; second, that the captain of the

---

* Published in the *New-York Daily Tribune* February 1, 1862.

Trent ought to be punished for his violation of English neutrality, as proclaimed by the Queen. In ordinary circumstances, the conduct of the British workingmen might have been anticipated from the natural sympathy the popular classes all over the world ought to feel for the only popular government in the world.

Under the present circumstances, however, when a great portion of the British working classes directly and severely suffers under the consequences of the Southern blockade; when another part is indirectly smitten by the curtailment of the American commerce, owing, as they are told, to the selfish "protective policy" of the Republicans; when the only remaining democratic weekly, *Reynolds's* paper, has sold itself to Messrs. Yancey and Mann and week after week exhausts its horsepowers of foul language in appeals to the working classes to urge the government, for their own interests, to war with the Union—under such circumstances, simple justice requires to pay a tribute to the sound attitude of the British working classes, the more so when contrasted with the hypocritical, bullying, cowardly, and stupid conduct of the official and well-to-do John Bull.

What a difference in this attitude of the people from what it had assumed at the time of the Russian complication! Then the *Times*, the [*Morning*] *Post*, and the other yellow plushes of the London press whined for peace, to be rebuked by tremendous war meetings all over the country. Now they have howled for war, to be answered by peace meetings denouncing the liberticide schemes and the proslavery sympathy of the government. The grimaces cut by the augurs of public opinion at the news of the pacific solution of the *Trent* case are really amusing.

In the first place, they must needs congratulate themselves upon the dignity, common sense, good will, and moderation daily displayed by them for the whole interval of a month. They were moderate for the first two days after the arrival of the *La Plata*, when Palmerston felt uneasy whether any legal pretext for a quarrel was to be picked. But hardly had the crown lawyers hit upon a legal quibble when they opened a charivari unheard of since the anti-Jacobin war. The dispatches of the English Government left Queenstown in the beginning of December. No official answer from Washington could possibly be looked for before the commencement of January. The new incidents arising in the interval told all in favor of the Americans. The tone of the transatlantic press, although the *Nashville* affair[1] might have roused its passions, was calm. All facts ascertained concurred to show that Captain Wilkes had acted on his own hook. The position of the Washington government was delicate. If it resisted the English demands, it

---

1. The *Nashville*, a Confederate privateer carrying war booty, entered Southampton, which was a violation of English neutrality.

would complicate the civil war by a foreign war. If it gave way, it might damage its popularity at home, and appear to cede to pressure from abroad. And the government thus placed, carried, at the same time, a war which must enlist the warmest sympathies of every man, not a confessed ruffian, on its side.

Common prudence, conventional decency, ought, therefore, to have dictated to the London press, at least for the time separating the English demand from the American reply, to abstain anxiously from every word calculated to heat passion, breed ill will, complicate the difficulty. But no! That "inexpressibly mean and groveling" press, as William Cobbett, and he was a connoisseur, calls it, really boasted of having, when in fear of the compact power of the United States, humbly submitted to the accumulated slights and insults of proslavery administrations for almost half a century, while now, with the savage exultation of cowards, they panted for taking their revenge on the Republican administration, distracted by a civil war. The record of mankind chronicles no self-avowed infamy like this.

One of the yellow plushes, Palmerston's private *Moniteur*—the *Morning Post*—finds itself arraigned on a most ugly charge from the American papers. John Bull has never been informed—on information carefully withheld from him by the oligarchs that lord it over him—that Mr. Seward, without awaiting Russell's dispatch, had disavowed any participation of the Washington cabinet in the act of Captain Wilkes. Mr. Seward's dispatch arrived at London on December 19. On the 20th of December the rumor of this "secret" spread on the Stock Exchange. On the 21st, the yellow plush of the *Morning Post* stepped forward to herald gravely that "the dispatch in question does not in any way whatever refer to the outrage on our mail packet."

In the *Daily News*, the *Morning Star*, and other London journals you will find yellow plush pretty sharply handled, but you will not learn from them what people out of doors say. They say that the *Morning Post* and the *Times*, like the *Patrie* and the *Pays*, dupe the public not only to mislead them politically, but to fleece them in the monetary line on the stock exchange, in the interest of their patrons.

The brazen *Times*, fully aware that during the whole crisis it had compromised nobody but itself, and given another proof of the hollowness of its pretensions of influencing the real people of England, plays today a trick which here, at London, only works upon the laughing muscles, but on the other side of the Atlantic might be misinterpreted. The "popular classes" of London, the "mob," as the yellow plush call them, have given unmistakable signs—have even hinted in newspapers —that they should consider it an exceedingly seasonable joke to treat Mason (by the bye, a distant relative of Palmerston, since the original Mason had married a daughter of Sir W. Temple), Slidell, & Co. with the same demonstrations Hainau received on his visit at Barclay's brewery. The *Times* stands aghast at the mere idea of such a shocking incident, and how does it try to parry it? It admonishes the people of England not to overwhelm Mason, Slidell, & Co. with any sort of public *ovation*. The *Times* knows that its article of today will form the laughingstock of all the taprooms of London. But never mind! People on the other side of the Atlantic may, perhaps, fancy that the magnanimity of the *Times* has saved them from the affront of public ovation to Mason, Slidell, & Co., while, in point of fact, the *Times* only intends saving those gentlemen from public insult!

So long as the *Trent* affair was undecided, the *Times*, the *Post*, the *Herald*, the *Economist*, the *Saturday Review*, in fact the whole of the fashionable hireling press of London, had tried its utmost to persuade John Bull that the Washington government, even if it willed, would prove unable to keep the peace, because the Yankee mob would not allow it, and because the Federal Government was a mob government. Facts have now given them the lie direct. Do they now atone for their malignant slanders against the American people? Do they at least confess the error which yellow plush, in presuming to judge of the acts of a free people, could not but commit? By no means. They now unanimously discover that the American Government, in not anticipating England's demands, and not surrendering the Southern traitors as soon as they were caught, missed a great occasion, and deprived its present concession of all merit. Indeed, yellow plush! Mr. Seward disavowed the act of Wilkes before the arrival of the English demands, and at once declared himself willing to enter upon a conciliatory course; and what did you do on similar occasions? When, on the pretext of impressing English sailors on board American ships—a pretext not at all connected with maritime belligerent rights, but a downright, monstrous usurpation against all international law—the *Leopard* fired its broadside at the *Chesapeake*, killed six, wounded twenty-one of her sailors, and seized the pretended Englishmen on board the *Chesapeake*, what did the English Government do? That outrage was perpetrated on the 22nd of June, 1807. The real satisfaction, the surrender of the sailors, etc., was only offered on November 8, 1812, five years later. The British Government, it is true, disavowed at once the act of Admiral Berkeley, as Mr. Seward did in regard to Captain Wilkes; but to punish the Admiral, it removed him from an inferior to a superior rank. England, in proclaiming her Orders in Council, distinctly confessed that they were outrages on the rights of neutrals in general, and of the United States in particular; that they were forced upon her as measures of retaliation against Napoleon, and that she would feel but too glad to revoke them whenever Napoleon should revoke his encroachments on neutral rights. Napoleon did revoke them, as far as the United States were concerned, in the spring of 1810. England persisted in her avowed outrage on the maritime rights of America. Her resistance lasted from 1806 to the 23rd of June, 1812—after, on the 18th of June, the United States had declared war against England. England abstained, consequently, in this case for six years, not from atoning for a confessed outrage, but from discounting it. And this people talk of the magnificent occasion missed by the American Government! Whether in the wrong or in the right, it was a cowardly act on the part of the British Government to back a complaint grounded on pretended technical blunder, and a mere error of procedure, by an ultimatum, by a demand for the surrender of the prisoners. The American Government might have reasons to accede to that demand; it could have none to anticipate it.

By the present settlement of the *Trent* collision, the question underlying the whole dispute, and likely to again occur—the belligerent rights of a maritime power against neutrals—has not been settled. I shall, with your permission, try to survey the whole question in a subsequent letter. For the present, allow me to add that, in my opinion, Messrs. Mason and Slidell have done great service to the Federal Government. There was an influential war party in England which, what for commercial, what for political reasons, showed itself eager for a fray with the United States. The *Trent* affair put that party to the test. It has failed. The war passion has been discontented on a minor issue, the steam has been let off, the vociferous fury of the oligarchy has raised the suspicions of English democracy, the large British interests connected with the United States have made a stand, the true character of the Civil War has been brought home to the working classes, and last, not least, the dangerous period when Palmerston rules singlehanded without being checked by Parliament is rapidly drawing to an end. That was the only time in which an English war for the slavocrats might have been hazarded. It is now out of question.

A London Workers' Meeting[*]

*Published in *Die Presse*, Vienna, February 2, 1862.

January 28, 1862

THE WORKING CLASS, which is such a preponderant constituent of a society that within living memory has not had a peasant estate, is not, as is well known, represented in Parliament. Nevertheless, it is not without political influence. No important innovation, no decisive measure has ever been carried out in this country without pressure from without, whether the Opposition needed such pressure against the government or the government needed it against the Opposition. By pressure from without, the Englishman understands large, extra-parliamentary people's demonstrations, which naturally cannot be staged without the lively participation of the working class. Pitt, in his anti-Jacobin war, knew how to use the masses against the Whigs. The Catholic Emancipation, the Reform Bill, the repeal of the Corn Laws, the Ten Hours' Bill, the war against Russia, the rejection of Palmerston's Conspiracy Bill[1] were all the fruit of stormy extra-parliamentary demonstrations, in which the working class, sometimes artificially incited, sometimes acting spontaneously, played the main role or—depending on circumstances—the role of spectator, now as *persona dramatis*, now as chorus. So much the more striking is the attitude of the English working class in regard to the American Civil War.

The distress among workers in the northern manufacturing districts, motivated by the blockade of the slave states which closed the factories or shortened the working hours, is unbelievable and increases daily. The other portions of the working class do not suffer to the

1. On February 8, 1858, Lord Palmerston introduced in the House of Commons a bill aimed at political refugees, and their conspiracies, in England; in consequence of a protest movement against it, the House defeated the Bill on February 12, which led to Palmerston's resignation.

same degree, but they suffer keenly from the repercussion of the crisis in the cotton industry on other branches of industry, from the reduction of exports of their own products to North America as a result of the Morrill Tariff[2] and the destruction of this export to the southern United States as a result of the blockade. At the present moment, English intervention in America has therefore become a bread-and-butter question for the working class. In addition, no means of inflaming its anger against the United States is scorned by the workers' "natural superiors." The only large and widely circulating workers' organ still in existence, *Reynolds's Newspaper*, was bought six months ago for the express purpose of repeating weekly in fuming diatribes the *ceterum censeo* [repeated resolve] of English intervention. The working class is therefore fully aware that the government is only waiting for the intervention cry from below, the pressure from without, in order to put an end to the American blockade and the distress in England. Under these circumstances, the obstinacy with which the working class keeps silent, or breaks its silence only to raise its voice in opposition to intervention and *for* the United States, is admirable. This is a splendid new proof of the indestructible soundness of the English popular masses, the soundness which is the secret of England's greatness and which, to speak in Mazzini's hyperbolic language, made the ordinary English soldier seem a demigod during the Crimean War and the Indian Insurrection.

The following report of a mass meeting of workers, which took place yesterday in Marylebone, the most populous London borough, may serve to characterize the "politics" of the working class:

Mr. Steadman, the chairman, opened the meeting with the remark that the business before it was to decide how the English people were to receive Messrs. Mason and Slidell. "It is to be considered whether these gentlemen came here to free the slaves from their chains or to forge a new ring for these chains."

Mr. Yates: "On the present occasion the working class ought not to keep silent. The two gentlemen who are sailing across the Atlantic to our land are agents of tyrannical, slaveholding states. They are in open rebellion against the lawful constitution of their country and come here to induce our government to recognize the independence of the slave states. It is the duty of the working class to voice its opinion now, if the English Government is not to believe that its foreign policy is a matter of indifference to us. We must show that the money expended by this people on the emancipation of the slaves[3]

---

2. The Morrill Tariff Act of March 2, 1861, and subsequent revisions, raised duties to an average of 47 percent.

3. When slavery was abolished in the British colonies in 1838, Parliament voted £10 million for the compensation of the slaveowners.

cannot be allowed to go to waste. If our government were acting honestly, it would be supporting the northern states heart and soul in the suppression of this terrible rebellion."

After a detailed defense of the northern states and the observation that "Mr. Lovejoy's violent tirade against England was provoked by the slanders of the English press," the speaker proposed the following motion: "This meeting resolves that Mason and Slidell, agents of the rebels, now en route from America to England, are wholly unworthy of the moral sympathies of the working class of this country, since they are slaveholders as well as the confessed agents of the despotic faction that at this moment is engaged in rebellion against the republic of the United States and is the sworn enemy of the social and political rights of the working class in all countries."

Mr. Whynne seconded the motion. However, it was self-evident that every personal insult to Mason and Slidell, during their stay in London, was to be avoided.

Mr. Nichols, a resident of the "extreme North of the United States," as he announced himself to be, but in fact sent to the meeting by Messrs. Yancey and Mann as *advocatus diaboli*, objected to the motion: "I am here because free speech prevails here. In our country the government has not permitted anybody to open his mouth for the past three months. Liberty has been crushed not only in the South, but also in the North. Many northerners are opposed to the war, but they dare not say so. No less than two hundred newspapers have been suppressed or their premises wrecked by mobs. The southern states have the same right to secede from the North as the United States had to separate from England."

Despite Mr. Nichols' eloquence, the first motion was carried unanimously. He then rose once more: "If you reproach Messrs. Mason and Slidell that they are slaveholders, the same would apply to Washington, Jefferson, etc."

Mr. Beales refuted Nichols in a detailed speech and then moved a second motion: "Whereas the *Times* and other misleading journals are making ill-concealed attempts to misrepresent English public opinion on all American affairs, to involve us in war with millions of our kinsmen on any pretext whatever, and to take advantage of the dangers now imperilling the republic to defame democratic institutions—

"Therefore this meeting considers it the particular duty of the workers, since they are not represented in the senate of the nation, to declare their sympathy with the United States in its gigantic struggle for maintenance of the Union, to denounce the base dishonesty and advocacy of slaveholding indulged in by the *Times* and kindred aristocratic journals, to express themselves most emphatically in favor of a policy of strictest nonintervention in the affairs of the United States, in favor of settling all disputes that may arise by commissioners or courts of arbitration appointed by both sides, to protest against the war policy of the organ of the stock-exchange sharks, and to manifest the warmest sympathy with the endeavors of the Abolitionists to bring about a final solution of the question of slavery."

This motion was adopted unanimously, as was also the concluding motion "to transmit copies of the resolutions adopted to the American Government through Mr. Adams as an expression of the sentiments and opinions of the working class in England."

Anti-Intervention Feeling* ·

January 31, 1862

LIVERPOOL's commercial greatness derives its origin from the *slave trade*. The only contributions with which Liverpool has enriched England's poetic literature are odes to the slave trade. Fifty years ago Wilberforce could set foot on Liverpool's soil only at the risk of his life. As in the preceding century the slave trade, so in the present century the trade in the product of slavery—cotton—formed the material foundation of Liverpool's greatness. No wonder, then, that Liverpool is the center of the English friends of Secession. It is in fact the *only* city in the United Kingdom where during the recent crisis it has been possible to organize a quasi-public meeting in favor of a war with the United States. And what does Liverpool say now? Let us listen to one of its great daily organs, the *Daily Post*.

In an editorial entitled, "The Cute Yankee," it is stated among other things:

> The Yankees, with their usual adroitness, contrived to convert a loss into a gain. In point of fact they have so managed affairs as to make England subservient to their advantage . . . Great Britain has the advantage of displaying her power (but to what end?). The Yankees were always in favor of the unlimited privilege of neutrals, but Great Britain was opposed to it (this privilege was contested to the limit during the Anti-Jacobin war, the Anglo-American War of 1812 to 1814, and again, more recently, in 1842, during the negotiations between Lord Ashburton and the Secretary of State, Daniel Webster). Now our opposition must cease. *The Yankee principle is virtually recognized*. Mr. Seward establishes the fact . . . (declares that England has given way in principle and through the *Trent* case the United States has obtained a concession

* Published in *Die Presse*, Vienna, February 4, 1862.

to secure which they had hitherto exhausted every means of diplomacy and of war in vain).

Even more important is the *Daily Post*'s admission of the revulsion
in public opinion, even in Liverpool:

> The Confederates have certainly done nothing to forfeit the
> good opinion entertained of them. Quite the contrary. They have
> fought manfully and made dreadful sacrifices. If they do not obtain
> their independence every one must admit that they deserve it . . .
> Public opinion, however, has now run counter to their claims. They
> are no longer the fine fellows they were six months ago. They are
> pronounced by implication to be a very sorry set.
>   . . . A reaction has in fact set in. The antislavery people, who,
> to use a vulgarism, shrunk in their shoes in the presence of popular
> excitement, now come forth to thunder big words against man-
> selling and the slaveowners of the Southern states . . . The walls
> of the town were yesterday posted with a great placard full of
> denunciation and angry invective, and a London evening paper, the
> *Sun*, remembered something to Mr. Mason's disadvantage . . . "the
> author of the accursed Fugitive Slave Law . . ." The Confederates
> have lost by the *Trent* affair. It was to be their gain; it has turned
> out to be their ruin. The sympathy of this country will be with-
> drawn from them and they will have to realize as soon as possible
> their peculiar situation. They have been very ill used but they will
> have no redress.[1]

From this admission by the Secession-friendly Liverpool daily, it is
easy to explain the altered language that some important organs of
Palmerston now suddenly use before the opening of Parliament. Thus
the *Economist* of last Saturday published an article under the title:
"Should the Blockade be Respected?"

It first proceeds from the axiom that the blockade is a mere *paper
blockade* and that its violation is therefore permitted by international
law. France demanded the blockade's forcible elimination. The practical resolution of the question lies, therefore, in the hands of England,
which has great and pressing motives for such a step. Specifically, it
needs American cotton. One may remark in passing that it is not quite
clear how a "mere paper blockade" can prevent the shipping of cotton.

"But nevertheless," cries the *Economist*, "England *must* respect the
blockade." Having motivated this judgment with a series of sophisms,
it finally comes to the gist of the matter:

> It would be undesirable in a case of this kind for our govern-
> ment to take any steps or to enter any course of action in which
> they would not carry the whole country cordially and spontaneously
> with them . . . Now we doubt whether the great body of the

---

1. The *Liverpool Daily Post*, January 13, 1862.

British people are yet prepared for any interposition which would have even the semblance of siding with, or aiding the establishment of, a slave republic. The social system of the Confederate States is based on slavery; the Federalists have done what they could . . . to persuade us that slavery lay at the root of the secession movement, and that they, the Federalists, were hostile to slavery—and slavery is our especial horror and detestation. . . .

But the real error of the popular movement is here: . . . it is the *restoration* and not the *dissolution* of the Union that would be the consolidation and perpetuation of Negro servitude, and it is in the independence of the South and not in her defeat that we can alone look with confidence for the early amelioration and ultimate extinction of the slavery we abhor . . . We hope soon to make this clear to our readers. But it is not clear yet. The majority of Englishmen still think otherwise; and as long as they do, any intervention on the part of our government which should place us in a position of actual opposition to the North, and inferential alliance with the South, would scarcely be supported by the hearty cooperation of the British nation.[2]

In other words: the attempt at such an intervention would overthrow the ministry. And this also explains why the *Times* pronounces itself so decidedly against any intervention and in favor of England's neutrality.

---

2. The *Economist*, January 25, 1862.

On the Cotton Crisis*

Early February, 1862

A FEW DAYS ago the annual meeting of the Manchester Chamber of Commerce took place. It represents Lancashire, the greatest industrial district of the United Kingdom and the main seat of British cotton manufacture. The chairman of the meeting, Mr. E. Potter, and the main speakers, Messrs. Bazley and Turner, represent Manchester and a part of Lancashire in the Lower House. From the proceedings of the meeting, therefore, we learn *officially* what attitude the great center of the English cotton industry will adopt in the "Senate of the Nation" in the face of the American crisis.

At last year's meeting of the Chamber of Commerce, Mr. Ashworth, one of England's greatest cotton barons, had celebrated with Pindaric exuberance the unparalleled expansion of the cotton industry during the past decade. In particular, he stressed that even the commercial crises of 1847 and 1857 had produced no decline in the export of English cotton yarns and textiles. He explained the phenomenon by the wonder-working powers of the free trade system introduced in 1846. Even then it sounded strange that this system, although unable to spare England the crises of 1847 and 1857, should be able to withdraw a particular branch of English industry, that of cotton, from the influence of that crisis. But what do we hear today? All the speakers, including Mr. Ashworth, admit that since 1858 an unprecedented glutting of the Atlantic markets has taken place and that in consequence of the enormous and steadily continuing overproduction, the present stagnation was bound to occur, even without the American Civil War, the Morrill Tariff, and the blockade. Whether without those aggravating circumstances the decline of last year's exports would have reached

---

* Published in *Die Presse*, Vienna, February 8, 1862.

as much as £6,000,000 naturally remains an open question, but it does not appear improbable when we hear that the main markets of Asia and Australia are stocked with sufficient English cotton manufactures for twelve months.

Thus, according to the admission of the Manchester Chamber of Commerce, which in this matter speaks with authority, the crisis in the English cotton industry has so far been the result not of the American blockade but of English overproduction. But what would be the consequences of a continuation of the American Civil War? To this question we again receive a unanimous answer: immeasurable suffering on the part of the working class and ruin for the smaller manufacturers.

"It is said in London," observed Mr. Cheatham, "that they still have plenty of cotton for continued production. But it is not merely a question of cotton. It is above all a question of *price*. At present prices the capital of the mill owners is being destroyed."

The Chamber of Commerce, nevertheless, declares itself decidedly *against any intervention* in the United States, although most of its members are sufficiently influenced by the *Times* to consider the dissolution of the Union to be unavoidable.

"The last thing," says Mr. Potter, "that we should do is recommend intervention. The last place where such a thing could be entertained is Manchester. Nothing would tempt us to recommend something that is morally wrong."

Mr. Bazley: "The American quarrel must be left to the strictest principle of nonintervention. The people of that big country must be undisturbed in settling their own affairs."

Mr. Cheatham: "The dominant opinion in this district is wholly opposed to intervention in the American quarrel. It is necessary to make a clear announcement on this, because in case of doubt, strong pressure would be put on the government by the other side."

What, then, does the Chamber of Commerce recommend? The English Government ought to remove all the obstacles that the administration uses to impede cotton cultivation in *India*. In particular, it ought to abolish the 10 percent import duty with which the English cotton yarns and fabrics are burdened in India. Hardly had the regime of the East India Company been done away with, hardly had the East Indies been incorporated into the British Empire, when Palmerston, through Mr. Wilson, introduced this import duty on English manufactures, and he did so at the very same time he sold Savoy and Nice for the Anglo-French commercial treaty. While the French market was opened to English industry to a certain extent, the Indian market was closed to it to a larger extent.

With reference to the above, Mr. Bazley remarked that since the introduction of that tax, great quantities of English machinery had been exported to Bombay and Calcutta, and factories had been erected there in the English style. These were preparing to snatch from the Indians their best cotton. If one adds 15 percent for freight to the 10 percent import duty, the rivals artificially brought into being at the initiative of the English government enjoy a protective duty of 25 percent.

In general, bitter resentment was expressed at the meeting of the magnates of English industry at the protectionist tendency spreading more and more in the colonies, especially in Australia. The gentlemen forget that for a century and a half the colonies vainly protested against the "colonial system" of the mother country. At that time the colonies demanded free trade. England insisted on prohibition. Now England preaches free trade, and the colonies find protection against England better suited to their interests.

The Debate in Parliament*

February 7, 1862

THE OPENING of Parliament was a lusterless ceremony. The absence of
the Queen and the reading of the Speech from the Throne by the
Lord Chancellor[1] banished all theatrical effect. The Speech from the
Throne itself is short without being striking. It recapitulates the *faits
accomplis* of foreign policy and, for an evaluation of it, refers to the
documents submitted to Parliament. Only one phrase created a certain
sensation, the one in which the Queen "trusts" that "there is no reason
to apprehend any disturbance of the peace of Europe." This phrase, in
fact, implies that European peace is relegated to the realms of hope and
faith.

The gentlemen who, in accord with parliamentary practice, moved
the Reply to the Speech from the Throne in the two houses had been
commissioned to this business by the ministers three weeks ago. In
conformance with the usual procedure, their Reply consists of a broad
echo of the Speech from the Throne and of fulsome eulogies which
the ministers bestow upon themselves in the name of Parliament. In the
year 1811, when Sir Francis Burdett anticipated the official movers of
the Address and seized the occasion to subject the Speech to a cutting
criticism, Magna Charta itself seemed to have been endangered. Since
that time no further enormity of the kind has occurred.

The interest of the debate on the Speech from the Throne is therefore limited to the "hints" of the official Opposition Clubs and the
"counter-hints" of the ministers. This time, however, the interest was
more academic than political. It was a question of the best funeral
oration on Prince Albert, who during his life found the yoke of the

---

* Published in *Die Presse*, Vienna, February 12, 1862.
1. William Ewart Gladstone.

English oligarchy by no means light. According to the *vox populi*, Derby and Disraeli have carried off the academic palms, the first as a natural speaker, the second as an artificial one.

The "business" part of the debate revolved around the United States, Mexico, and Morocco.

In regard to the United States, the Outs praised the policy of the Ins (the *beati possidentes* [blessed possessors]). Derby, the Conservative leader in the House of Lords, and Disraeli, the Conservative leader in the House of Commons, opposed, not the cabinet but each other.

Derby in the first place expressed his dissatisfaction with the absence of "pressure from without." He "admired," he said, the stoic and dignified behavior of the factory workers. In regard to the mill owners, however, he must exclude them from his commendation. For them the American disturbance had been unusually opportune, since overproduction and glutting of all markets had in any case imposed on them a shrinking of trade.

Derby went on to make a violent attack on the Union Government, which had "exposed itself and its people to the most undignified humiliation" and had not acted like "gentlemen," because it had not taken the initiative in voluntarily surrendering Mason, Slidell, & Co., and had not made amends. His seconder in the House of Commons, Mr. Disraeli, immediately understood how very damaging Derby's attack was to the ministerial hopes of the Conservatives. He therefore declared to the contrary: "When I consider the great difficulties which the statesmen of North America have to encounter, I must venture to say that they have met these manfully and courageously."

On the other hand—with the consistency customary to him—Derby protested against the "new doctrines" of maritime law. England had ever upheld belligerent rights against the pretensions of neutrals. Lord Clarendon, to be sure, had made a "dangerous" concession at Paris in 1856. Happily, this had not yet been ratified by the crown, so that "it did not change the position of international law." On the other hand, Mr. Disraeli, manifestly in collusion with the ministry, avoided touching on this point at all.

Derby approved of the nonintervention policy of the ministry. The time to recognize the Southern Confederacy has not *yet* come, but he demands authentic documents to judge "to what extent the blockade is effective and hence legally binding." Lord John Russell, on the other hand, declared that the Union Government had employed a sufficient number of ships in the blockade, but had not everywhere carried it out consistently. Mr. Disraeli does not wish to permit himself any judgment on the nature of the blockade, but demands ministerial papers for enlightenment. He warns against any premature recognition of the Confederacy, the more so since England is compromising itself at present by threatening an American state (Mexico), the independence of which it was the first to recognize.

After the United States, it was Mexico's turn, No member of Parliament condemned a war without declaration of war, but condemned intervention in the internal affairs of a country under the shibboleth of "nonintervention policy," and the coalition of England with France and Spain in order to intimidate a semidefenseless country. The Outs, as a matter of fact, merely indicated that they are reserving Mexico to themselves as a pretext for party maneuvers. Derby demanded documents on both the convention among the three powers and the mode of carrying it out. He approves the convention because—in his opinion —the right way was for each of the contracting parties to enforce its claims *independently* of the others. Certain public rumors made him fear that at least one of the powers—Spain—intended operations transcending the limits of the treaty. As if Derby really believed that great power Spain capable of the audacity of acting counter to the will of England and France! Lord John Russell replied: The three powers pursued the same aim and would anxiously avoid hindering the Mexicans in regulating their own political affairs.

In the Lower House, Mr. Disraeli defers any judgment before scrutinizing the documents submitted. Nevertheless, he finds "the announcements of the government suspicious." The independence of Mexico was first recognized by England. This recognition recalls a memorable policy—the Anti-Holy-Alliance policy—and a memorable man, Canning. What singular occasion, therefore, impelled England to strike the first blow against this independence? Moreover, the intervention has changed its pretext within a very short time. Originally it was a question of satisfaction for wrong done to English subjects. Now there are whispers about introducing new governmental principles and setting up a new dynasty. Lord Palmerston refers to the papers submitted and to the convention that prohibits the "subjugation" of Mexico by the allies, or the imposition of a form of government unpalatable to the people. At the same time, however, he reveals a secret diplomatic hiding place. He has it from hearsay that a party in Mexico desires the transformation of the republic into a monarchy. He does not know the strength of that party. He, for his part, "only desires that some form of government be set up in Mexico with which foreign governments may treat." He desires, therefore, to set up a "new" government system. He declares the nonexistence of the present government. He claims for the alliance of England, France, and Spain the prerogative of the Holy Alliance to decide on the existence or nonexistence of foreign governments. "That is the utmost," he adds modestly, "which the government of Great Britain is desirous of obtaining." Nothing more!

The last "open question" of foreign policy concerned Morocco. The English Government has concluded a convention with Morocco in order to enable the latter to pay off its debt to Spain, a debt that Spain could never have imposed on Morocco without England's permission. Certain persons, it seems, have advanced Morocco money to pay the installments to Spain, thus cutting off from the latter a pretext for the further occupation of Tetuán and a renewal of the war. The English Government has in one way or another guaranteed these persons the interest on their loan and, in its turn, takes over the administration of Morocco's customs houses as security. Derby found this manner of insuring the independence of Morocco "rather strange," but elicited no answer from the ministers. In the Lower House, Mr. Disraeli went into the transaction further, explaining that it was "to some extent unconstitutional," in that the ministry had imposed new financial obligations on England behind Parliament's back. Palmerston simply referred him to the "documents" submitted.

Home affairs were hardly touched upon. Derby merely warned against "disturbing" controversial questions, such as parliamentary reform, out of regard "for the state of mind of the Queen." He is ready to pay his tribute regularly to the English working class, on condition that it suffers its exclusion from popular representation with the same abstemious stoicism as it does the American blockade.

It would be a mistake to infer from the idyllic opening of Parliament an idyllic future. Quite the contrary! Dissolution of Parliament or dissolution of the ministry is the motto of this year's session. Opportunity to substantiate these alternatives will be found later.

American Affairs*

February 26, 1862

PRESIDENT LINCOLN never ventures a step forward before the turn of circumstances and the general call of public opinion forbid further delay. But once "Old Abe" has convinced himself that such a turning point has arrived, he surprises friend and foe alike by a sudden operation carried out as quietly as possible. Thus recently, in the most unpretentious way, he has executed a coup which half a year ago would perhaps have cost him the presidential chair and even a few months ago would have called forth a storm of debate. We mean the removal of McClellan from his post as commander-in-chief of all the Union armies. First of all, Lincoln replaced Secretary of War Cameron with an energetic and ruthless lawyer, Mr. Edwin Stanton. Stanton then issued an order of the day to Generals Buell, Halleck, Butler, Sherman, and other commanders of whole departments or heads of expeditions, informing them that in the future they would receive all orders, public and private, direct from the War Department and that they, for their part, would have to report direct to the War Department. Finally, Lincoln issued some orders in which he signed himself with his constitutionally proper attribute, "Commander-in-Chief of the Army and Navy." In this "quiet" manner, "the young Napoleon"[1] was deprived of the supreme command he had hitherto held over *all* the armies and was reduced to the command of the Army of the Potomac, although the *title* of "commander-in-chief" was left to him. The successes in Kentucky, Tennessee, and on the Atlantic Coast have favorably inaugurated Lincoln's assumption of the supreme command.

---

* Published in *Die Presse*, Vienna, March 3, 1862.

1. McClellan's followers in the Democratic party called him "the young Napoleon" because he became supreme commander of the Union armies at the age of thirty-four, in 1861.

The post of commander-in-chief, hitherto held by McClellan, has been bequeathed by England to the United States and corresponds approximately to the dignity of a *Grand Connétable* [Grand Constable] in the old French army. During the Crimean War even England discovered the inappropriateness of this old-fashioned institution. Hence a compromise took place, whereby some of the attributes hitherto pertaining to the commander-in-chief were transferred to the secretary of war.

The necessary material is still lacking for an evaluation of McClellan's Fabian tactics on the Potomac. But that his influence acted as a brake on the general conduct of the war is beyond doubt. One can say of McClellan what Macaulay says of Essex: "The military mistakes of Essex sprang largely from political compunction. He was honestly, but by no means warmly attached to the cause of Parliament, and next to a great defeat he feared nothing so much as a great victory."[2]

McClellan, like most of the Regular Army officers who were trained at West Point, is more or less bound by *esprit de corps* to his old comrades in the enemy camp. They share the same jealousy of the parvenus among the "civilian soldiers." In their view, the war must be conducted in a purely businesslike manner, with the constant objective of restoring the Union to its old basis, and hence free from all revolutionary tendencies in matters of principle. A fine conception of a war that is essentially a war of principles! The first generals of the English Parliament fell into the same error.

"But," says Cromwell in his speech to the Rump Parliament on July 4, 1653, "how changed everything was as soon as men took the lead who professed a principle of godliness in religion!"

The *Washington Star*, McClellan's special organ, declares in one of its latest issues: "The aim of all General McClellan's military combinations is the restoration of the Union exactly as it existed before the outbreak of the rebellion."

No wonder, therefore, that on the Potomac, under the eyes of the supreme general, the army was trained to catch slaves! Only recently, by special order, McClellan expelled the Hutchinson family of musicians from the camp, because they sang antislavery songs.

Apart from such "antitendency" demonstrations, McClellan covered the traitors in the Union Army with his protective shield. Thus, for example, he promoted Maynard to a higher post, although Maynard, as the papers published by the investigating committee of the House of Representatives prove, worked as an agent of the Secessionists. From General Patterson, whose treachery was decisive in the Manassas defeat, to General Stone, who effected the defeat at Ball's Bluff in direct

2. Thomas Babington Macaulay, *Critical and Historical Essays* Vol. I (London, 1870).

agreement with the enemy, McClellan knew how to keep every traitor from a court-martial, indeed, mostly also from dismissal. The investigating committee of the Congress has revealed the most surprising facts in this respect. Lincoln resolved to prove by an energetic step that with his assumption of the supreme command, the hour of the traitors in epaulets had struck, and that a turning point in the war policy had come. At his order, General Stone was arrested in his bed on February 10, at two o'clock in the morning, and transported to Fort Lafayette. A few hours later appeared the order for his arrest, signed Stanton, charging high treason and ordering judgment by court-martial. Stone's arrest and trial took place without prior communication to General McClellan.

McClellan was obviously determined that, so long as he himself remained in a state of inaction and wore his laurels merely in advance, he would permit no other general to forestall him. Generals Halleck and Pope had agreed upon a combined movement to force General Price, who had already been saved from Frémont once by intervention of Washington, to a decisive battle. A telegram from McClellan forbade them to deliver the blow. By a similar telegram General Halleck was "ordered back" from Fort Columbus, at a time when this fort stood half under water. McClellan had expressly forbidden the generals in the West to correspond with each other. Each of them was obliged first to address himself to Washington, as soon as a combined movement was intended. President Lincoln has now given them back the necessary freedom of action.

How profitable McClellan's general war policy was for the Secession is best proved by the panegyric that the *New-York Herald* constantly lavishes upon him. He is a hero after the *Herald*'s own heart. The notorious Bennett, proprietor and editor-in-chief of the *Herald*, had formerly controlled the administrations of Pierce and Buchanan through his "special representatives," alias correspondents, in Washington. Under Lincoln's administration he sought to win the same power again, in a roundabout way, by having his "special representative," Dr. Ives, a man of the South and a brother of an officer who had deserted to the Confederacy, insinuate himself into McClellan's favor. Under McClellan's patronage, great liberties must have been allowed this Ives at the time when Cameron was at the head of the War Department. He obviously expected Stanton to guarantee him the same privileges, and accordingly, on February 8, found himself in the War Office, where the Secretary of War, his chief secretary, and some members of Congress were consulting about war measures. He was shown the door. He got up on his hind legs, and finally beat a retreat with the threat that the *Herald* would open fire on the present War Department in case the latter withdrew his "special privilege" of confidences to

him—particularly from the War Department—about cabinet delibera-
tions, telegrams, public communications, and war news. Next morning,
February 9, Dr. Ives assembled McClellan's whole general staff for a
champagne breakfast at his house. But misfortune moves fast. A noncommissioned officer and six men entered, seized the mighty Ives, and
brought him to Fort McHenry, where, as the order of the Secretary
of War expressly states, he is "to be kept under strict watch *as a spy*."

The Mexican Imbroglio*

February 15, 1862

THE BLUE BOOK on the intervention in Mexico, just published, contains the most damning exposure of modern English diplomacy with all its hypocritical cant, ferocity against the weak, crawling before the strong, and utter disregard of international law. I must reserve for another letter the task of forwarding, by a minute analysis of the dispatches exchanged between Downing Street and the British representatives in Mexico, the irrefragable proof that the present imbroglio is of English origin, that England took the initiative in bringing about the intervention, and did so on pretexts too flimsy and self-contradictory to even veil the real but unavowed motives of her proceedings. The infamy of the means employed in starting the Mexican intervention is only surpassed by the anile imbecility with which the British Government affects to be surprised at and slink out of the execution of the nefarious scheme planned by themselves. It is the latter part of the business I propose dealing with for the present.

On the 13th of December, 1861, Mr. Istúriz, the Spanish Ambassador at London, submitted to John Russell a note including the instructions sent by the Captain General of Cuba to the Spanish commanders, at the head of the expedition to Mexico. John Russell shelved the note and kept silent. On the 23rd of December, Mr. Istúriz addresses him a new note, professing to explain the reasons that had induced the Spanish expedition to leave Cuba before the arrival of the English and French forces. John Russell again shelves the note and persists in his taciturn attitude. Mr. Istúriz, anxious to ascertain whether that protracted restraint of speech so unusual in the verbose upshoot of the house of Bedford means possible mischief, urges a personal interview, which is

---

* Published in the *New-York Daily Tribune* March 10, 1862.

granted to him, and takes place on the 7th of January. John Russell had now for more than a month been fully acquainted with the one-sided opening of the operations against Mexico on the part of Spain. A month had almost passed since the event had been officially communicated to him by Mr. Istúriz. With all that, in his personal interview with the Spanish Ambassador, John Russell breaks no word breathing the slightest displeasure or astonishment at "the precipitate steps taken by General Serrano," nor leave his utterances the faintest impression on the mind of Mr. Istúriz that all was not right, and that the Spanish proceedings were not fully approved of by the British Government. The Castilian pride of Mr. Istúriz shuns, of course, any notion of Spain being played with by her powerful allies and made a mere cat's-paw of. Yet the time of the meeting of Parliament approached, and John Russell had now to pen a series of dispatches, especially intended, not for international business, but for Parliamentary consumption. Accordingly, on the 16th of January, he pens a dispatch inquiring, in rather angry tones, about the one-sided initiative ventured upon by Spain. Doubts and scruples, which for longer than a month had slumbered in his bosom, and had not even matured into symptoms of existence, on the 7th of January, during his personal interview with Mr. Istúriz, all at once disturb the serene dream of that confident, sincere, and unsuspecting statesman. Mr. Istúriz feels thunderstruck, and in his reply, dated January 18, somewhat ironically reminds His Excellency of the opportunities missed by him of giving vent to his posthumous spleen. He pays in fact His Excellency in his own coin, assuming in his justification of the initiative taken by Spain, the same air of naïveté Lord John Russell affected in his request for an explanation. "The Captain General of Cuba," says Mr. Istúriz, "came too early because he was fearful of arriving too late at Vera Cruz." "Besides," and here he pinches Lord John, "the expedition had been for a long time ready on every point," although the Captain General, till the middle of December, was "unacquainted with the details of the treaty, and with the point fixed for the meeting of the squadrons." Now, the treaty was not concluded before the 20th of November. If, then, the Captain General had his expedition for a long time "ready in every point before the middle of December," the orders originally sent out to him from Europe for starting the expedition had not waited upon the treaty. In other words, the original agreement between the three powers, and the steps taken in its execution, did not wait upon the treaty, and differed in their "details" from the clauses of the treaty, which, from the beginning, were intended not as a rule of action, but only as decent formulas, necessary to conciliate the public mind to the nefarious scheme. On the 23rd of January John Russell replies to Mr. Istúriz in a rather bluff note, intimating to him that "the British Government was *not entirely* satisfied with the explanation offered," but at the same time would not suspect Spain of the foolhardiness of presuming to act in the teeth of England and France. Lord John Russell, so sleepy, so inactive, for a whole month, becomes all life and wide awake as the parliamentary session rapidly draws near. No time is to be lost. On the 17th of January he has a personal interview with Count Flahault, the French Ambassador at London. Flahault broaches to him the ill-omened news that his master considered it necessary "to send an additional force to Mexico," that Spain by her precipitate initiative had spoiled the mess; that "the allies must now advance to the interior of Mexico, and that not only the forces agreed upon would now prove insufficient for the operation, but that the operation itself would assume a character in regard to which Louis Bonaparte could not allow the French forces to be in a position of inferiority to those of Spain, or run the risk of being compromised." Now Flahault's argumentation was anything but conclusive. If Spain had overstepped the convention, a single note to Madrid from the quarters of St. Tours and the Tuileries would have sufficed to warn her off her ridiculous pretensions, and drive her back to the modest part imposed upon her by the convention. But no. Because Spain had broken the convention—a breach merely formal and of no consequence, since her premature arrival at Vera Cruz changed nothing in the professed aim and purpose of the expedition—because Spain had presumed to cast anchor at Vera Cruz in the absence of the English and French forces, there remained no other issue open to France but to follow in the track of Spain, break also the convention, and augment, not only her expeditionary forces, but change the whole character of the operation. There was, of course, no pretext needed for the Allied Powers to let the murder out, and, on the very outset of the expedition, set at naught the pretexts and purposes upon which it was started. Consequently, John Russell, although he "regrets the step" taken by France, endorses it by telling Count Flahault that "he had no objection to offer, on behalf of Her Majesty's Government, to the *validity* of the French *argument*." In a dispatch dated January 20, he forwards to Earl Cowley, the English Ambassador at Paris, the narrative of this his interview with Count Flahault. The day before, on the 19th of January, he had penned a dispatch to Sir F. Crampton, the English Ambassador at Madrid—that dispatch being a curious medley of hypocritical cant addressed to the British Parliament, and of sly hints to the Court of Madrid as to the intrinsic value of the liberal slang so freely indulged in. "The proceedings of Marshal Serrano," he says, "are calculated to produce some uneasiness," not only because of the precipitate departure of the Spanish expedition from Havana, but also because "of the tone of the proclamations issued by the Spanish Government." But, simultaneously, the *bon homme* suggests to the Madrid Court a plausible excuse for their apparent breach of the convention. He is fully convinced that the Madrid Court means no harm; but, then, commanders, at a distance from Europe, are sometimes "rash," and require "to be very closely watched." Thus good man Russell volunteers his services, in order to shift the responsibility from the Court at Madrid to the shoulders of indiscreet Spanish commanders "at a distance," and even out of the reach of good man Russell's sermonizing. Not less curious is the other part of his dispatch. The Allied Forces are not to preclude the Mexicans from their right "of choosing their own government," thus intimating that there exists "no government" in Mexico; but that, on the contrary, not only new governors, but even "a new form of government," must so be chosen by the Mexicans under the auspices of the Allied invaders. Their "constituting a new government" would "delight" the British Government; but, of course, the military forces of the invaders must not falsify the general suffrage which they intend calling the Mexicans to for the installation of a new government. It rests, of course, with the commanders of the armed invasion to judge what form of new government is or is not "repugnant to the feelings of Mexico." At all events, good man Russell washes his hands in innocence. He dispatches foreign dragoons to Mexico, there to force the people into "choosing" a new government; but he hopes the dragoons will do the thing gently, and be very careful in sifting the political feelings of the country they invade. Is it necessary to expatiate one moment upon this transparent farce? Apart from the context of good man Russell's dispatches, read the *Times* and the *Morning Post* of October, six weeks before the conclusion of the sham convention of November 30, and you will find the English Government prints to foretell all the very same untoward events Russell feigns to discover only at the end of January, and to account for by "the rashness" of some Spanish ambassadors at a distance from Europe.

The second part of the farce Russell had to play was the putting on the tapis of the Archduke Maximilian of Austria as the Mexican King, held *in petto* by England and France.

On the 24th of January, about ten days before the opening of Parliament, Lord Cowley writes to Lord Russell that not only Paris gossip was much busied with the Archduke, but that the very officers going with the reenforcements to Mexico pretended that the expedition was for the purpose of making the Archduke Maximilian King of Mexico. Cowley thinks it necessary to interpellate Thouvenel upon the delicate subject. Thouvenel answers him, that it was not the French Government, but Mexican emissaries, "come for the purpose, and gone to Vienna," that had set on foot such negotiations with the Austrian Government.

Now, at last, you expect unsuspecting John Russell, who even five days ago, in his dispatch to Madrid, had harped upon the terms of the convention, who still later, in the royal speech of February 6, had proclaimed "the redress" of wrongs sustained by European subjects the exclusive motive and purpose of the intervention—you expect him now at last to fly into a passion and to fret and foam at the very idea of his kind-natured confidence having been played such unheard-of pranks with. Nothing of the sort! Good man Russell receives Cowley's gossip on the 26th of January, and on the following day he hastens to sit down and write a dispatch volunteering his patronage of the Archduke Maximilian's candidature for the Mexican throne.

He informs Sir C. Wyke, his representative at Mexico, that the French and Spanish troops will march "at once" to the city of Mexico; that Archduke Maximilian "is said" to be the idol of the Mexican people, and that, if such be the case, "there is nothing in the convention to prevent his advent to the throne of Mexico."

There are two things remarkable in these diplomatic revelations: first, the fool Spain is made of; and second, that there never passes the slightest thought through Russell's mind that he cannot wage war upon Mexico without a previous declaration of war, and that he can form no coalition for that war with foreign powers, except on the ground of a treaty binding upon all parties. And such are the people who have fatigued us for two months with their hypocritical cant on the sacredness of, and their homage to, the strict rules of international law!

The Secessionists' Friends in the Lower House–Recognition of the American Blockade*

March 8, 1862

Parturiunt montes! [The mountains have labored (and brought forth a mouse)!] Since the opening of Parliament, the English friends of Secessia have threatened a "motion" on the American blockade. The motion has finally been introduced in the Lower House in the very modest form of a resolution in which the government is urged "to submit further documents on the state of the blockade"—and even this insignificant motion was rejected without the formality of a roll call.

Mr. Gregory, the Member for Galway, who moved the resolution, had in the parliamentary session of last year, shortly after the outbreak of the Civil War, already introduced a motion for recognition of the Southern Confederacy. To his speech of this year a certain sophistical adroitness is not to be denied. But the speech suffers from the unfortunate circumstance that it falls into two parts, of which one cancels the other. One part describes the disastrous effects of the blockade on the English cotton industry and therefore demands the elimination of the blockade. The other part proves from the papers submitted by the ministry, among them two petitions by Messrs. Yancey, Mann, and Mason, that the blockade does not exist at all, except on paper, and therefore should no longer be recognized. Mr. Gregory spiced his argument with successive quotations from the *Times*. The *Times*, for whom a reminder of its oracular pronouncements is at this moment altogether inconvenient, thanks Mr. Gregory in an editorial in which it holds him up to public ridicule.

Mr. Gregory's motion was supported by Mr. Bentinck, an ultra-Tory who for two years has vainly tried to bring about a secession from Mr. Disraeli in the Conservative camp.

It was in and of itself a ludicrous spectacle to see the alleged

* Published in *Die Presse*, Vienna, March 12, 1862.

interests of English industry represented by Gregory, the representative of Galway, an insignificant seaport in the west of Ireland, and by Bentinck, the representative of Norfolk, a purely agricultural district.

Mr. Forster, a representative of Bradford, one of the centers of English industry, rose to oppose them both. Forster's speech deserves closer examination, since it strikingly proves the nullity of the rhetoric on the character of the American blockade given currency by the friends of Secession in Europe. First, he said, the United States has observed all formalities required by international law. It has declared no port in a state of blockade without prior proclamation, without special notice of the moment of its commencement, or without fixing the fifteen days after whose expiration entrance and departure of foreign neutral ships shall be forbidden.

The talk about the legal "ineffectiveness" of the blockade rests, therefore, only on the allegedly frequent cases in which it has been broken through. Before the opening of Parliament, it was said that 600 ships had broken through it. Mr. Gregory now reduces the number to 400. His evidence rests on two lists handed to the government, the one on November 30 by the Southern commissioners Yancey and Mann, the other, the supplementary list, by Mason. According to Yancey and Mann, more than 400 ships broke through from the time of the proclamation of the blockade to August 20, running the blockade either incoming or outgoing. According to customs house reports, however, the total number of incoming and outgoing ships amounts to only 322. Of this number, 119 departed *before* the declaration of the blockade, 56 *before* the expiration of the time period of fifteen days. There remain 147 ships. Of these 147, 25 were river boats that sailed from inland waters to New Orleans, where they lay idle; 106 were coastal vessels; with the exception of three ships, all these were, in the words of Mr. Mason himself, "quasi-inland" vessels. Of the 106, 66 sailed between Mobile and New Orleans. Anyone who knows this coast knows how absurd it is to call the sailing of a ship behind lagoons, when it hardly touches the open sea and merely creeps along the coast, a breach of the blockade. The same applies to the ships between Savannah and Charleston, where they sneak between islands along narrow tongues of land. According to the testimony of the English consul, Bunch, these flat-bottomed boats appeared for only a few days on the open sea. After subtracting 106 coastal vessels, there remain 16 departures for foreign ports; of these, 15 were for American ports, mainly Cuba, and one for Liverpool. The "ship" that landed in Liverpool was a schooner, and so were all the rest of the "ships," with the exception of one sloop. There has been much talk, exclaimed Mr. Forster, of sham blockade. Is this list of Messrs. Yancey and Mann not a sham list? Forster subjected the supplementary list of Mr. Mason to a similar analysis, and showed further that the number of cruisers that slipped out amounted to only three or four, whereas in the last Anglo-American war no fewer than 516 American cruisers broke through the English blockade and harried the English seaboard. "The blockade has been, on the contrary, wonderfully effective from its commencement."

Further proof is provided by the reports of the English consuls, above all, by the current prices in the South. On January 11 the price of cotton in New Orleans offered a premium of 100 percent for export to England; the profit on import of salt amounted to 1,500 percent and the profit on contraband of war has been incomparably higher. Despite this alluring prospect of profit, it has been just as impossible to ship cotton to England as salt to New Orleans or Charleston. In fact, however, Mr. Gregory does not complain that the blockade is ineffective, but that it is too effective. He demands that an end be put to it, and with it, an end to the crippling of industry and commerce. One reply suffices: "Who urges this House to break the blockade? The representatives of the suffering districts? Does this cry resound from Manchester, where the factories have to close, or from Liverpool, where from lack of freight the ships lie idle in the docks? On the contrary. It resounds from Galway and is supported by Norfolk."

On the side of the friends of Secession, Mr. Lindsay, a big shipbuilder of North Shields, made himself conspicuous. Lindsay offered his shipyards to the Union, and for this purpose he traveled to Washington, where he experienced the vexation of seeing his business propositions rejected. Since that time, he has turned his sympathies to the land of Secessia.

The debate was concluded with a detailed speech by Sir R. Palmer, the Solicitor-General, who spoke in the name of the government. He provided legally well-grounded proof of the force and sufficiency of the blockade in international law. On this occasion, in fact, he tore to pieces—and was upbraided for it by Lord Cecil—the "new principles" proclaimed at the Paris Convention of 1856. Among other things, he expressed his astonishment that Gregory and Company had the audacity to appeal to the authority of Mr. de Hautefeuille in a British Parliament. The latter, indeed, is a brand-new "authority" discovered in the Bonapartist camp. Hautefeuille's articles in the *Revue Contemporaine*[1] on the maritime law of neutrals show the most complete ignorance or *mauvaise foi* [bad faith] at higher command.

With the complete fiasco of the Parliamentary friends of Secession on the blockade question, all prospect of a breach between England and the United States is eliminated.

---

1. A pro-Bonapartist bimonthly published in Paris.

The American Civil War (I)*

FROM WHATEVER standpoint one regards it, the American Civil War presents a spectacle without parallel in the annals of military history. The vast extent of the disputed territory; the far-flung fronts of the lines of operation; the numerical strength of the hostile armies, whose creation derived barely any support from previous organizational bases; the fabulous costs of these armies; the manner of their administration and the general tactical and strategic principles with which the war is waged—all these are new in the eyes of the European onlooker.

The Secessionist conspiracy, organized long before its outbreak, protected and supported by Buchanan's administration, gave the South an advantage by which alone it could hope to achieve its aim. Endangered by its slave population and by a strong Unionist element among the whites themselves, with a population of free men one-third the size of the North, but more ready to attack, thanks to the multitude of adventurous idlers that it harbors—for the South, everything depended on a swift, bold, almost foolhardy offensive. If the Southerners succeeded in capturing St. Louis, Cincinnati, Washington, Baltimore, and perhaps also Philadephia, they could count on a panic, during which diplomacy and bribery could secure recognition of the independence of all the slave states. If this first attack failed, at least at the decisive points, their position must worsen daily, simultaneously with the development of the strength of the North. This point was correctly understood by the men who had organized the secessionist conspiracy in a truly Bonapartist spirit. They opened the campaign in a corresponding manner. Their bands of adventurers overran Missouri and Tennessee, while their more regular troops invaded East Virginia

---

* Written in collaboration with Frederick Engels. Published in *Die Presse*, Vienna, March 26, 1862.

and prepared a *coup de main* against Washington. With the miscarriage of this coup, the Southern campaign was lost *from a military standpoint*.

The North came to the theater of war reluctantly, sleepily, as was to be expected from its higher industrial and commercial development. The social machinery was incomparably more complicated here than in the South, and it required far more time to give its movement this unaccustomed direction. The enlistment of three-month volunteers was a great, but perhaps unavoidable, mistake. It was the policy of the North first to remain on the defensive at all decisive points, to organize its forces, to train them through operations on a small scale and without risking decisive battles, and finally, as soon as the organization was sufficiently strengthened and the traitorous element was at the same time more or less removed from the army, to pass to an energetic, unrelenting offensive and, above all, to reconquer Kentucky, Tennessee, Virginia, and North Carolina. The transformation of citizens into soldiers was bound to take more time in the North than in the South. Once effected, one could count on the individual superiority of the Northern man.

By and large, and allowing for the mistakes that sprang more from political than from military sources, the North acted in accordance with those principles. The guerrilla warfare in Missouri and West Virginia, while it protected the Unionist populations, accustomed the troops to field service and to fire, without exposing them to decisive defeats. The great disgrace of Bull Run was to some extent the result of the earlier mistake of enlisting volunteers for three months. It was senseless to allow a strong position, on difficult terrain, possessed by an enemy hardly inferior in numbers, to be attacked by raw recruits in the front lines. The panic which took possession of the Union Army at the decisive moment—and its cause has not yet been clarified—could surprise no one who was to some extent familiar with the history of people's wars. Such things happened very often to the French troops in 1792–95, but nevertheless did not prevent them from winning the battles of Jemappes and Fleurus, Montenotte, Castiglione, and Rivoli.[1] The jokes of the European press over the Bull Run panic had only one excuse for their silliness—the previous bragging of a part of the North American press.

The six months' respite that followed the defeat at Manassas was utilized by the North better than by the South. Not only were the Northern ranks filled up in greater measure than the Southern ones.

---

1. On November 6, 1792, the French republican troops defeated the Austrians at Jemappes (Belgium); on June 26, 1794, they defeated them at Fleurus (Belgium); on April 12, 1796, at Montenotte (Italy); on August 5, 1796, at Castiglione (Italy); and on January 14-15, 1797, at Rivoli (Italy).

Their officers received better instructions; the discipline and training of the troops did not encounter the same obstacles as in the South. Traitors and incompetents were more and more removed, and the period of the Bull Run panic already belongs to the past. The armies on both sides are, of course, not to be measured by the standard of great European armies or even by that of the former Regular Army of the United States. Napoleon could in fact drill battalions of raw recruits in the depots during the first month, have them march during the second month, and lead them against the enemy during the third month; but then every battalion received a sufficient stiffening of officers and noncommissioned officers, every company some old soldiers, and on the day of battle the new troops were brigaded together with veterans and, so to speak, framed by them. All these conditions were lacking in America. Without the considerable mass of military experience that emigrated to America as a result of the European revolutionary commotions of 1848–49, the organization of the Union Army would have required even a much longer time. The very small number of killed and wounded in proportion to the sum total of the troops engaged (usually one out of twenty) proves that most of the engagements, even the most recent ones in Kentucky and Tennessee, were mainly fought with firearms at fairly long range, and that the occasional bayonet attacks either soon stopped before the enemy fire or put the enemy to flight before it came to hand-to-hand encounter. In the meantime, the new campaign has been opened under more favorable auspices with the successful advance of Buell and Halleck through Kentucky and Tennessee.

After the reconquest of Missouri and West Virginia, the Union opened the campaign with the advance into Kentucky. Here the Secessionists held three strong positions, fortified camps: Columbus on the Mississippi on their left, Bowling Green in the center, Mill Springs on the Cumberland River on their right. Their lines stretched more than three hundred miles from west to east. The extension of this line cut off the possibility of the three corps' affording each other mutual support, and offered the Union troops the chance to attack each one individually with superior forces. The great mistake in the disposition of the Secessionists sprang from the attempt to hold all they occupied. A single strongly fortified central camp, chosen as the field of battle for a decisive engagement and held by the main body of the army, would have defended Kentucky incomparably more effectively. It must have either attracted the main force of Unionists or placed the latter in a dangerous position should they attempt to march on without regard to so strong a troop concentration.

Under the given circumstances, the Unionists resolved to attack those three camps in succession, to maneuver their enemy out of them, and to force him to accept battle in open country. This plan, which violated all the precepts of the arts of war, was carried out with speed and energy. Toward the middle of January one corps of about 15,000 Unionists marched on Mill Springs, which was occupied by 20,000 Secessionists. The Unionists maneuvered in such a way that it led the enemy to believe that it had to deal with a weak reconnoitering corps. General Zollicoffer quickly fell into the trap, broke out of fortified camp, and attacked the Unionists. He soon convinced himself that a superior force confronted him. He fell, and his troops suffered a complete defeat, like the Unionists at Bull Run. But this time the victory was exploited in quite a different fashion. The defeated army was closely pursued until it reached its camp at Mill Springs broken, demoralized, without field artillery or baggage. This camp was pitched on the northern bank of the Cumberland River, so that in the event of another defeat the troops had no retreat open to them except across the river by way of a few steamers and river boats. We find in general that nearly all Secessionist camps were pitched on the *enemy* side of the stream. Taking up such a position is not only according to rule, but also very practical when there is a bridge in the rear. In such a case the camp serves as the bridgehead and gives its holders the chance to throw their fighting forces at will on both banks of the stream and thus maintain complete command of them. On the other hand, without a bridge in the rear, a camp on the enemy side of the stream cuts off retreat after an unlucky engagement and forces the troops to capitulate, or exposes them to massacre and drowning, as befell the Unionists at Ball's Bluff on the enemy side of the Potomac, whither the treachery of General Stone had sent them.

When the defeated Secessionists reached their camp at Mill Springs they immediately understood that an enemy attack on their fortifications must be repulsed, or capitulation must follow in a very short time. After the experience of the morning they had lost confidence in their powers of resistance. Hence when next day the Unionists advanced to attack the camp, they found that the enemy had taken advantage of the night to cross the stream, leaving the camp, baggage, artillery, and supplies behind them. In this way the extreme right of the Secessionists' line was pushed back to Tennessee, and East Kentucky, where the mass of the population is hostile to the slaveholders' party, was reconquered for the Union.

At the same time—toward the middle of January—preparations began for dislodging the Secessionists from Columbus and Bowling Green. A strong flotilla of mortar vessels and ironclad gunboats was held in readiness, and the news was spread in all directions that it was to serve as a convoy to a large army marching along the Mississippi from Cairo to Memphis and New Orleans. But all the demonstrations on the Mississippi were merely mock maneuvers. At the decisive moment the gunboats were brought to the Ohio River and from there to the Tennessee River, up which they sailed as far as Fort Henry. This place, together with Fort Donelson on the Cumberland River, formed the second line of defense of the Secessionists in Tennessee. The position was well chosen, for in the event of a retreat behind the Cumberland the latter stream would have covered its front and the Tennessee its left flank, while the narrow strip of land between the two streams was sufficiently covered by both the above-mentioned forts. The swift action of the Unionists, however, broke through the second line itself, before the left wing and the center of the first line were attacked.

In the first week of February the Unionists' gunboats appeared before Fort Henry, which surrendered after a short bombardment. The garrison escaped to Fort Donelson, since the land forces of the expedition were not strong enough to encircle the place. Now gunboats again sailed down the Tennessee, upstream to the Ohio, and thence up the Cumberland as far as Fort Donelson. A single gunboat sailed boldly up the Tennessee through the very heart of the state of Tennessee, skirting the state of Mississippi and pushing on as far as Florence, in North Alabama, where a series of swamps and banks (known by the name of Muscle Shoals) prevented further navigation. This fact, that a single gunboat made this long voyage of at least 150 miles and then returned, without suffering any kind of attack, proves that Union sentiment prevails along the river and will be very useful to the Union troops should they penetrate that far.

The boat expedition up the Cumberland now combined its movements with those of the land forces under Generals Halleck and Grant. The Secessionists at Bowling Green were deceived over the movements of the Unionists. Hence they remained quietly in their camp, while a week after the fall of Fort Henry, Fort Donelson was surrounded on the land side by 40,000 Unionists and threatened on the river side by a strong flotilla of gunboats. Like the camp at Mill Springs and Fort Henry, Fort Donelson had the river lying in its rear, without a bridge for retreat. It was the strongest place the Unionists had hitherto attacked. The works were constructed with the greatest care; furthermore, the place was capacious enough to accommodate the 20,000 men who occupied it. On the first day of the attack, the gunboats silenced the fire of the batteries trained on the river side and bombarded the interior of the defense works, while the land troops drove back the enemy outposts and forced the main body of the Secessionists to seek shelter right under the cannons of their own defense works. On the second day, the gunboats, which had suffered severely the day before, seem to have accomplished   little.

The land troops, on the contrary, had to fight a long and, in places, hot battle with the columns of the garrison, which sought to break through the right wing of the enemy to secure their line of retreat to Nashville. Nevertheless, an energetic attack by the Unionist right wing on the Secessionists' left wing, together with considerable reinforcements that the Unionists' left wing received, decided the victory in favor of the attackers. Various outworks were stormed. The garrison, forced into its inner lines of defense, without a chance of retreat and clearly not in a position to withstand an attack the next day, surrendered unconditionally on the following morning.

The American Civil War (II)*

WITH FORT DONELSON, the enemy's artillery, baggage, and military supplies fell into the hands of the Unionists; 30,000 Secessionists surrendered on the day of its capture, 1,000 more the next day, and as soon as the outposts of the victors appeared before Clarksville, a town that lies farther up the Cumberland River, it opened its gates. Here, too, considerable supplies for the Secessionists had been piled up.

The capture of Fort Donelson presents only one riddle: the flight of General Floyd with 5,000 men on the second day of the bombardment. These fugitives were too numerous to be smuggled away in steamboats during the night. With some precautionary measures on the part of the attackers, they could not have got away.

Seven days after the surrender of Fort Donelson, Nashville was occupied by the Federals. The distance between the two places amounts to about a hundred English miles, and a march of fifteen miles a day, on extremely wretched roads, during the most unfavorable season of the year, redounds to the honor of the Union troops. On receipt of the news of the fall of Fort Donelson, the Secessionists evacuated Bowling Green; one week later they left Columbus and fell back to a Mississippi island forty-five miles south. Thus Kentucky was completely recaptured for the Union. But Tennessee can be held by the Secessionists only if they invite a big battle and win it. In fact, they are said to have concentrated 65,000 men for this purpose. In the meantime nothing prevents the Unionists from bringing a superior force against them.

The leadership of the Kentucky campaign from Somerset to Nashville deserves the highest praise. The reconquest of so extensive a

---

* Written in collaboration with Frederick Engels. Published in *Die Presse*, Vienna, March 27, 1862.

[189]

territory, the advance from the Ohio to the Cumberland in a single month, shows an energy, decisiveness, and speed that have seldom been attained by the regular armies of Europe. One compares, for example, the slow advance of the Allies from Magenta to Solferino in the year 1859[1]—without pursuit of the retreating enemy, without endeavor to cut off his stragglers or in any way to envelop and encircle whole bodies of his troops.

Halleck and Grant in particular offer fine examples of decisive military leadership. Without the slightest regard for either Columbus or Bowling Green, they concentrated their forces at the decisive points, Fort Henry and Fort Donelson, captured them quickly and energetically, and thereby made Columbus and Bowling Green untenable. Then they promptly marched on Clarksville and Nashville, without giving the retreating Secessionists time to take up new positions in North Tennessee. During this rapid pursuit the corps of Secessionist troops in Columbus was completely cut off from the center and right wing of its army. English papers have criticized this operation unjustly. Even if the attack on Fort Donelson had failed, the Secessionists, kept busy by General Buell in Bowling Green, could not have detached sufficient men to enable the garrison to follow the repulsed Unionists into open country or to endanger their retreat. Columbus, on the other hand, was so far away that it could not interfere at all with Grant's movements. In fact, after the Unionists had cleared Missouri of the Secessionists, Columbus became an entirely useless post for the latter. The troops who constituted their garrison had to greatly hasten their retreat to Memphis or even to Arkansas, to escape the danger of an inglorious laying down of their arms.

In consequence of the clearing of Missouri and the reconquest of Kentucky, the theater of war has so far narrowed that the various armies can to a certain extent cooperate along the whole line of operations to achieve definite results. In other words, the war only now assumes a *strategic* character, and the geographic configuration of the country acquires a new interest. It is now the task of the Northern generals to find the Achilles heel of the cotton states.

Until the capture of Nashville, no common strategy was possible between the Army of Kentucky and the Army of the Potomac. They were much too far apart. They stood in the same front line, but their lines of operations were entirely different. Only with the victorious advance into Tennessee did the movements of the Army of Kentucky become important for the whole theater of war.

The American newspapers influenced by McClellan are making a great to-do over the anaconda-like envelopment theory. According

1. At the battles of Magenta (June 4, 1859) and Solferino (June 24), the French, allied with the Sardinians, defeated the Austrians.

to this, a vast line of armies is to envelop the rebels, gradually constrict its coils, and finally strangle the enemy. This is pure childishness. It is a rehash of the so-called *Cordon* system,[2] invented in Austria around 1770, which was employed against the French from 1792 to 1797 with such great stubbornness and such constant failure. At Jemappes, Fleurus, and particularly at Montenotte, Millesimo, Dego, Castiglione, and Rivoli, the knockout blow was dealt to this system. The French cut the "anaconda" in two by attacking at a point where they had concentrated superior forces. Then the pieces of the "anaconda" were chopped to bits one after another.

In well-populated and more or less centralized states, there is always a center whose occupation by the enemy would break the national resistance. Paris is a shining example. But the slave states possess no such center. They are sparsely populated, with few big cities and all of these on the seacoast. One therefore asks: Does there, nevertheless, exist a military center of gravity whose capture would break the backbone of their resistance, or are they, as Russia still was in 1812, unconquerable without, in a word, occupying every village and every patch of ground along the whole periphery?

Cast a glance at the geographic configuration of Secessia, with its long coastline on the Atlantic Ocean and its long coastline on the Gulf of Mexico. So long as the Confederates held Kentucky and Tennessee, the whole formed a great compact mass. The loss of those two states drives an immense wedge into their territory, separating the states on the North Atlantic Ocean from those on the Gulf of Mexico. The direct route from Virginia and the two Carolinas to Texas, Louisiana, Mississippi, and partly even to Alabama leads through Tennessee, which is now occupied by the Unionists. The *only* route, after the complete capture of Tennessee by the Union, that links the two sections of the slave states goes through Georgia. This proves that *Georgia is the key to Secessia.* With the loss of Georgia, the Confederacy would be cut into two sections which would have lost all connection with each other. A reconquest of Georgia by the Secessionists, furthermore, would be hardly thinkable, for the Unionist fighting forces would be concentrated in a central position, while their adversaries, divided into two camps, would have scarcely sufficient forces to put forth a united attack.

Would the conquest of all of Georgia, together with the seacoast of Florida, be required for such an operation? By no means. In a land where communication, particularly between distant points, depends much more on railroads than on highways, the seizure of railroads suffices. The southernmost railroad line between the states on the Gulf

---

2. The system whereby the troops were distributed at equal strength along the whole front line.

of Mexico and the Atlantic Coast goes through Macon and Gordon near Milledgeville.

The occupation of these two points would therefore cut Secessia in two and enable the Unionists to beat one part after the other. From the above, one sees at the same time that no Southern republic is viable without the possession of Tennessee. Without Tennessee, the vital point of Georgia lies only ten days' march from the border; the North would certainly have its fist at the throat of the South, and at the slightest pressure the South would have to yield or fight anew for its life, under circumstances in which a single defeat would cut off every prospect of success.

From the foregoing considerations, it follows: The Potomac is *not* the most important position of the theater of war. The capture of Richmond and the advance of the Army of the Potomac farther south —difficult because of the many streams that cut across the line of march—could produce a tremendous moral effect. Purely militarily, they would decide *nothing*.

The decision of the campaign belongs to the Kentucky army, now in Tennessee. On the one hand, this army is closest to the decisive points; on the other hand, it occupies a territory without which the Secession is not viable. Hence this army would have to be strengthened at the expense of all the rest and the sacrifice of all minor operations. Its next point of attack would be Chattanooga and Dalton on the Upper Tennessee, the most important railroad centers of the entire South. After their occupation, the connection between the eastern and western states of Secessia would be restricted to the connecting lines in Georgia. The further question would then be one of cutting off another railroad line to Atlanta and Georgia, and finally of destroying the last connection between the two sections by the capture of Macon and Gordon.

If, on the contrary, the "anaconda" plan were followed, then, despite all single successes and even one on the Potomac, the war would be prolonged indefinitely, while the financial difficulties together with diplomatic complications would acquire new scope.[3]

---

3. Instead of following the "anaconda" plan, the North finally did what Marx and Engels suggested in this article. In 1864 General Sherman's March to the Sea through Georgia cut the Confederacy in half and thus hastened its defeat. The South surrendered in April, 1865.

An International *Affaire Mirès**

April 28, 1862

A MAJOR THEME in local diplomatic circles is France's appearance in Mexico. One finds it puzzling that Louis Bonaparte should have increased the expeditionary troops at the moment when he promised to reduce them, and that he should want to go forward while England pulls back. It is exact knowledge here that the impetus for the Mexican expedition came from the Cabinet of St. James's, and not from the Tuileries. It is no less known that Louis Bonaparte likes to carry out all his undertakings, but particularly his overseas adventures, under English aegis. The restored Empire, one knows, has not yet copied the trick of its original, of quartering the French armies in the capitals of modern Europe. On the other hand, as a *pis aller* [last resort], it has led them to the capitals of old Europe, to Constantinople, Athens, and Rome, and even to Peking into the bargain. Should the theatrical effect of an excursion to the capital of the Aztecs be lost, and the opportunity for military archaeological collections *à la* Montauban? But if one considers only the present state of French finance and the future serious conflicts with the United States and England to which Louis Bonaparte's advance into Mexico may lead, one is obliged to reject without further ado the foregoing interpretation of his proceedings, which is favored by various British papers.

At the time of the Convention of July 17, 1861,[1] when the claims of the English creditors were to be settled, but the English plenipotentiary demanded at the same time an examination of the entire list of the Mexican debts or misdeeds, Mexico's foreign minister put the debt

---

* Published in *Die Presse*, Vienna, May 2, 1862.

1. On July 17, 1861, the Mexican Congress postponed payment of foreign debts for two years—an act that gave England, France, and Spain the pretext for intervention in Mexico.

[193]

to France at $200,000, hence a mere bagatelle of some £40,000. The account now drawn up by France, on the other hand, by no means confines itself to these modest limits.

Under the Catholic administration of Zuloaga and Miramón, an issue of Mexican state bonds to the amount of $14,000,000 was contracted through the medium of the Swiss banking house of J. B. Jecker & Co. The whole sum realized by the first issue of these bonds came to only 5 percent of the nominal amount, or $700,000. The total sum of the bonds issued very soon fell into the hands of prominent Frenchmen, among them relatives of the Emperor and fellow operators of *"haute politique."* The house of Jecker & Co. let these gentlemen have the aforesaid bonds far below their original nominal price.

Miramón contracted this debt at a time when he found himself in possession of the capital city. Later, after he had sunk to the role of a mere guerrilla chieftain, he again caused to be issued, through his so-called Finance Minister, Senor Peza-y-Peza, state bonds to the nominal value of $38,000,000. Once more it was the house of Jecker & Co. that negotiated the issue, but this time it limited its advances to the modest sum of barely $500,000, or from 1 to 2 percent on the dollar. Again the Swiss bankers knew how to dispose of their Mexican property as quickly as possible, and again the bonds fell into the hands of those "prominent" Frenchmen, among whom were some of the Imperial Court's habitués whose names will live on in the annals of the European stock exchanges as long as the *Affaire Mirès*.

Hence this debt of $52,000,000, of which not even $4,200,000 have so far been advanced, the administration of President Juárez declines to recognize: on the one hand, because he knows nothing about it, and on the other hand, because Messrs. Miramón, Zuloaga, and Peza-y-Peza possessed no constitutional authority for the contraction of such a state debt. The above-mentioned "prominent" Frenchmen, however, knew how to put through the opposite opinion at the decisive place. Lord Palmerston, for his part, was opportunely informed by some members of Parliament that the whole affair would lead to highly adverse interpellations in the Lower House. Among other things, what was to be feared was the question whether British land and sea power might be employed to support certain *rouge-et-noir*[2] politicians on the other side of the Channel. Palmerston, therefore, seized eagerly on the Conference of Orizaba[3] to withdraw from a business that threatens to besmirch like an international *Affaire Mirès*.

---

2. Red and black, the colors of roulette; reckless gambling.
3. The conference of Orizaba, Mexico, was held in the spring of 1862; representatives of England, France, and Spain participated.

The English Press and the Fall of New Orleans*

May 16, 1862

UPON THE ARRIVAL of the first reports of the fall of New Orleans,[1] the *Times*, the *Herald*, the *Standard*, the *Morning Post*, the *Daily Telegraph*, and other English "sympathizers" with the southern "niggerdrivers" proved strategically, tactically, philologically, exegetically, politically, morally, and fortificationally that the news was one of the "canards" that Reuters, Havas, Wolff, and their understrappers so often let fly. The natural defenses of New Orleans, it was said, had not only been strengthened by newly constructed forts but also by underwater infernal machines of all sorts and by ironclad gunboats. Then there was the Spartan mood of New Orleans and its deadly hate for Lincoln's mercenaries. Finally, was it not before New Orleans that England had suffered a defeat which brought its second war against the United States (1812–14) to an ignominious end? Hence there was no reason to doubt that New Orleans would immortalize itself for the "Southland" as a second Saragossa or Moscow.[2] In addition, it harbored 15,000 bales of cotton, with which it was easy to light an inextinguishable, self-consuming fire, quite apart from the fact that in 1814 the properly dampened bales of cotton proved themselves to be more indestructible by gunfire than the earthworks of Sevastopol. It was therefore clear as daylight that the fall of New Orleans was a case of the well-known Yankee boastfulness.

When the first reports were confirmed two days later by steamers arriving from New York, the bulk of the proslavery press persisted in

---

* Published in *Die Presse*, Vienna, May 20, 1862.
  1. Union troops entered New Orleans on May 1, 1862.
  2. The Spanish city of Saragossa withstood French sieges from June to August, 1808, and from December to February, 1809, when it capitulated. In September, 1812, the Russians left a burning Moscow to the invading French troops under Napoleon.

its skepticism. The *Evening Standard* especially was so sure in its un-
belief that in the same number it published a first editorial which
proved in black and white the impregnability of the Crescent City,
while its "latest news" announced in large type the fall of the impreg-
nable city. The *Times*, however, which has always held discretion to
be the better part of valor, tacked. It still doubted, but at the same
time it prepared itself for any eventuality, since New Orleans was a
city of "rowdies" and not of heroes. This time the *Times* was right.
New Orleans is a settlement of the dregs of French *Bohème*—in the
true sense of the word, a French convict colony—and never, with the
change of time, has it denied its origins. Only *post festum* [belatedly]
did the *Times* acquire this widely known information.

Finally, however, the *fait accompli* struck even the most complete
doubting Thomas. What to do? The English proslavery press now
proves that the fall of New Orleans is an advantage for the Confederates and a defeat for the Federals.

The fall of New Orleans permitted General Lovell to reinforce
with his troops the army of Beauregard, who was the more in need
of reinforcement since 160,000 men (rather an exaggeration) were
said to have been concentrated on his front by Halleck and, on the
other side, General Mitchel had cut Beauregard's communication with
the east by breaking the railroad connection of Memphis with Chattanooga, that is, with Richmond, Charleston, and Savannah. After this
severance (which long before the Battle of Corinth we characterized
as a strategically necessary move), Beauregard had no railroad connection from Corinth except that with Mobile and New Orleans. After
New Orleans fell, and he had to depend on the single railroad to Mobile,
he naturally could no longer procure the necessary provisions for his
troops, hence he fell back on Tupelo, and in the judgment of the
English proslavery press, his capacity for provisioning is, of course,
heightened by the entry of Lovell's troops!

On the other hand, the same oracles remark, the yellow fever will
grind down the Federalists in New Orleans, and finally, even if the
city itself is no Moscow, is not its mayor a Brutus? Only read (*cf.* the
New York [*Herald*]) his melodramatically brave words to Commodore Farragut. "Brave words, sir, brave words!" But hard words break
no bones.

The press organs of the southern slaveholders, however, do not
visualize the fall of New Orleans as optimistically as their English
comforters. One sees this from the following extracts.

The *Richmond Dispatch* says: "What has become of the ironclad
gunboats, the *Mississippi* and the *Louisiana*, from which we expected
the deliverance of the Crescent City? In respect to their effect on the
enemy, these ships might just as well have been ships of glass. It is

useless to deny that the fall of New Orleans is a heavy blow. The Confederate Government is thereby cut off from West Louisiana, Texas, Missouri, and Arkansas."

The *Norfolk Day Book* remarks: "This is the most serious defeat since the beginning of the war. It augurs privation and want for all classes of society and, what is worse, it threatens the supplies for our army."

The *Daily Intelligencer* [Atlanta, Georgia] laments: "We expected a different result. The approach of the enemy was no surprise attack; it had been long foreseen, and we had been promised that should he even pass near Fort Jackson, formidable artillery emplacements would force him to withdraw or assure his annihilation. In all this we have deceived ourselves, as on every occasion when defenses were supposed to guarantee the safety of a place or a town. It appears that modern inventions have annihilated the defensive capacity of fortified works. Ironclad gunboats demolish them or sail past them undisturbed. Memphis, we fear, will share the fate of New Orleans. Would it not be folly to deceive ourselves with hope?"

Finally, the *Petersburg Express:* "The capture of New Orleans by the Federals is the most extraordinary and the most fateful event of the whole war."

A Treaty Against the Slave Trade*

May 18, 1862

THE TREATY for the suppression of the slave trade, concluded between the United States and England in Washington on April 7 of this year, is now communicated to us *in extenso* by the American newspapers. The main points of this important document are as follows: The right of search is reciprocal, but can be carried out only by such warships of both sides as have received special authorization for this purpose from one of the contracting powers. From time to time, the contracting powers supply one another with complete statistics about the portions of their navies that are assigned to keep watch on the traffic in Negroes. The right of search can be exercised against merchantmen only within a distance of two hundred miles from the African coast, south of 32 degrees north latitude, and within thirty nautical miles from the coast of Cuba. Search, be it of English ships by American cruisers or American ships by English cruisers, does not take place in that part of the sea (that is, three nautical miles from the coast) which belongs to English or American territory; no more does it take place before the ports or settlements of foreign powers.

Mixed courts, composed half of Englishmen and half of Americans, sitting in Sierra Leone, Capetown, and New York, will pass judgment on the prize ships. In case of a ship's condemnation, her crew will be handed over to the jurisdiction of the nation under whose flag the ship sailed, insofar as this can be done without extraordinary cost. Not only the crew (including the captain, helmsman, etc.), but also the owners of the ship will then incur the penalties customary to the country. Compensation of merchantmen that have been acquitted by the mixed courts is to be paid within a year by the power under whose flag the capturing warship sailed. Not only the presence of captive Negroes is

* Published in *Die Presse,* Vienna, May 22, 1862.

regarded as legal ground for seizing ships, but also specially made arrangements in the ship's construction for the traffic in Negroes—manacles, chains, and other instruments for the securing of Negroes, and finally, stores of provisions that bear no relation to the needs of the ship's company. A ship on which such suspicious articles are found has to furnish proof of her innocence and even in the event of acquittal cannot claim compensation.

The commander of a cruiser who exceeds the authority conferred on him by the treaty is to be subjected to punishment by his respective government. Should the commander of a cruiser of one of the contracting powers harbor a suspicion that a merchantman under escort by one or more warships of the other contracting power carries Negroes on board, or has been engaged in the African slave trade, or is equipped for this trade, he has to communicate his suspicion to the commander of the escort and, in company with him, search the suspected ship; the latter is to be conducted to the place of residence of one of the mixed courts if, in accordance with the treaty, it falls under the category of suspicious ships. The Negroes found on board the condemned ships are placed at the disposal of the government under whose flag the seizure was made. They are to be set at liberty immediately and remain free under guarantee of the government in whose territory they find themselves. The treaty can be terminated only after ten years. It remains in force for a full year from the period of the notice given by one of the contracting parties.

The traffic in Negroes has received a mortal blow with this Anglo-American treaty—the result of the American Civil War. The effect of the treaty will be completed by the bill recently introduced by Senator Sumner, which repeals the law of 1808 dealing with the traffic in Negroes on the coasts of the United States, and punishes as a crime the transport of slaves from one United States port to another. This bill in large measure paralyzes the trade that the Negro-producing states (border slave states) carry on with the Negro-consuming states (the slave states proper).

The Situation in the American Theater of War*

May 23–25, 1862

THE CAPTURE of New Orleans, as the detailed reports now arrived show, is distinguished as an almost unparalleled deed of naval valor. The Unionists' navy consisted only of wooden ships: some six warships, each with fourteen to twenty-five cannon, supported by a large squadron of gunboats and mortar boats. This fleet had before it two forts that blocked the passage of the Mississippi. Within range of the hundred cannon of these forts the river was barred by a strong chain, behind which were massed torpedoes, incendiary floats, and other instruments of destruction. These first obstacles had therefore to be overcome in order to pass between the forts. On the farther side of the forts, however, was a second formidable line of defense made up of ironclad gunboats, among them the *Manassas*, an iron ram, and the *Louisiana*, a powerful floating battery. After the Unionists had bombarded the two forts that completely commanded the river for six days with no effect, they decided to brave their fire, force the iron barrier in three divisions, sail up the river, and risk battle with the "ironsides." The bold venture succeeded. As soon as the flotilla landed before New Orleans, the victory was naturally won.

Beauregard now has nothing more to defend in Corinth. His position there made sense only so long as it covered Mississippi and Louisiana, and especially New Orleans. He now finds himself strategically in the position that a lost battle would leave him no choice but to disband his army into guerrillas, for without a big city, where railroads and provisions are concentrated, in the rear of his army, he can no longer hold masses of men together.

McClellan has proved indisputably that he is a military incompetent

* Written in collaboration with Frederick Engels. Published in *Die Presse*, Vienna, May 30, 1862.

who, having been elevated by favorable circumstances to a commanding and responsible position, wages war not in order to defeat the enemy, but rather in order not to be defeated by the enemy and thereby forfeit his own usurped greatness. He comports himself like the old so-called "maneuvering generals," who excused their anxious avoidance of any tactical decision on the ground that by strategic envelopment they forced the enemy to give up his positions. The Confederates always escape him, because at the decisive moment he never attacks them. Thus—although their plan of retreat had already been announced ten days before, even in the New York papers (for example, the *Tribune*)—he let them quietly retire from Manassas to Richmond. Then he divided his army and flanked the Confederates strategically, while with one body of troops he established himself before Yorktown. A war of sieges always affords a pretext for wasting time and avoiding battle. No sooner had he concentrated a military force superior to that of the Confederates than he let them retire from Yorktown to Williamsburg and from there farther, without forcing them to join battle. Never has a war been waged so wretchedly. If the rear-guard action near Williamsburg ended in defeat for the troops of the Confederate rear instead of a second Bull Run for the Union troops, McClellan was entirely innocent of this result.

After a march of about twelve miles (English) in a twenty-four-hour downpour and through veritable seas of mud, 8,000 Union troops under General Heintzelmann (of German descent, but born in Pennsylvania) arrived near Williamsburg and encountered only weak enemy pickets. As soon, however, as he had assured himself of their numerically inferior strength, he had sent from his picked troops at Williamsburg reinforcements that gradually swelled the number of his men to 25,000. By nine o'clock in the morning the battle was joined in earnest; by half past twelve General Heintzelmann discovered that the engagement was going in favor of the enemy. He sent messenger after messenger to General Kearny, who was eight miles to his rear, but, owing to the complete "dissolution" of the road because of the rain, the latter advanced only slowly. For a full hour Heintzelmann remained without reinforcements and the Seventh and Eighth New Jersey regiments, which had exhausted their stock of powder, began to run for the woods on both sides of the road. Heintzelmann now had Colonel Menill and a squadron of Pennsylvania cavalry take up a position on both fringes of the forest, with the threat of firing on the fugitives. This brought the latter once more to a standstill.

In addition, order was further restored by the example of a Massachusetts regiment, which had likewise exhausted its powder but which now fixed bayonets to its muskets and calmly awaited the enemy. Finally, Kearny's vanguard under Brigadier Berry (from the State of

Maine) came in sight. Heintzelmann's army received its rescuers with a wild "Hurrah"; he had the regimental band strike up "Yankee Doodle," and Berry's fresh forces formed a line of nearly half a mile in length in front of his exhausted troops. After preliminary musket fire, Berry's brigade made a bayonet charge at the double and drove the enemy from the battlefield back to his earthworks, the largest of which, after repeated attacks and counterattacks, remained in the hands of the Union troops. Thus the equilibrium of the battle was restored. Berry's arrival saved the Unionists. The arrival of Jameson's and Birney's brigades at four o'clock decided the victory. At nine o'clock in the evening, the retreat of the Confederates from Williamsburg began; on the following day they continued it—in the direction of Richmond —hotly pursued by Heintzelmann's cavalry. Between six and seven in the morning after the battle, Heintzelmann had already caused Williamsburg to be occupied by General Jameson. The rear guard of the fleeing enemy had evacuated the town from the opposite end only half an hour before. Heintzelmann's battle was an infantry battle in the true sense of the word. Artillery hardly came into play. Musket fire and bayonet attacks were decisive. If the Congress in Washington wanted to pass a vote of thanks, it should have been to General Heintzelmann, who saved the Yankees from a second Bull Run, and not to McClellan, who in his usual fashion avoided the "tactical decision" and permitted the numerically weaker foe to escape for the third time.

The Confederate army in Virginia has better chances than Beauregard's army, first because it is facing a McClellan instead of a Halleck, and second, because the many rivers on its line of retreat flow crosswise from the mountains to the sea. Nevertheless, in order to avoid being broken up into bands *without a battle,* its generals will be forced sooner or later to accept a decisive battle, exactly as the Russians had to fight at Smolensk and Borodino against the best judgment of the generals. Wretched as McClellan's generalship has been, the constant retreats, accompanied by abandonment of artillery, munitions, and other military supplies, and simultaneously the small, unlucky rearguard actions—all these have in any case badly demoralized the Confederates, as will become evident on the day of a decisive battle. We come, therefore, to the summary:

If Beauregard or Jefferson Davis should lose a decisive battle, his armies would dissolve into bands. If one of them should win a decisive battle, which is altogether improbable, the dissolution of their armies would at best be deferred. They are in no position to make even the slightest lasting use of a victory. They cannot advance twenty English miles without coming to a standstill and again awaiting a renewed enemy offensive.

It still remains to examine the chances of a guerrilla war. But it is

(Above) The Second Battle of the Wilderness, May 10, 1864. (Below) The Battle of Shiloh Church, near Pittsburg Landing, Tenn., on April 6-7, 1862.
THE GRANGER COLLECTION

Civil War gunboats. (Top) gunboat flotilla, 1862. (Center, left) A mortar-boat. (Center, right) The Louisiana. *(Bottom) The* New Era.
PICTURE COLLECTION NYPL

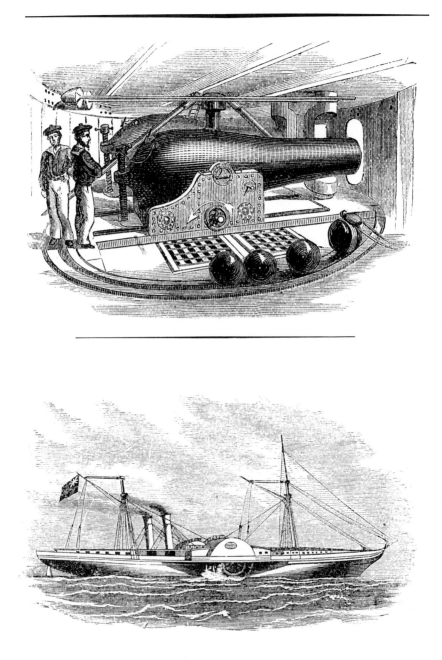

(Above) Interior of the Monitor's *turret. (Below) A blockade runner.*

Henry C. Carey, American economist. THE GRANGER COLLECTION

(Top, left) The Abolitionist John Brown. (Top, right) John Caldwell Calhoun of South Carolina. (Bottom, left) Robert Toombs, Secretary of State of the Confederacy. (Bottom, right) Alexander Hamilton Stephens, Vice-President of the Confederacy. THE GRANGER COLLECTION

To Abraham Lincoln
President of the United States
of America

Sir

We congratulate the American People upon your Re-election by a large Majority.

If resistance to the Slave power was the reserved Watchword of your first election, the triumphant Warcry of your Re-election is, Death to Slavery.

From the commencement of the titanic American Strife, the Working men of Europe felt instinctively that the Star spangled Banner carried the Destiny of their class. The Contest for the territories which opened the dire epopee, Was it not to decide whether the virgin soil of immense tracts should be wedded to the Labour of the Emigrant, or prostituted by the Tramp of the Slave Driver?

When an Oligarchy of 300,000 Slaveholders dared to inscribe, for the first time in the annals of the World, Slavery on the Banner of Armed Revolt: when on the very spots where hardly a century ago the idea of one great democratic Republic had first sprung up, Whence the first Declaration of the Rights of Man was issued, and the first impulse given to the European Revolution of the 18th Century; When on those very spots counter revolution, with systematic thoroughness, gloried in rescinding "the Ideas entertained at the time of the formation of the old Constitution" and maintained "Slavery to be a beneficent Institution, indeed the only Solution of the great problem of the relation of Labour to Capital", and cynically proclaimed property in Man "the corner stone of the new Edifice". Then the Working Classes of Europe understood at once, even before the fanatic partisanship of the Upper Classes for the confederate gentry had given its dismal warning, that the Slaveholder's Rebellion was to sound the tocsin for a general holy Crusade of Property against Labour, and that for the Men of Labour, with their hopes for the future, even their past conquests were at stake in that tremendous Conflict on the other side of the Atlantic. Everywhere they bore therefore patiently the hardships imposed upon them by the Cotton crisis, opposed enthusiastically the Pro Slavery Intervention, importunities of their betters; and from most parts of Europe contributed their quota of blood to the good cause.

While the Working Men, the true political power of the North, allowed Slavery to defile their own Republic, while before the Negro, mastered and sold without his concurrence, they boasted it the highest prerogative of the white skinned Labour to sell himself and choose his own Master, they were unable to attain the true freedom of Labour or to support their European Brethren in their struggle for Emancipation, but this barrier to progress has been swept off by the red sea of Civil War.

The Working Men of Europe feel sure that as the American War of Independence initiated a new era of ascendency for the Middle Class, so the American Anti Slavery War will do for the Working Classes. They consider it an earnest of the epoch to come, that it fell to the lot of Abraham Lincoln, the single minded Son of the Working Class, to lead his Country through the matchless struggle for the rescue of an enchained Race and the Reconstruction of a Social World.

Signed on behalf of The International Working Men's Association the Central Council.

(Opposite page) Congratulatory letter sent to President Lincoln by the International Working Men's Association. (Above) Henry George, American economist. THE GRANGER COLLECTION

Joseph Hooker, Major General, USA. Photographed by Mathew Brady during the Civil War. THE GRANGER COLLECTION

George Brinton McClellan, Major General, USA. Photographed by Mathew Brady during the Civil War. THE GRANGER COLLECTION

William Tecumseh Sherman, Major General, USA. Photographed by Mathew Brady during the Civil War. THE GRANGER COLLECTION

Union generals. (Top, left) Samuel P. Heintzelman, Major General. (Top, right) Henry Wager Halleck, Major General. (Center, left) William Starke Rosecrans, Major General. (Center, right) John Pope, Major General. (Bottom, left) Winfield Scott, Lieutenant General. (Bottom, right) A. McDowell McCook, Major General. PICTURE COLLECTION NYPL

Banner of the South Carolina secession convention. PICTURE COLLECTION NYPL

(Top) Confederate flag. (Center) Confederate ten-dollar note. (Bottom) Confederate State Department seal. PICTURE COLLECTION NYPL

(Top, left) Thomas Jonathan ("Stonewall") Jackson, Lieutenant General, CSA. (Top, right) Governor Beriah Magoffin of Kentucky. (Center) Senator Andrew P. Butler of South Carolina. (Bottom, left) John Cabell Breckinridge, Major General, CSA. (Bottom, right) Pierre G. T. Beauregard, General, CSA.

(Top, left) Howell Cobb, Major General, CSA. (Top, right) John Hunt Morgan, Brigadier General, CSA. (Center) John B. Floyd, Brigadier General, CSA. (Bottom, left) Felix K. Zollicoffer, Brigadier General, CSA. THE GRANGER COLLECTION

The man with the (carpet) bags. Cartoon by Thomas Nast.
THE GRANGER COLLECTION

precisely in this war of the slaveholders that it is most amazing how little, or rather how nonexistent, has been the participation of the population. In the year 1813 the communications of the French were constantly interrupted and harrassed by Colomb, Lützow, Chernyshev, and twenty other leaders of insurgents and Cossacks. In 1812 the Russian population completely vanished before the French line of march; in 1814 the French peasants armed themselves and killed the patrols and stragglers of the Allies; but here nothing happens at all. People resign themselves to the fortune of the big batttles and console themselves with "*Victrix causa diis placuit, sed victa Catoni.*"[1] The boast about the war at sea dissolves into vapor. There can hardly be any doubt, to be sure, that the "white trash," as the planters themselves call the poor whites, will attempt guerrilla warfare and brigandage. But such an attempt will very quickly transform the property-owning planters into Unionists. They themselves will call the troops of the Yankees to their aid. The alleged burnings of cotton, etc., on the Mississippi rest exclusively on the testimony of two Kentuckians, who are said to have come to Louisville—surely not up the Mississippi. The conflagration in New Orleans was easily organized. The fanaticism of the New Orleans merchants is explained on the ground that they were obliged to take a mass of Confederate Treasury bonds for hard cash. The conflagration at New Orleans will be repeated in other cities; assuredly there will be some other burnings, but such theatrical coups can only bring the split between the planters and the "white trash" to a head, and therewith, *finis Secessiae!*

---

1. "The victorious cause pleased the gods, but that of the vanquished pleased Cato": Lucan, *Pharsalia.*

English Humanity and America*

June 14, 1862

HUMANITY in England, like liberty in France, has now become an article of export for the traders in politics. We recall the time when Czar Nicholas had Polish ladies flogged by soldiers and when Lord Palmerston found the moral indignation of a few parliamentarians over the event to be "unpolitical." We recall that about a decade ago a revolt broke out on the Ionian Islands which induced the English governor there to have a not inconsiderable number of Greek women flogged. *Probatum est* [It is approved], said Palmerston and his Whig colleagues who were then in office. Only a few years ago official documents of Parliament showed that the tax collectors in India employed coercive means against the wives of the ryots, the infamy of which forbids further detailing. Palmerston and colleagues, to be sure, did not dare to justify these atrocities, but what an outcry they would have made if a *foreign* government had dared to proclaim publicly its indignation over these English infamies and to indicate, in no uncertain terms, that it would intervene if Palmerston and colleagues did not immediately disavow the Indian tax officials. But Cato the Censor himself could not watch over the morals of the Roman citizens more anxiously than the English aristocrats and their ministers do over the "humanity" of the war-waging Yankees.

The ladies of New Orleans, yellow beauties, tastelessly decked out in jewels, and somewhat comparable to the women of the ancient Mexicans, except that they do not devour their slaves *in natura* [in the flesh], are this time—previously it was the harbors of Charleston—the occasion of a British-aristocratic display of humanity. The Englishwomen (they are, however, not ladies, nor do they own slaves) who are starving in Lancashire have hitherto inspired no parliamentary utter-

* Published in *Die Presse*, Vienna, June 20, 1862.

ance; the cry of distress of the Irishwomen who, with the progressive elimination of the small tenant farmers in green Erin, are thrown half naked into the street and hunted from house to house as if the Tartars had invaded, has hitherto called forth a single echo from Lords, Commons, and Her Majesty's Government—homilies on the absolute rights of landed property. But the ladies of New Orleans!

This, of course, is another matter. These ladies were far too enlightened to participate in the tumult of war, like the goddesses of Olympus, or to cast themselves into the flames, like the women of Sagunt.[1] They have invented a new and undangerous mode of heroism, one that could have been invented only by female slaveholders, and especially in a land where the free portion of the population consists of shopkeepers by vocation, tradesmen in cotton or sugar or tobacco, and does not keep slaves, like the *cives* [citizens] of the world of antiquity. After their men had run away from New Orleans or had crept into their back closets, these ladies rushed into the streets to spit in the faces of the victorious Union troops or to stick out their tongues at them or, like Mephistopheles, in general to make "an indecent gesture," accompanied by insulting words. These Megaeras believed they could be ill-bred "with impunity."

This was their heroism. General Butler issued a proclamation in which he notified them that they would be treated as streetwalkers if they continued to act as streetwalkers. Butler, indeed, has the makings of a lawyer, but seems not to have properly studied English statute law. Otherwise, by analogy with the laws imposed by Castlereagh on Ireland,[2] he would have forbidden them to set foot on the street at all. Butler's warning to the "ladies" of New Orleans has aroused such moral indignation in Earl Carnarvon, Sir J. Walsh (who played so ridiculous and hateful a role in Ireland), and Mr. Gregory, who was already demanding recognition of the Confederacy a year ago, that the Earl in the Upper House, and the knight and the man "without a handle to his name" in the Lower House, interpellated the ministry with a view to inquiring what steps it intended to take in the name of insulted "humanity." Russell and Palmerston both castigated Butler, both expected that the government in Washington would disavow him, and the very softhearted Palmerston—who behind the back of the Queen, without the foreknowledge of his colleagues, merely out of "human" admiration, recognized the *coup d'état* of December 1851[3] (when "ladies" were actually shot dead, while others were raped by

---

1. In 219 A.D., after Hannibal captured the besieged city of Sagunt, in Spain, the inhabitants incinerated themselves.

2. In 1801 Castlereagh's government instituted martial law in Ireland, after having suppressed an Irish uprising that began in 1798.

3. Louis Bonaparte's *coup d'état* of December 2, 1851, in which he made himself Emperor.

Zouaves)—this same sensitive Viscount declared Butler's warning to be an "infamy." Indeed, ladies—and ladies who actually own slaves—were not even to be allowed to vent their anger and their malice on common Union troops, peasants, artisans, and other rabble with impunity! It is "infamous."

In the public here, nobody is deceived by this humanity farce. It is meant partly to bring forth and partly to strengthen the sentiment for intervention, on the part of France in the first place. After the first melodramatic outbursts the knights of humanity in the Upper and Lower Houses, as if on command, also threw away their emotional mask. Their declamation served merely as a prologue to the question whether the Emperor of the French had come to an understanding with the English Government in regard to mediating, and whether the latter, as they hoped, had received such an offer favorably. Russell and Palmerston both declared that they knew nothing of the offer. Russell declared that the present moment was highly unfavorable for mediation. Palmerston, more cautious and reserved, contented himself with saying that at the *present* moment the English government had no intention of mediating.

The plan is that during the recess of the English Parliament, France should play her role of mediator, and in the autumn, if Mexico is secure, should initiate her intervention. The lull in the American theater of war again awakened the intervention speculators in St. James's and the Tuileries from their marasmus. That lull itself is due to a strategic error in the Northern conduct of the war. If after its victory in Tennessee the Kentucky army had advanced rapidly on the railroad centers in Georgia, instead of allowing itself to be sidetracked southward down the Mississippi, Reuter & Co. would have been cheated of their business in "intervention" and "mediation" rumors. However that may be, Europe can wish nothing more ardently than that the *coup d'état* should make an attempt "to restore order in the United States" and "save civilization" there too.

A Suppressed Debate on Mexico and the Alliance with France*

July 16, 1862

ONE OF the most singular English parliamentary devices is the count-out. What is the count-out? If there are fewer than forty members present in the Lower House, they do not form a quorum, that is, an assembly capable of making decisions. If an independent parliamentarian introduces a bill that is equally annoying to both oligarchic fractions, the Ins and the Outs (those in office and those in opposition) come to an agreement that on the day of the debate parliamentarians on both sides will be gradually lacking, alias absenting themselves. When the emptying of the benches has reached the necessary maximum, the government whip—that is, the parliamentarian entrusted with party discipline by the current ministry—gives a wink to the brother previously chosen for this purpose. Brother parliamentarian rises and quite nonchalantly asks the chairman to have the House counted. The count takes place and, lo! it is discovered that fewer than forty members are assembled. Herewith the proceedings come to an end. The obnoxious motion is shelved, without the government party or the opposition party having put itself in the awkward and compromising position of being forced to vote it down.

At yesterday's session the count-out was brought up in an interesting manner. Lord R. Montagu had, for that day, given notice of a motion that dealt with the communication of new diplomatic documents on the intervention in Mexico. He began his speech with the following words: "Last Saturday the latest Blue Book on Mexico was presented to the House, which thus must be intending to debate the Mexican affair now. I *know* that the government party and the opposition party have agreed to set aside my motion. I hope that the sense

---

* Published in *Die Presse*, Vienna, July 20, 1862.

of duty of the House will not tolerate such a maneuver in so important a matter."

But Lord R. Montagu reckoned without the host. After he himself had spoken, Layard had replied to him on behalf of the government, and Fitzgerald had delivered himself of some official chatter on behalf of the Tories, Kinglake (a Liberal member) rose. The prelude to his speech concluded with the following words: "The whole series of negotiations, disclosed by the documents submitted, offers a striking example of the manner in which the French Government uses its relations with this country as a means of propping up the imperial throne.

"For the French Government it is of decisive importance to divert the French people's attention from affairs at home by showing how it is engaged in great undertakings abroad, in agreement with one of the great respectable powers."

Hardly had Kinglake uttered these words when an "honorable" member of the House moved that the House be "*counted*." And behold! The House had dwindled to only thirty-three members. Lord Montagu's motion was killed by the same count-out which he had protested against at the opening of the debate.

Apart from Kinglake's interrupted speech, only that of Lord Montagu had a substantive interest. Lord R. Montagu's speech contains the following important explanation of the facts of the case: "Sir Charles Wyke has concluded a treaty with Mexico. Out of servility to Louis Bonaparte, this treaty was not ratified by Lord John Russell. Sir Charles Wyke concluded the said treaty after France, through her connection with Almonte, the leader of the reactionary party, had entered a path that abrogated the joint convention between England, France, and Spain. Lord John Russell himself declared in an official dispatch that this treaty satisfied all legitimate demands of England. In his correspondence with Thouvenel, however, he promised, in compliance with Bonaparte's wish, *not* to ratify the treaty for the time being. He allowed Thouvenel to communicate this decision to the *Corps Législatif*. Indeed, Lord Russell demeaned himself so far as to promise Thouvenel that he would break off all communication with Sir Charles Wyke until July 1, 1862—a period that gave Thouvenel time to reply. Thouvenel answered that Bonaparte did not contest England's right to act in isolation, but disapproved of the Anglo-Mexican treaty concluded by Sir Charles Wyke. Whereupon Russell ordered Wyke to withhold ratification of the treaty."

England, added Lord Montagu, lends her influence to collect the fraudulent claims on the Mexican Treasury that Morny "and perhaps also persons of higher standing in France" have obtained for themselves through the medium of the Swiss stock-exchange swindler Jecker.

"The whole Mexican deal," he continued, "was begun without the previous knowledge of Parliament. The first extraparliamentary war was waged in 1857. Palmerston defended it on the ground that it would be waged in Asia. The same principle is now applied to America. It will finally be applied to Europe. The parliamentary regime thus becomes a mere farce, in that with the loss of control over wars, the people's representatives lose control over the purse."

Lord Montagu concluded with the words: "I accuse the ministry of having allied us with the murderer of liberty in France, in that it now enables this unprincipled adventurer to plant a despotism in a foreign country. Our fate is tied to a man who calls forth the abhorrence of humanity and the vengeance of heaven."

A Criticism of American Affairs*

August 4, 1862

THE CRISIS which at the moment dominates conditions in the United States results from two causes: military and political.

If the last campaign had been waged according to a *single* strategic plan, the main army of the West must then, as previously explained in these columns, have availed itself of its successes in Kentucky and Tennessee to penetrate Georgia through northern Alabama, in order to seize the railroad centers at Decatur, Milledgeville, etc. Thereby the connection with the eastern and western armies of the Secessionists would have been broken and their mutual support rendered impossible. Instead, the Kentucky army marched down the Mississippi, southward in the direction of New Orleans, and its victory near Memphis had no other result than to dispatch the great part of Beauregard's troops to Richmond, so that the Confederates there now suddenly confronted McClellan—who had not exploited the defeat of the enemy's troops at Yorktown and Williamsburg, but who, on the other hand, had from the first split his own fighting forces—with a superior army in a superior position. McClellan's generalship, already described by us previously, was in itself sufficient to assure the downfall of the strongest and best disciplined army. Finally, War Minister Stanton committed an inexcusable mistake. To make an impression abroad, he suspended recruiting after the conquest of Tennessee, and thus condemned the army to constant weakening, precisely when it most needed reinforcements for a rapid, decisive offensive. Despite the strategic blunders and despite McClellan's generalship, with a steady influx of recruits, the war, if not decided now, would nevertheless have been rapidly nearing a victorious decision. Stanton's step was the more

* Published in *Die Presse*, Vienna, August 9, 1862.

[210]

disastrous in that the South was just then enlisting all men from eighteen to thirty-five and thus staking everything on a single card. It is these men, trained in the meantime, who give the Confederates the upper hand and secure them the initiative almost everywhere. They held down Halleck, drove Curtis from Arkansas, beat McClellan, and under Stonewall Jackson gave the signal for the guerrilla raids that already reach as far as the Ohio.

The military causes are partly connected with the political ones. It was the influence of the Democratic party that elevated an incompetent like McClellan, because he was once an adherent of Breckinridge, to the position of commander-in-chief of all the fighting forces of the North. It is anxious regard for the wishes, advantages, interests of the spokesmen of the border slave states that has hitherto blunted the Civil War's points of principle and, so to speak, deprived it of its soul. The "loyal" slaveholders of those border states saw to it that the Fugitive Slave Acts, dictated by the South, were maintained and the sympathies of the Negroes for the North so forcibly suppressed that no general could dare to put a Negro company in the field, and that finally slavery was transformed from the Achilles' heel of the South into its invulnerable horny hide. Thanks to the slaves, who perform all productive labors, the entire battle-ready manhood of the South can be led into the field!

At the present moment, when the Secession's stock is rising, the spokesmen of the border states increase their claims. However, Lincoln's appeal[1] to them, in which he threatens them with inundations by the Abolitionist party, shows that things are taking a revolutionary turn. Lincoln knows what Europe does not know, that it is by no means apathy or yielding under pressure of defeat that caused his request for 300,000 recruits to meet with such a cold echo. New England and the Northwest, which had supplied the main body of troops, are determined to force on the government a revolutionary waging of the war and to inscribe on the star-spangled banner the battle slogan: "Abolition of Slavery." Lincoln yields only hesitantly and cautiously to this pressure from without, but knows that he is incapable of offering resistance to it for long. Hence his imploring appeal to the border states to give up the institution of slavery voluntarily and under conditions of a favorable contract. He knows that it is only the continuation of slavery in the border states that has hitherto left slavery untouched in the South and has prohibited the North from applying the great radical remedy. But he is mistaken if he imagines that the "loyal" slaveholders can be moved by well-meaning speeches and rational arguments. They will yield only to force.

---

1. Lincoln's letter of July 12, 1862, to the members of the border states in Congress.

Up to now we have witnessed only the first act of the Civil War—the *constitutional* waging of war. The second act, the *revolutionary* waging of war, is at hand.

In the meantime, the first session of the Congress, which has now adjourned, has decreed a series of important measures, which we will briefly summarize here.

Apart from its financial legislation, it has passed the Homestead Act,[2] which the Northern masses had long vainly striven for; by this act a portion of the public lands is given gratis for cultivation to settlers, native or immigrants. The Congress has abolished slavery in the District of Columbia and the national capital, with monetary compensation to the former slaveholders. Slavery has been declared "forever impossible" in all the *territories* of the United States.[3] The act under which the new state of West Virginia was admitted into the Union prescribes abolition of slavery by stages and declares all Negro children born after July 4, 1863, to be born free. The conditions of gradual emancipation are entirely borrowed from the law enacted seventy years ago in Pennsylvania for the same purpose.[4] By a fourth act, all slaves owned by rebels are to be emancipated as soon as they fall into the hands of the republican army. Another law, which is now being executed *for the first time*, provides that these emancipated Negroes may be militarily organized and sent into the field against the South. The independence of the Negro republics of Liberia and Haiti has been recognized,[5] and finally, a treaty for the abolition of the slave trade has been concluded with England.

Thus no matter how the dice may fall in the fortune of battle, it can now be said with certainty that Negro slavery will not outlive the Civil War for long.

---

2. The Homestead Act was passed on May 20, 1862.

3. In June, 1862, Lincoln signed a bill ending slavery and involuntary servitude in all the territories.

4. The Pennsylvania law providing for the gradual emancipation of slaves was passed in 1780.

5. Liberia and Haiti were granted diplomatic recognition in June, 1862.

Russell's Protest Against American Insolence*

August 20, 1862

AMONG the English, Lord John Russell is known as a "letter writer." In his latest letter to Mr. Stuart he complains of the insults against "Old England" by North American newspapers. *Et tu, Brute!* It is impossible to speak face to face with any respectable Englishman who does not raise his hands high and clap them over this tour de force! It is well known that in the years 1789–1815 English journalism was unsurpassed in its attacks of hateful rage against the French nation. And still, in recent years it has surpassed this tradition by its "malignant brutality" against the United States! A few recent examples may suffice.

"We owe," says the *Times*, "our whole moral weight to our kinsmen (the Southern slaveholders), who are fighting so bravely and perseveringly for their freedom, against a mongrel race of robbers and oppressors."

The *New York Evening Post* (the Abolitionist organ) comments on this: "Are these English squibblers, these descendants of Britons, Danes, Saxons, Celts, Normans, and Dutch, of such pure blood that all other peoples appear to be mongrels compared to them?"

Shortly after the publication of the above citation, the *Times*, in heavy Garamond type, called President Lincoln a "respectable buffoon," his cabinet a "gang of scoundrels and rascals," and the Army of the United States an "army whose officers are Yankee swindlers and whose common soldiers are German thieves." And Lord John Russell, not sufficiently satisfied with the laurels of his letters to the Bishop

---

* From an article in *Die Presse*, Vienna, August 24, 1862.

of Durham and to Sir James Hudson at Turin,[1] dares to speak, in his letter to Stuart, of "insults by the North American press."

Still, it is natural that trees do not grow up to heaven. Malevolent impertinence and hateful rancor to the contrary, official England will keep the peace with the "Yankee swindlers," and will restrict its deep sympathies for the noble-minded Southern sellers of human blood to blotting-paper rhetoric and isolated smuggling ventures, for an increase in the price of grain is not to be fooled with, and any conflict with the Yankees would now add food famine to cotton famine.

England has long since ceased to live on its own grain production. In the years 1857, 1858, and 1859, she imported £66,00,000 worth of grain flour; in the years 1860, 1861, and 1862 the import amounted to £118,000,000. In regard to the weight of cereals and flour, in 1858 it was 10,278,774 quarters; in 1860, 14,484,976 quarters; and in 1861, 16,094,914 quarters. Thus in the last five years alone the import of grain rose by 50 percent.

In fact, England now imports practically half of her grain requirements from abroad. And there is every probability that in the coming year this import will be increased by at least 30 percent, we mean 30 percent in cost price, as the very ample harvest in the United States will prevent too high a rise in the price of grain. But that this year's shortage of cereals will amount to from one-fourth to one-fifth of the average is as good as proved in the detailed reports which the *Mark Lane Express* [*and Agricultural Journal*] and the *Gardeners' Chronicle and Agricultural Gazette* published from all the agricultural districts. As when Lord Brougham said after the peace of 1815 that England's debt of a billion pounds to Europe was a guarantee of the latter's "good behavior," so this year's harvest shortage offers the United States the best guarantee that England will not "break the Queen's peace." . . .

---

1. On November 4, 1850, Russell, then Prime Minister, wrote to the Bishop of Durham against the "usurping actions" of Pope Pius IX. On October 27, 1860, Russell, then Foreign Minister, wrote to Hudson, the British envoy to Turin, approving Sardinia's annexation of southern Italy.

Abolitionist Demonstrations in America*

August 22, 1862

IT WAS previously observed in these columns that President Lincoln, legally cautious, constitutionally conciliatory, by birth a citizen of the border slave state of Kentucky, withdraws only painfully from the control of the "loyal" slaveowners, seeks to avoid any open breach with them, and precisely thereby calls forth a conflict with the parties of the North which are consistent in principle and are pushed more and more into the foreground by events. The speech that Wendell Phillips delivered at Abington, Massachusetts, on the occasion of the anniversary of the emancipation of the slaves in the British West Indies, may be regarded as a prologue to this conflict.

Wendell Philips is, next to Garrison and G. Smith, the leader of the Abolitionists in New England. For thirty years, unremittingly and in danger of his life, he has proclaimed the emancipation of the slaves as his battle cry, regardless equally of the persiflage of the press, the enraged howls of the paid rowdies, and the conciliatory remonstrances of worried friends. He is acknowledged, even by his opponents, to be one of the greatest orators of the North, combining an iron character with powerful energy and purest conviction. The London *Times*—and what could characterize this magnanimous paper more strikingly? —today denounces Wendell Phillips' speech at Abington to the government in Washington. It is an "abuse" of freedom of speech.

"Anything more violent," says the *Times*, "is scarcely possible to imagine and anything more daring in time of civil war was never perpetrated in any country by any sane man who valued his life and liberty. In reading the speech it is scarcely possible to avoid the conclusion that the speaker's object was to force the government to prosecute him."

* Published in *Die Presse*, Vienna, August 30, 1862.

And the *Times*, in spite, or perhaps because, of its hatred for the Union Government, does not seem at all averse to taking over the role of public prosecutor!

In the present state of affairs, Wendell Phillips' speech is of greater importance than a battle bulletin. We therefore condense its most striking passages: [1]

> I believe Mr. Lincoln is conducting this war, at present, with the purpose of saving slavery . . . Mr. Lincoln is intentionally waging a *political* war . . . When Mr. Lincoln, by an equivocal declaration, nullifies General Hunter, . . . he does it because he is afraid of Kentucky . . . He believes in the South . . . I had a friend who went to Port Royal, went among the Negro huts, and saw the pines that were growing between them shattered with shells and cannon balls. He said to the Negroes: "When those balls came, were you here?" "Yes." "Didn't you run?" "No, massa, we knew they were not meant for us." . . . Every Southern traitor on the other side of the Potomac can say of McClellan's cannon ball, if he ever fires one, "We know it is not meant for us." . . . I do not say that McClellan is a traitor, but I say this, that if he had been a traitor from the crown of his head to the sole of his foot, he could not have served the South better than he has done since he was commander-in-chief [applause] . . . There is more danger today that Washington will be taken than Richmond . . . Every man who under the present policy loses his life in the swamps of the South, and every dollar sent there to be wasted, only prolongs a murderous and wasteful war, waged for no purpose whatever . . . Such an aimless war I call wasteful and murderous. Better that the South should go today, than that we should prolong such a war . . . A hundred and twenty-three thousand men a year, and I suppose, a million of dollars a day, and a government without a purpose!
>
> You say, "Why not end the war?" We cannot. Jefferson said of slavery, "We have got the wolf by the ears; we can neither hold him nor let him go." That was his figure. We have now got the South—this wolf—by the ears; we *must* hold her; we cannot let her go . . . Let the South go tomorrow, and you have not got peace. Intestine war here, border war along the line, aggression and intrigue on the part of the South! She has lived with us for seventy years, and kept us constantly in turmoil. Exasperated by suffering, grown haughty by success, the moment she goes off, is such a neighbor likely to treat us any better, with our imaginary line between us, than she has treated us for seventy years while she held the scepter? The moment we ask for terms, she counts it victory,

---

1. Phillips' speech, given at Abington, Mass., August 1, 1862, is published, under the title "The Cabinet," in his *Speeches, Lectures and Letters, Series I* (Boston, 1864), pp. 448-63. Marx's condensation, presented in direct quotes, while conveying the general sense, took some liberties with the original. The passages cited here—including the material in brackets—are directly from Phillips' book.

and the war in another shape goes on. You and I are never to see peace, we are never to see the possibility of putting the army of this nation, whether it be made up of nineteen or thirty-four states, on a peace footing, until slavery is destroyed . . . As long as you keep a tortoise at the head of the government, you are digging a pit with one hand and filling it with the other . . . Until the whole nation endorses the resolution of the New York Chamber of Commerce, "Better every rebel dies than one loyal soldier" [applause], and begs of the government, demands of the government, to speak that word which is victory and peace—until we do that, we shall have no prospect of peace. . . .

If Jefferson Davis is a sane man, if he is a sagacious man, and has the power to control his army, he will never let it take Washington; for he knows as well as we do, that shelling the dome of that Capitol to ashes, that the Capitol in flames or surmounted with the rebel flag, would be the fiery cross to melt the North into unity, and to demand emancipation [applause]. . . . I do not believe Jefferson Davis, while he is able to control his forces, will ever allow them to take Washington. He wants time. If we float on until the fourth of March, 1863, England could hardly be blamed if she did acknowledge the South. . . .

The President, judged by both proclamations that have followed the late confiscation act of Congress, has no mind whatever. He has not uttered a word which gives even a twilight glimpse of any antislavery purpose. He may be honest—nobody cares whether the tortoise is honest or not; he has neither insight, nor prevision, nor decision. It is said in Washington streets that he long ago wrote a proclamation abolishing slavery in the state of Virginia, but McClellan bullied him out of it. It is said, too—what is extremely probable—that he has more than once made up his mind to remove McClellan, and Kentucky bullied him out of it. . . .

This war is to go on. There will be drafting in three months or six.[2] . . . But even that will not make Lincoln declare for emancipation. We shall wait one year or two, if we wait for him, before we get it. In the meantime what an expense of blood and treasure each day! It is a terrible expense that democracy pays for its mode of government. If we lived in England now, if we lived in France now, a hundred men, convinced of the exigency of the moment, would carry the nation here or there . . . Democracy, when it moves, has to carry the whole people with it. The minds of nineteen millions of people are to be changed and educated. Ministers and politicians have been preaching to them that the Negro will not fight, that he is a nuisance, that slavery is an ordination of God, that the North ought to bar him out with statutes. The North wakes up, its heart poisoned, its hands paralyzed with these

---

2. Phillips' forecast was virtually accurate; seven months after his speech, Congress passed the First Conscription Act (March 3, 1863).

ideas, and says to its tortoise President, "Save us, but not through the Negro!"....

With chronic Whig distrust and ignorance of the people, Lincoln halts and fears . . . He is not a genius . . . I will tell you what he is. He is a first-rate *second-rate* man [laughter]. He is one of the best specimens of a second-rate man, and he is honestly waiting, like any other servant, for the people to come and send him on any errand they wish. . . . He is as good as the average North, but not a leader, which is what we need. In yonder grove, July after July, in years just past, the Whigs of this Commonwealth lavished their money to fire guns once every minute to smother the [antislavery] speeches that we made on our platform. You remember it. The sons of those men are dying in the South because their fathers smothered the message which, heeded, might have saved this terrible lesson to the nation [sensation]. Who shall say that God is not holding to their lips the cup which they poisoned? . . . We are not to shrink from the idea that this is a political war; it must be. But its politics is a profound faith in God and the people, in justice and liberty, as the eternal safety of nations as well as of men [applause]. It is of that Lincoln should make his politics, planting the cornerstone of the new Union in the equality of every man before the law, and justice to all races [renewed applause]....

I asked the lawyers of Illinois, who had practiced law with Mr. Lincoln for twenty years, "Is he a man of decision, is he a man who can say no?" They all said: "If you had gone to the Illinois bar, and selected the man least capable of saying no, it would have been Abraham Lincoln. He has no stiffness in him." I said to the bankers and the directors of railroads in Chicago, "Is McClellan a man who can say no?" and they said: ". . . McClellan never answered a question while he was here. If there was one to be decided, he floated until events decided it. He was here months, and never decided a single question that came up in the management of the Illinois Central."[3] These are the men we have put at the at the head of the Union, and for fourteen months they have been unable to say yes or no . . . I had a private letter from a captain in McClellan's army in the Peninsula, in which he said: "We have had five chances to enter Richmond; we might have done it after Yorktown, after Williamsburg, and after Seven Pines . . . no troops in front of us, we ourselves in full condition for an advance. Instead of that, we sat down and dug.". . .

The most serious charge I have against the President, the only thing that makes a film upon his honesty . . . is this: that, while I do not believe that in his heart he trusts McClellan a whit more than I do, from fear of the border states and Northern conserva-

3. In January, 1857, McClellan, a West Point graduate in engineering, resigned his commission and became chief engineer of the Illinois Central Railroad; he was appointed major general of Ohio Volunteers in April, 1861.

tism he keeps him at the head of the army . . . and if, twenty years hence, he renders up an account of his stewardship to his country, you . . . will see him confess that this whole winter he never believed in McClellan's ability . . . If this rebellion cannot shake the North out of her servility, God will keep her in constant agitation until He does shake us into a self-respecting, courageous people, fit to govern ourselves [applause]. This war will last just long enough to make us over into men, and when it has done this, we shall conquer with as much ease as the lion takes the tiniest animal in his grip. If Mr. Lincoln could only be wakened to the idea . . . that God gives him the thunderbolt of slavery with which to crush the rebellion . . . victory would be easy. . . .

On Events in North America*

October 7, 1862

THE BRIEF campaign in Maryland[1] has decided the fate of the American Civil War, even though the fortunes of war of both contending parties may yet be in the balance for a shorter or longer period of time. It has already been pointed out in this newspaper that the struggle for the border slave states is the struggle for the domination of the Union, and in this conflict, the Confederacy, although it began under the most favorable circumstances, which have never again recurred, has been defeated.

Maryland was rightly considered the head, and Kentucky the arm, of the slaveholders' party in the border states. Maryland's metropolis, Baltimore, has hitherto been kept "loyal" only by means of a state of siege. It was an accepted dogma, not only in the South but also in the North, that the appearance of the Confederates in Maryland would serve as the signal for a popular mass rising against "Lincoln's satellites." The question here was not only one of military success, but of a moral demonstration that would electrify the Southern elements in all the border states and draw them forcibly into their vortex.

With the occupation of Maryland, Washington would fall, Philadelphia would be endangered, and New York no longer safe. The

---

* Published in *Die Presse*, Vienna, October 12, 1862.
1. The Maryland campaign began on September 4, 1862. On September 17, at Antietam, near Sharpsburg, 51,844 Confederates under General Lee engaged 75,316 Federals under General McClellan. In the bloody battle that resulted, the Confederates lost 13,724 men (2,700 killed, 9,024 wounded, and about 2,000 missing), as against 12,410 Federal losses (2,108 killed, 9,549 wounded, 753 missing): Thomas L. Livermore, *Numbers and Losses in the Civil War in America, 1861–1865* (1901). Lee withdrew to Virginia, thus giving the Union a technical victory. As Marx pointed out, Antietam was a turning point in the Civil War. See his letter to Engels October 29, 1862 (page 262).

simultaneous invasion of Kentucky,[2] the most important border state because of its population, position, and economic sources, was, considered by itself, only a diversion. If, however, it had been supported by decisive successes in Maryland, it would have led to suppression of the Union party in Tennessee, outflanked Missouri, secured Arkansas and Texas, threatened New Orleans, and, above all, carried the war to Ohio, the central state of the North, whose possession would assure control of the North as much as that of Georgia would that of the South. A Confederate army in Ohio would cut off the western parts of the Northern states from the eastern, and fight the enemy from its own center. After the defeat of the main rebel army in Maryland, the invasion of Kentucky, carried out with little energy, and nowhere meeting with popular sympathy, shrank to an insignificant guerrilla move. Even the capture of Louisville now only caused the "giants of the West"—the bands of troops from Iowa, Illinois, Indiana, and Ohio —to unite into an "avalanche" comparable to the one that came crashing down on the South during the first glorious Kentucky campaign.

Thus the Maryland campaign showed that the waves of Secession lacked the powerful thrust to strike across the Potomac and into the Ohio. The South was limited to the defensive; whereas any possibility for success lay *only in the offensive*. Deprived of the border states, squeezed between the Mississippi in the West and the Atlantic Ocean in the East, it has won nothing—except a graveyard.

One must not for a moment forget that the Southerners possessed, and politically dominated, the border states at the time they raised the banner of rebellion. What they demanded was the territories. With the loss of the territories, they lost the border states.

And yet the invasion of Maryland was risked under the most favorable circumstances. A series of ignominious and unheard-of defeats on the part of the North; the Federal Army demoralized; "Stonewall" Jackson the hero of the day; Lincoln and his administration a general laughingstock; the Democratic party in the North newly strengthened and already counting on a "Jefferson Davis" presidential candidacy; France and England at the point of loudly proclaiming the legitimacy of the slaveholders, whom they had already recognized within themselves! "*E pur si muove.*" ["And still it moves."] Nevertheless, in world history reason does conquer.

More important than the Maryland campaign is Lincoln's Proclamation. The figure of Lincoln is *sui generis* in the annals of history. No initiative, no idealistic eloquence, no buskin, no historic drapery. He always presents the most important act in the most insignificant

2. The Confederate troops which invaded Kentucky September 12, 1862, were defeated at Perryville October 8.

form possible. Others, when dealing with square feet of land, proclaim it a "struggle for ideas." Lincoln, even when he is dealing with ideas, proclaims their "square feet." Hesitant, resistant, unwilling, he sings the bravura aria of his role as though he begged pardon for the circumstances that force him "to be a lion." The most awesome decrees, which will always remain historically remarkable, that he hurls at the enemy all resemble, and are intended to resemble, the trite summonses that one lawyer sends to an opposing lawyer, the legal chicaneries and pettifogging stipulations of an *actiones juris* [court case].[3] His most recent proclamation—the Emancipation Proclamation[4]—the most significant document in American history since the founding of the Union and one which tears up the old American Constitution, bears the same character.

Nothing is easier than to point out, as do the English Pindars of slavery—the *Times*, the *Saturday Review*, and *tutti quanti* [all the rest]—what is aesthetically repulsive, logically inadequate, officially burlesque, and politically contradictory in Lincoln's major actions and policies. Nevertheless, in the history of the United States and of humanity, Lincoln will take his place directly next to Washington! Nowadays, when the most insignificant event on this side of the Atlantic Ocean takes on an air of melodrama, is it entirely without significance that in the New World what is significant should appear dressed in a workaday coat?

Lincoln is not the offspring of a people's revolution. The ordinary play of the electoral system, unaware of the great tasks it was destined to fulfill, bore him to the summit—a plebeian, who made his way from stone-splitter to senator in Illinois,[5] a man without intellectual brilliance, without special greatness of character, without exceptional importance—an average man of good will. Never has the New World scored a greater victory than in the demonstration that with its political and social organization, average men of good will suffice to do that which in the Old World would have required heroes to do!

Hegel once remarked that in reality comedy is above tragedy, the humor of reason above its pathos.[6] If Lincoln does not possess the pathos of historical action, he does, as an average man of the people, possess its humor. At what moment did he issue the Proclamation that, as of January 1, 1863, slavery is abolished in the Confederacy? At the very moment when, in its Congress at Richmond, the

---

3. See also Marx's letter to Engels, October 29, 1862, where he makes the same point (page 262).

4. The Emancipation Proclamation, effective January 1, 1863, was announced on September 23, 1862.

5. Lincoln, the "rail-splitter," was not a senator but a congressman (1847-49).

6. "The Principle of Tragedy, Comedy and Drama," in Hegel's *Vorlesungen über Ästhetik* [*Lectures on Esthetics*], Book III, Sec. A.

Confederacy, as an independent state, decided on "peace negotiations." At the very moment when the slaveholders of the border states believed that, with the incursion of the Southerners into Kentucky, the "peculiar institution" would be about as secure as their control over their *Landsmann*,[7] President Abraham Lincoln at Washington.

7. Countryman—in this instance, fellow southerner; a reference to Lincoln's southern (Kentucky) birth.

On the Situation in America*

November 4, 1862

GENERAL BRAGG, who commands the Southern army in Kentucky—the other fighting forces of the South ravaging the state are merely guerrilla bands—when he irrupted into this border state, issued a proclamation that throws light on the latest combined moves of the Confederacy. Bragg's proclamation, directed at the states of the Northwest, assumes his success in Kentucky as a matter of course and manifestly calculates on the eventuality of a victorious penetration into Ohio, the central state of the North. In the first place he declares the Confederacy's readiness to guarantee free navigation on the Mississippi and the Ohio. The guarantee acquires meaning only when the slaveowners find themselves in possession of the border states. At Richmond, therefore, it was assumed that simultaneous incursions of Lee into Maryland and of Bragg into Kentucky would secure possession of the border states in one stroke. Bragg then goes on to prove the justification of the South, which fights only for its independence, but otherwise wants peace; but the real, characteristic point of the proclamation is the offer of a separate peace with the northwestern states, the invitation to them to secede from the Union and join the Confederacy, since the economic interests of the Northwest and the South are in harmony, just as those of the Northwest and the Northeast are inimical. One sees: Hardly does the South think itself safely in possession of the border states when it officially blurts out its more far-reaching object of a reconstruction of the Union, to the exclusion of the New England states.

Like the invasion of Maryland, however, that of Kentucky has also failed: as the former in the battle of Antietam Creek, so the latter in the battle of Perryville, near Louisville. As there, so here too the

---
* Published in *Die Presse*, Vienna, November 10, 1862.

Confederates found themselves on the offensive, in that they attacked the advance guard of Buell's army. The Federals owed their victory to the commander of the advance guard, General McCook, who withstood the far superior forces of the enemy long enough to give Buell time to lead his main body into the field. There is not the slightest doubt that the defeat at Perryville will entail the evacuation of Kentucky. The most considerable guerrilla band, composed of fanatical partisans of the slave system in Kentucky and led by General Morgan, has been annihilated at Frankfort (between Louisville and Lexington) at almost the same time. Finally, there must be added the decisive victory of Rosecrans at Corinth, which makes imperative the hastiest retreat of General Bragg's defeated invasion army.

Thereby the Confederate campaign for the reconquest of the lost border slave states, undertaken on a large scale, with military skill and under the most favorable conditions, has come completely to grief. Apart from the immediate military results, these battles contribute in another way to the elimination of the main difficulty. The foothold of the slave states proper in the border states naturally depends on the slave element of the latter, the same element that forces diplomatic and constitutional considerations on the Union Government in its struggle against slavery. But this element is in practice being destroyed by the Civil War itself in the border states, the main arena of the Civil War. Great numbers of slaveholders are constantly migrating to the South with their "black chattels," to bring their property to safety. After each defeat of the Confederates, this migration is renewed on a larger scale.

One of my friends, a German officer[1] who has fought variously in Missouri, Arkansas, Kentucky, and Tennessee under the star-spangled banner, writes me that this migration is wholly reminiscent of the exodus from Ireland in 1847 and 1848. Furthermore, the energetic portion of the slaveholders, the youth on the one hand, the political and military leaders on the other, separate themselves from the bulk of their class, in that they either form guerrilla bands in their own states, and are annihilated as guerrilla bands, or they leave home and incorporate themselves in the army or administration of the Confederacy. Hence the result: on the one hand, an immense diminution of the slave element in the border states, where it always had to contend with the "encroachments" of competing free labor; on the other hand, removal of the energetic portion of the slaveowners and their white following. There is left behind only a sediment of "moderate" slaveowners, who will soon eagerly grasp the pile of ill-gotten money offered them by Washington for the redemption of their "black chattels," whose value will at any rate be lost as soon as the southern

---

1. Joseph Weydemeyer.

market for their sale is closed. Thus the war itself leads to a solution through the actual overthrow of the form of society in the border states.

For the South, the favorable season for waging war is over; for the North, it is beginning, in that the inland rivers are now navigable again and the combination of land and sea warfare, already attempted once with so much success, is once more practicable. The North had utilized the interim period zealously. "Ironclads," ten in number, for the rivers of the West, are rapidly nearing completion; to this must be added twice as many semiarmored vessels for shallow waters. In the East, many new armor-plated ships have already left the yards, while others are still under construction. All of them will be ready by January 1, 1863. Ericsson, the inventor and builder of the *Monitor*, is directing the construction of nine new ships on the same model. Four of them are already "afloat."

On the Potomac, in Tennessee and Virginia, as well as at different points in the South—Norfolk, New Bern, Port Royal, Pensacola and New Orleans—the army daily receives fresh reinforcements. The first levy, of 300,000 men, which Lincoln promulgated in July, has been fully provided and is in part already in the theater of war. The second levy, of 300,000 men for nine months, is gradually assembling. In some states conscription has been done away with by voluntary enlistment; in none does it meet with serious difficulties. Ignorance and hatred have decried conscription as an unheard-of event in the history of the United States. Nothing could be more false. During the War of Independence and the second war with England (1812–14) large bodies of troops were conscripted—indeed, even in various small wars with the Indians—without this ever having encountered opposition worth mentioning.

It is a remarkable fact that during the present year Europe has furnished the United States with an emigrant contingent of approximately 100,000 souls and that half these emigrants consist of Irishmen and Britons. At the recent congress of the English "Association for the Advancement of Science" at Cambridge, the economist Merivale had to remind his countrymen of a fact which the *Times*, the *Saturday Review*, the *Morning Post*, and the *Morning Herald*, not to speak of the *dei minorum gentium* [gods of lesser importance], have so completely forgotten, or want to make England forget, namely, the fact that the majority of the English surplus population finds a new home in the United States.

Symptoms of Dissolution in the
Southern Confederacy*

November 7, 1862

THE ENGLISH press is more Southern than the South itself. While it sees everything in the North as black and everything in the land of the "nigger" as white, those in the slave states do not by any means rock themselves with the "joy of victory" celebrated by the *Times*.

The Southern press unanimously raises an outcry of complaint over the defeat of Corinth[1] and accuses Generals Price and Van Dorn of "incompetence and arrogance." The *Mobile Advertiser* mentions one regiment, the 42nd Alabama, which went into battle 530 men strong on Friday [October 3], had 300 men left on Saturday, and on Sunday evening had only 10 men left. The rest were killed, captured, wounded, or missing. The Virginia papers speak the same way.

"It is clear," says the *Richmond Whig*, "that our Mississippi campaign has failed in its immediate objective." "It is to be feared," says the *Richmond Enquirer*, "that the effect of this battle will have the most damaging influence on our campaign in the West."

This misgiving has been realized, as is shown by Bragg's evacuation of Kentucky and the Confederates' defeat at Nashville.

From the same source, the newspapers of Virginia, Georgia, and Alabama, we receive interesting information about the conflict between the central government at Richmond and the governments of the individual slave states. This was occasioned by the latest conscription act, in which the Congress extended the military service obligation beyond the normal age. In Georgia, a certain Levingood was drafted, and upon his refusal to serve he was arrested by an agent of the Con-

---

* Published in *Die Presse*, Vienna, November 14, 1862.

1. In the two-day battle at Corinth, in northwestern Mississippi (on the Tennessee line), which began on October 3, 1862, the Confederates were defeated and forced to retreat.

federacy, J. P. Bruce. Levingood appealed to the highest Court in
Elbert County (Georgia), which ordered the immediate release of the
prisoner. According to the very far-reaching arguments of the decision:

> In the introductory paragraph of the Constitution of the Con-
> federacy, it is specifically stated that the individual states are
> sovereign and independent. In what sense could this apply to
> Georgia, if every militiaman were to be forcibly removed from the
> control of his own commander? If the Congress at Richmond can
> pass a conscription act with exceptions, what is to prevent it from
> passing a conscription act without exceptions, and thereby to draft
> the governor, the legislature, the judiciary, and thus make an end
> to all the state governments? . . . For this and other reasons, it is
> hereby ordained and decided that the conscription act of the Con-
> gress is null and void and without lawful validity. . . .

Thus the state of Georgia forbade conscription within its borders,
and the government of the Confederacy did not dare prohibit the
prohibition.

In Virginia there is a similar collision between the "separate
state" and the "Confederation of Separate States." The ground of the
conflict is the effort of the state government to take away the right
of Mr. Jefferson Davis' agent to recruit Virginia militiamen and incorporate them into the Confederate army. In this connection there
was a sharp exchange of letters between the Secretary of War and
General J. G. Floyd, the infamous creature who, as President Buchanan's Secretary of War, had prepared for the Secession and in addition had considerable sums of the U. S. Treasury "secede" into his
private coffer. This notorious Secession chief, known in the North
as "Floyd the Thief," now comes forth as the champion of the rights
of Virginia against the Confederacy. The *Richmond Examiner*, speaking of the correspondence between Floyd and the Secretary of War,
says, among other things:

> The whole correspondence is a good illustration of the resistance
> and enmity which our state (Virginia) and its army have to suffer
> at the hands of those who abuse the power of the Confederacy at
> Richmond. But everything has its limits, and the patience of the
> state will not tolerate a repetition of the injustice much longer.
> Virginia has provided nearly all the weapons, munitions, and war
> supplies that won the battles of Bethel and Manassas. It contributed
> to the Confederate service, out of its own armories and arsenals,
> 73,000 rifles and muskets, 233 artillery pieces, and a magnificent
> arms factory. Its manpower capable of bearing arms has been de-
> pleted to the last dregs in the service of the Confederacy; it was
> forced to drive the enemy from its western borders by its own

efforts, and is it not, therefore, outrageous that the creatures of the Confederate government now dare to play their game with it?

In Texas, too, the repeated removal of its adult manpower to the East has aroused opposition to the Confederacy. On September 30, Mr. Oldham, the representative from Texas, protested in the Congress at Richmond:

> In the wild-goose expedition of Subley, 3,500 of Texas' picked troops were sent to their destruction on the barren plains of New Mexico. The result was to draw the enemy to our borders, which he crossed in the winter. You transported the best troops from Texas to east of the Mississippi, dragged them to Virginia, used them in the most dangerous points, where they have been decimated. Three-fourths of each Texas regiment sleep in their graves or have had to be released because of sickness. If this government continues to draw out of Texas the manhood capable of bearing arms in order to keep those regiments at their normal strength, Texas will be ruined, irrevocably ruined. This is unjust and unpolitical. My constituents have to defend their families, property, and home. In their name, I protest against transporting men from west of the Mississippi to the East, a policy that lays open their own land to the incursions of the enemy from north, east, west, and south.

Two things emerge from these reports taken from the Southern journals. First, the forcible measures of the Confederate Government to fill the ranks of the Army have overstrained the bowstring. The military resources are drying up. Secondly, and this is decisive, the doctrine of "state's rights," which the usurpers at Richmond invoked constitutionally to justify secession, is already beginning to turn its point against them. This is how poorly Mr. Jefferson Davis has succeeded in "making a nation out of the South," in the boastful words of its English admirer, Gladstone.[2]

---

2. Quoted from a speech by Chancellor of the Exchequer William Ewart Gladstone, at Newcastle, on October 7, 1862.

The Election Results in
the Northern States*

November 18, 1862

THE ELECTIONS are in reality a defeat for the government in Washington.[1] The old leaders of the Democratic party have cleverly exploited the ill feeling over financial ineptitude and military clumsiness, and there is no doubt that the state of New York, officially in the hands of the Seymours, Woods, and Bennetts, could become a center of dangerous intrigues. Still, one must not exaggerate the importance of this reaction. The present Republican House of Representatives continues, and the recently elected successors will not take their seats until December, 1863. The elections, insofar as they affect the Congress in Washington, are thus merely the prelude to a demonstration. No governors were chosen in any state except New York. Hence the Republican party finds itself at the head of the individual states, as it has been before. The election victories of the Republicans in Massachusetts, Iowa, Illinois, and Michigan balance to some extent the losses in New York, Pennsylvania, Ohio, and Indiana.

A closer analysis of the "Democratic" gains leads to an entirely different result from the one now trumpeted by the English newspapers. The *city* of New York, with a strongly seditious Irish mob, hitherto an active participant in the slave trade, the seat of the American money market and full of owners of southern plantation mortgages, has always been decisively "Democratic," just as Liverpool is still Tory today. The *country districts* of New York State this time voted Republican, as they have done since 1856, but not with the same zeal as in 1860. Furthermore, a large portion of its men eligible to vote are in the field. If one combines the city and country districts, the

---

* Published in *Die Presse*, Vienna, November 23, 1862.
1. In the congressional elections of November, 1862, while the Republicans retained the majority in the House (102 to 75 Democrats) and the Senate (36 to 8 Democrats), they lost a number of seats in New York and in the Northwest.

Democratic majority in the state of New York amounts to only 8,000 to 10,000 votes.

In Pennsylvania, which has long oscillated first between Whigs and Democrats and later between Democrats and Republicans, the Democratic majority amounts to merely 3,500 votes; in Indiana the majority is even smaller; in Ohio, where the majority is 8,000, the Democratic leaders shown to be in sympathy with the South, as, for example, the notorious Vallandigham, have lost their seats in Congress. The Irishman sees in the Negro a dangerous competitor. The efficient farmers in Indiana and Ohio hate the Negro second only to the slaveowner. For them he is the symbol of slavery and the debasement of the working class, and the Democratic press threatens them daily with an inundation of their territories by the "nigger." In addition, the discontent with the sorry conduct of the war in Virginia was loudest in those states that had provided the largest contingents of volunteers.

All this, however, does not touch upon the main point. At the time of Lincoln's election (1860), there was neither a Civil War nor was the question of Negro emancipation the order of the day. The Republican Party, at that time thoroughly separated from the party of the Abolitionists, aimed in the election of 1860 at nothing but a protest against the extension of slavery in the territories, but at the same time it proclaimed noninterference with that institution where it already existed legally. If the *emancipation of slaves* had been a campaign slogan, Lincoln would then have been absolutely defeated. Emancipation was decisively rejected.

It is quite different in the case of the recently concluded elections. The Republicans made common cause with the Abolitionists. They declared themselves emphatically in favor of immediate emancipation, be it for its own sake or as a means of ending the rebellion. Once this circumstance is considered, then the pro-Administration majority in Michigan, Illinois, Massachusetts, Iowa, and Delaware, and the very considerable minority in the states of New York, Ohio, and Pennsylvania that voted for it, appear equally surprising. Before the war, such a result was impossible, even in Massachusetts. It requires only energy on the part of the Administration and of the Congress which convenes next month, for the Abolitionists, now identical with the Republicans, to retain everywhere the moral and numerical preponderance. Louis Bonaparte's interventionist appetites[2] are giving them an "external" support. The only danger is the retention of such generals as McClellan, who, apart from their incompetence, are self-declared proslavery men.

---

2. On October 30, 1862, the French Government of Napoleon III proposed to England and Russia that the three powers take combined steps to lift the Northern blockade and open Southern ports to European commerce. Russia rejected the proposal on November 8, and England followed suit.

The Removal of McClellan*

November 24, 1862

McClellan's removal! is Lincoln's answer to the election victory of the Democrats.

The Democratic journals had stated with the most positive assurance that the election of Seymour as governor of New York State would mean the immediate revocation of the Proclamation in which Lincoln declared the abolition of slavery in Secessia as of January 1, 1863. Their prophetic blotting paper had hardly left the press when their favorite general—their favorite because "next to a great defeat, he most feared a decisive victory"[1]—was deprived of his command and returned to private life.

One recalls that to this Proclamation of Lincoln, McClellan had replied with a counterproclamation, an order of the day to his army in which he, to be sure, forbade any demonstration against the President's measure, but at the same time let slip the fateful words: "The remedy for political errors . . . is to be found only in the action of the people at the polls."[2] McClellan, at the head of the main army of the United States, thus appealed from the President to the impending elections. He threw the weight of his position into the scales. Making allowance for a *pronunciamento* in the Spanish manner, he could not have demonstrated his hostility to the President's policy more strikingly. Hence after the Democratic electoral victory the only choice left to Lincoln was either to sink to the level of a tool of the pro-slavery compromise party or, by removing McClellan, take away its base of support in the army.

* Published in *Die Presse*, Vienna, November 29, 1862.
1. A quotation from Macaulay, *Critical and Historical Essays* (Vol. I, London, 1870).
2. McClellan's General Order 163, October 7, 1862.

McClellan's removal at the *present* moment is therefore a political demonstration. Nevertheless, it had become inescapable. Halleck, the commander-in-chief, in a report to the Secretary of War, had charged McClellan with direct insubordination. For shortly after the defeat of the Confederates in Maryland, on October 6, Halleck ordered the crossing of the Potomac, particularly as the lower water level of the Potomac and its tributaries favored military operations at the time. Despite the order, McClellan remained immovable, under the pretext of his army's inability to march because of lack of provisions. Halleck, in the report mentioned, proves that this was a hollow subterfuge, that, compared with the Western Army, the Eastern Army enjoyed great privileges in regard to commissariat and that the supplies still lacking could have been received just as well south as north of the Potomac. A second report links up with this report of Halleck's; in it the committee appointed to inquire into the surrender of Harpers Ferry to the Confederates accuses McClellan of having concentrated the Union troops stationed near that arsenal in an inconceivably slow way—he let them march only six English miles (about one and a half German miles) a day—for its relief. Both reports, that of Halleck and that of the committee, were in the President's hands *before* the Democrats' election victory.

McClellan's generalship has been described in these columns so repeatedly that here it suffices merely to recall how he sought to substitute strategical envelopment for tactical decision and how indefatigable he was in discovering considerations of general-staff wisdom that forbade him either to take advantage of victories or to anticipate defeats. The brief Maryland campaign has cast a false halo about his head. Here, however, we have to consider the facts that he received his general marching orders from General Halleck, who also drew up the plan of the first Kentucky campaign, and that victory on the battlefield was due exclusively to the bravery of the subordinate generals, in particular of General Reno, who fell in battle, and of Hooker, who has not yet recovered from his wounds. Napoleon once wrote to his brother Joseph that on the battlefield there was danger at all points alike and one ran into its jaws most surely when one sought to avoid it. McClellan seems to have grasped this axiom, but without the application that Napoleon suggested to his brother. Throughout his whole military career McClellan has *never* been on the battlefield, *never* found himself under fire, a peculiarity that General Kearny strongly stresses in a letter which his brother published after Kearny, fighting under Pope's command, had fallen in one of the battles before Washington.

McClellan understood how to hide his mediocrity under a mask of restrained earnestness, laconic reticence, and dignified reserve. His very shortcomings secured him the unshakable confidence of the Democratic party in the North and "loyal recognition" on the part of the Secessionists. Among the higher officers of his army he gained supporters through the formation of a general staff of dimensions hitherto unheard of in the annals of military history. Some of the older officers, who had belonged to the old Union Army and had been trained in the Academy at West Point, found in him a point of support for their rivalry with the newly emerged "civilian generals" and for their secret sympathies with the "comrades" in the enemy camp. The common soldier, finally, knew his military qualities only from hearsay, while for the rest he ascribed to him all the merits of the commissariat and was able to tell many glorious tales of his reserved affability. McClellan possessed one single gift of a supreme commander —that of assuring himself of popularity with his army.

McClellan's successor, Burnside, is too little known to have a judgment pronounced on him. He belongs to the Republican party. Hooker, on the other hand, who assumes command of the army corps that had been specifically under McClellan, is incontestably one of the ablest blades in the Union. "Fighting Joe," as the troops call him, played the largest part in the successes in Maryland. He is an *Abolitionist*.

The same American newspapers which bring us the news of McClellan's removal report utterances of Lincoln in which he declares emphatically that he will not deviate a hair's breadth from his Proclamation.

"He"—the *Morning Star* rightly observes—"has by successive exhibitions of firmness taught the world to know him as a slow but solid man, who advances with excessive caution, but does not go back. Each step of his administrative career has been in the right direction and has been stoutly maintained. Starting from the resolution to exclude slavery from the territories, he has come within sight of the ulterior result of all antislavery movements—its extirpation from the whole soil of the Union—and has already reached the high vantage ground at which the Union ceased to be responsible for the enslavement of a single human being."[3]

3. November 22, 1862.

English Neutrality – The Situation in the Southern States*

THE NEGOTIATIONS between the cabinet here and the government in Washington over the corsair *Alabama*[1] are still pending, while fresh negotiations on the renewed fitting out of Confederate warships in English ports have already begun. Professor Francis W. Newman, one of the theoretical representatives of English radicalism, has published in today's *Morning Star* a letter in which, among other things, he says:

> When the American Consul at Liverpool had got opinion of counsel as to the illegality of the *Alabama* and sent his complaint to Earl Russell, the law officers of the crown were consulted and they, too, condemned it as illegal. But so much time was lost in this process that the pirate meanwhile escaped . . . Is our government going to wink a second time at the successors of the *Alabama* escaping? Mr. Gladstone has made me fear that they are: in that speech of his at Newcastle he said that he had been informed that the rebel President, whom he panegyrized, was *"soon to have a navy."* Did this allude to the navy his Liverpool friends are building? . . .

Among the papers that arrived from America today, the *Richmond Examiner*, organ of the Confederacy, is perhaps the most interesting. It contains a detailed article on the situation. . . .

---

* From an article in *Die Presse*, Vienna, December 4, 1862.

1. A Confederate cruiser built and armed in England for raiding on Northern commerce.

Address of the International Working Men's Association to President Lincoln*

Sir:

We congratulate the American people upon your reelection by a large majority.[1] If resistance to the Slave Power was the reserved watchword of your first election, the triumphant war cry of your reelection is, Death to Slavery.

From the commencement of the titanic American strife the workingmen of Europe felt instinctively that the star-spangled banner carried the destiny of their class. The contest for the territories which opened up the dire epopee, was it not to decide whether the virgin soil of immense tracts should be wedded to the labor of the emigrant or prostituted by the tramp of the slavedriver?

When an oligarchy of 300,000 slaveholders dared to inscribe for the first time in the annals of the world "slavery" on the banner of Armed Revolt, when on the very spots where hardly a century ago the idea of one great Democratic Republic had first sprung up, whence the first Declaration of the Rights of Man was issued, and the first impulse given to the European revolution of the eighteenth century; when on those very spots counterrevolution, with systematic thoroughness, gloried in rescinding "the ideas entertained at the time of the formation of the old constitution," and maintained slavery to be a "beneficent institution," indeed, the only solution of the great problem

---

* From the minutes of the Central Council of the International, November 29, 1864: "Dr. Marx then brought up the report of the Subcommittee, also a draft of the address which had been drawn up for presentation to the people of America congratulating them on their having reelected Abraham Lincoln as President. The Address is as follows and was unanimously agreed to . . ." Marx wrote the document in English. See his letter to Engels December 2, 1864 (page 272).

1. In the presidential election of 1864, Lincoln received 55 percent of the votes cast—2,206,938 (212 electoral votes)—against 1,803,787 (21 electoral votes) for General George B. McClellan, the Democratic candidate.

of "the relation of labor to capital," and cynically proclaimed property in man "the cornerstone of the new edifice,"—then the working classes of Europe understood at once, even before the fanatic partisanship of the upper classes for the Confederate gentry had given its dismal warning, that the slaveholders' rebellion was to sound the tocsin for a general holy crusade of property against labor, and that for the men of labor, with their hopes for the future, even their past conquests were at stake in that tremendous conflict on the other side of the Atlantic. Everywhere they bore therefore patiently the hardships imposed upon them by the cotton crisis, opposed enthusiastically the proslavery intervention—importunities of their betters—and, from most parts of Europe, contributed their quota of blood to the good cause.

While the workingmen, the true political powers of the North, allowed slavery to defile their own republic, while before the Negro, mastered and sold without his concurrence, they boasted it the highest prerogative of the white-skinned laborer to sell himself and choose his own master, they were unable to attain the true freedom of labor, or to support their European brethren in their struggle for emancipation, but this barrier to progress has been swept off by the red sea of Civil War.

The workingmen of Europe feel sure that as the American War of Independence initiated a new era of ascendancy for the middle class, so the American Antislavery War will do for the working classes. They consider it an earnest of the epoch to come, that it fell to the lot of Abraham Lincoln, the single-minded son of the working class, to lead his country through the matchless struggle for the rescue of an enchained race and the reconstruction of a social world.[2]

Signed on behalf of the International Working Men's Association, the Central Council:
Longmaid, Worley, Whitlock, Fox, Blackmore, Hartwell, Pidgeon, Lucraft, Weston, Dell, Nieass, Shaw, Lake, Buckley, Osborne, Howell,

---

2. From the concluding minutes of the Central Council: "A long discussion then took place as to the mode of presenting the Address and the propriety of having a M. P. with the deputation; this was strongly opposed by many members who said workingmen should rely on themselves and not seek for extraneous aid.

"The Secretary stated he had corresponded with the American Minister and he, the Secretary, had no doubt that if Mr. Adams was asked that he would appoint a time to receive the deputation.

"It was then proposed by Whitlock, seconded by Eccarius, and carried unanimously: That the Secretary correspond with the United States Minister asking him to appoint a time for receiving the deputation, such deputation to consist of the members of the Central Council.

"Mr. Wheeler proposed, Le Lubez seconded: That the names of all those who are present be appended to the Address, also those who are absent and are willing to endorse the views set forth in the Address." The Address was signed by the Council's fifty-seven members and sent to Adams. It was published in the London *Daily News* December 23, 1864, in *Reynolds's Newspaper* December 25, and then in German newspapers: *Der Social-Demokrat*, December 30, 1864; *Berliner Reform*, January 5, 1865; and *Hermann*, January 7, 1865.

Carter, Wheeler, Stainsby, Morgan, Grossmith, Dick, Denoual, Jourdain, Morrissot, Leroux, Bordage, Bocquet, Talandier, Dupont, L. Wolff, Aldovrandi, Lama, Solustri, Nusperli, Eccarius, Wolff, Lessner, Pfänder, Lochner, Kaub, Bolleter, Rybczinski, Hansen, Schantzenbach, Smales, Cornelius, Petersen, Otto, Bagnagatti, Setacci; George Odger, President of Council; *P. V. Lubez,* Corresponding Secretary for France; *Karl Marx,* Corresponding Secretary for Germany; *G. P. Fontana,* Corresponding Secretary for Italy; *J. E. Holtorp,* Corresponding Secretary for Poland; *H. F. Jung,* Corresponding Secretary for Switzerland; *William R. Cremer,* Honorary General Secretary. 18, Greek Street, Soho.

Ambassador Adams' Reply to the Address to President Lincoln*

To Mr. W. R. Cremer, Honorary Secretary of The International Working Men's Association, London.

Legation of the United States

London, January 28, 1865

Sir:

I am directed to inform you that the address of the Central Council of your Association, which was duly transmitted through this Legation to the President of the United States, has been received by him.

So far as the sentiments expressed by it are personal, they are accepted by him with a sincere and anxious desire that he may be able to prove himself not unworthy of the confidence which has been recently extended to him by his fellow citizens and by so many of the friends of humanity and progress throughout the world.

The Government of the United States has a clear consciousness that its policy neither is nor could be reactionary, but at the same time it adheres to the course which it adopted at the beginning, of abstaining everywhere from propagandism and unlawful intervention. It strives to do equal and exact justice to all states and to all men and it relies upon the beneficial results of that effort for support at home and for respect and good will throughout the world.

Nations do not exist for themselves alone, but to promote the welfare and happiness of mankind by benevolent intercourse and example. It is in this relation that the United States regard their cause in the present conflict with slavery-maintaining insurgents as the cause of human nature, and they derive new encouragement to per-

---

* The letter was published in the London *Times* February 6, 1865. For Marx's comment on it, see his letter to Engels of February 10, 1865 (page 273).

[239]

severe from the testimony of the workingmen of Europe that the national attitude is favored with their enlightened approval and earnest sympathies.

I have the honor to be, sir, your obedient servant.

Charles Francis Adams

Address of the International Working Men's Association to President Johnson*

Sir:

The demon of the "peculiar institution," for the supremacy of which the South rose in arms, would not allow his worshipers to honorably succumb in the open field. What he had begun in treason, he must needs end in infamy. As Philip II's war for the Inquisition bred a Gérard, thus Jefferson Davis's proslavery war a Booth.

It is not our part to call words of sorrow and horror, while the heart of two worlds heaves with emotion. Even the sycophants who, year after year, and day by day, stick to their Sisyphus work of morally assassinating Abraham Lincoln, and the great Republic he headed, stand now aghast at this universal outburst of popular feeling, and rival with each other to strew rhetorical flowers on his open grave. They have now at last found out that he was a man, neither to be browbeaten by adversity, nor intoxicated by success, inflexibly pressing on to his great goal, never compromising it by blind haste, slowly maturing his steps, never retracing them, carried away by no surge of popular favor, disheartened by no slackening of the popular pulse, tempering stern acts by the gleams of a kind heart, illuminating scenes dark with passion by the smile of humor, doing his titanic work as humbly and homely as Heaven-born rulers do little things with the grandiloquence of pomp and state; in one word, one of the rare men who succeed in becoming great, without ceasing to be good. Such, indeed, was the modesty of this great and good man, that the world only discovered him a hero after he had fallen a martyr.

To be singled out by the side of such a chief, the second victim

* Written by Marx between May 2 and 9, 1865, and adopted by the General Council of the International on May 9. Published in the *Bee-Hive* newspaper May 20, 1865.

to the infernal gods of slavery, was an honor due to Mr. Seward.[1] Had
he not, at a time of general hesitation, the sagacity to foresee and the
manliness to foretell "the irrepressible conflict"? Did he not, in the
darkest hours of that conflict, prove true to the Roman duty to never
despair of the Republic and its stars? We earnestly hope that he and his
son will be restored to health, public activity, and well-deserved
honors within much less than "ninety days."

After a tremendous civil war, but which, if we consider its vast
dimensions, and its broad scope, and compare it to the Old World's
Hundred Years' Wars, and Thirty Years' Wars, and Twenty-three
Years' Wars, can hardly be said to have lasted ninety days, yours, sir,
has become the task to uproot by the law what has been felled by the
sword, to preside over the arduous work of political reconstruction
and social regeneration. A profound sense of your great mission will
save you from any compromise with stern duties. You will never forget that, to initiate the new era of the emancipation of labor, the
American people devolved the responsibilities of leadership upon two
men of labor—the one Abraham Lincoln, the other Andrew Johnson.[2]

Signed, on behalf of the International Working Men's Association,
London, May 13, 1865, by the Central Council—
*Charles Kaub, Edward Coulson, F. Lessner, Carl Pfänder, N. P. Hansen,
Karl Schapper, William Dell, George Lochner, George Eccarius, John
Osborne, P. Petersen, A. Janks, H. Klimosch, John Weston, H. Bol-
leter, B. Lucraft, J. Buckley, Peter Fox, N. Salvatella, George Howell,
Bordage, A. Valltier, Robert Shaw, J. H. Longmaid, W. Morgan, G. W.
Wheeler, J. D. Nieass, W. C. Worley, D. Stainsby, F. de Lassassie, J.
Carter; Emile Holtorp,* Secretary for Poland; *Karl Marx,* Secretary for
Germany; *H. Jung,* Secretary for Switzerland; *E. Dupont,* Secretary
for France; *J. Whitlock,* Financial Secretary; *G. Odger,* President;
W. R. Cremer, Hon. Gen. Secretary.

---

1. Secretary of State William Henry Seward was gravely wounded the same
evening Lincoln was assassinated.

2. For an account of Marx's increasing disillusionment with Johnson, see his
letters to Engels of June 24, 1865, and April 23, 1866; to F. Lafargue November
12, 1866; and to Vermorel August 27, 1867 (pages 274–75).

Address to the National Labor Union of the United States*

Fellow-workmen:

In the initiatory program of our Association we stated: "It was not the wisdom of the ruling classes, but the heroic resistance to their criminal folly by the working classes of England that saved the West of Europe from plunging headlong into an infamous crusade for the perpetuation and propagation of slavery on the other side of the Atlantic."[1] Your turn has now come to stop a war, the clearest result of which would be, for an indefinite period, to hurl back the ascendant movement of the working class on both sides of the Atlantic.

We need hardly tell you that there exist European powers anxiously bent upon hurrying the United States into a war with England. A glance at commercial statistics will show that the Russian export of raw produce, and Russia has nothing else to export, was rapidly giving

---

* From the minutes of the General Council of the International, May 11, 1869: "Citizen Marx then rose and said that most members would have seen a letter from Professor Goldwin Smith in the *Bee-Hive* respecting the impression made in America by the speech of Senator Sumner, and he, Citizen Marx, had received letters to the same effect from America and he thought it was a proper occasion for the Council to appeal to the workingmen of America to put a stop to these menaces of the Republican party. With this intention he had drawn up an address to the National Labor Union of the United States which, if approved of by the Council, should be adopted and sent to America."

Marx wrote the address in English. It was published as a pamphlet in London, on May 12, 1869. The National Labor Union was organized in Baltimore on August 20, 1866, with the objective of achieving an eight-hour day; the Union collapsed in failure in 1872. On April 13, 1869, Senator Charles Sumner, radical Republican, had demanded that the United States claim two billion dollars for damages inflicted by British violation of neutrality during the Civil War. The English historian Goldwin Smith argued in his letter of May 8 that Sumner's speech would stop British immigration to the United States.

1. See "Inaugural Address of the International Working Men's Association," in *Karl Marx on the First International*, Karl Marx Library, Vol. III.

way before American competition, when the Civil War suddenly turned the scales. To convert the American plowshares into swords would just now rescue from impending bankruptcy that despotic power which your Republican statesmen have, in their wisdom, chosen for their confidential adviser. But quite apart from the particular interests of this or that government, is it not the general interest of our common oppressors to turn our fast-growing international cooperation into an internecine war?

In a congratulatory address to Mr. Lincoln on his reelection as President, we expressed our conviction that the American Civil War would prove of as great import to the advancement of the working class as the American War of Independence had proved to that of the middle class. And, in point of fact, the victorious termination of the antislavery war has opened a new epoch in the annals of the working class. In the states themselves, an independent working-class movement, looked upon with an evil eye by your old parties and their professional politicians, has since that date sprung into life.[2] To fructify it wants years of peace. To crush it, a war between the United States and England is wanted.

The next palpable effect of the Civil War was, of course, to deteriorate the position of the American workman. In the United States, as in Europe, the monster incubus of a national debt was shifted from hand to hand, to settle down on the shoulders of the working class.[3] The prices of necessaries, says one of your statesmen, have since 1860 risen 78 percent, while the wages of unskilled labor rose 50 percent, those of skilled labor 60 percent only. "Pauperism," he complains, "grows now in America faster than population." Moreover, the sufferings of the working classes set off as a foil the newfangled luxury of financial aristocrats, shoddy aristocrats, and similar vermin bred by wars. Yet for all this the Civil War did compensate by freeing the slave and the consequent moral impetus it gave to your own class movement. A second war, not hallowed by a sublime purpose and a great social necessity, but of the Old World's type, would forge chains for the free laborer instead of tearing asunder those of the slave. The accumulated misery left in its track would afford your capitalists at once the motive and the means to divorce the working class from its bold and just aspirations by the soulless sword of a standing army.

On you, then, devolves the glorious task to prove to the world that now at last the working classes are bestriding the scene of history no

2. Between 1870 and 1872, out of a total of approximately 13,000,000 gainfully employed workers, about 300,000 were trade-union members, or about 2.3 percent of the labor force.

3. The U. S. Census shows that in 1860 the Federal debt was $64,844,000, or $2.06 per capita; in 1869 it was $2,545,000,111, or $65.17 per capita.

longer as servile retainers, but as independent actors, conscious of their own responsibility, and able to command peace where their would-be masters shout war.[4]

In the name of the General Council of the International Working Men's Association,

British nationality:

R. Applegarth, carpenter; *M. J. Boon*, engineer; *J. Buckley*, painter; *J. Hales*, elastic web-weaver; *Harriet Law; B. Lucraft*, chair-maker; *J. Milner*, tailor; *G. Odger*, shoemaker; *J. Ross*, bootcloser; *R. Shaw*, painter; *Cowell Stepney; J. Warren*, trunk-maker; *J. Weston*, hand-rail maker.

French nationality:

E. Dupont, instrument maker; *Jules Johannard*, lithographer; *Paul Lafargue.*

German nationality:

G. Eccarius, tailor; *F. Lessner*, tailor; *W. Limburg*, shoemaker; *Karl Marx.*

Swiss nationality:

H. Jung, watchmaker; *A. Müller*, watchmaker.

Belgian nationality:

M. Bernard, painter.

Danish nationality:

J. Cohn, cigarmaker.

Polish nationality:

Zabicki, compositor.

B. Lucraft, Chairman; *Cowell Stepney*, Treasurer; *J. George Eccarius*, General Secretary.

---

4. From the concluding minutes of the General Council: "Citizen Odger took objection to the word *vermin.*

"Citizen Lucraft rather preferred it and Citizen Marx stated that no other word could be substituted without altering the context.

"After some conversation the Address was adopted upon the proposition of Citizen Dupont seconded by Citizen Odger.

"It was agreed that all the Council members should sign it and that their occupation should be stated."

The Civil War and the Paris Commune*

From the first sketch of The Civil War in France:

He [Thiers] compares himself with Lincoln and the Parisians with the rebellious Southern slaveholders. The Southerners fought for the enslavement of labor and the territorial separation of the United States. Paris fights for the emancipation of labor and the separation of the parasite-politician Thiers, the would-be slaveholder of France, from power!

From the second sketch of The Civil War in France:

He compares himself with Lincoln and the Parisians with the rebellious Southern slaveholders. The men of the Southern states desired the territorial separation of the United States—in the interest of the enslavement of labor. But Paris desires the separation of M. Thiers, and the interests he represents, from power—in the interest of the emancipation of labor.

---

* From sketches for *The Civil War in France,* written April–May, 1871. For the complete text of *The Civil War in France,* see *Karl Marx on Revolution,* Karl Marx Library, Vol. I.

Personal Letters

From letter to Frederick Engels (in Manchester)
LONDON, JANUARY 11, 1860

. . . In my opinion, the biggest things now happening in the world are, on the one hand, the American slave movement, started by the death of [John] Brown, and the slave movement in Russia, on the other. . . .

I have just seen in the *Tribune* that there has been a new slave uprising in Missouri, naturally suppressed. But the signal has now been given. If things gradually get serious, what will become of Manchester? . . .

From letter to Lion Philips (in Zaltbommel)
LONDON, MAY 6, 1861

Dear Uncle:

. . . Here in London there reigns great consternation about the course of events in America.[1] It is feared that the acts of violence perpetrated not only by the seceded states but also by the eight pro-secession central or border states—namely, Virginia, Kentucky, Missouri, North Carolina, Tennessee, Arkansas, Maryland, and Delaware—have made *every compromise* impossible. There is no doubt that in the beginning of the struggle the scales will be tilted in favor of the South, where the class of propertyless white adventurers forms an inexhaustible reservoir of martial militia. But in the long run, of course, the

1. In mid-December, 1860, South Carolina seceded from the Union. It was soon followed by Georgia, Florida, Mississippi, Alabama, Louisiana, and Texas. See Marx's letter to Engels July 1, 1861, and Marx's article, "The American Question in England," in the *New-York Daily Tribune*, October 11, 1860 (page 53).

North will win, for in case of necessity it can play the last card, that of a slave uprising. The great difficulty for the North is the question, how to get their forces to the South?[2] Even an unopposed march at the rate of 15 miles per day would be a trying thing at the present time of year; but Charleston, the closest vulnerable point, is 544 miles from Washington, 681 from Philadelphia, 771 from New York, and 994 from Boston, and the three latter cities are the main bases of operation against the South. Montgomery, the seat of the Secessionist Congress, is 910, 1050, 1130, and 1350 miles respectively from the above-named cities. A land march, therefore, seems to be out of the question. (Northern use of the railroad would merely lead to its destruction.) Hence only the sea route and sea warfare remain, but this can easily lead to complications with foreign powers. This evening the English Ministry will state in the House of Commons the attitude it plans to take in such an eventuality.

For me personally, the American events are, of course, rather harmful, as for the time being the transatlantic readers have eyes and ears only for their own story. Still, I have received advantageous offers from the Vienna *Presse*, which I will accept, after some ambiguous points have been cleared up. I am to do the writing from London. My wife is particularly opposed to our moving to Berlin, as she does not wish to have our daughters introduced to the Countess Hatzfeldt circle, which would be difficult to avoid. . . .

Your devoted nephew,
K. MARX

From letter to Ferdinand Lassalle (in Berlin)
LONDON, MAY 29, 1861

Dear Lassalle:
     . . . My American correspondence, due to the conditions there, is suspended for the time being, until European relationships have again become of interest to the transatlantics.

As a result of the American crisis, there is an extraordinary unease among the Paris workers. Ditto in Lyons.

The whole official English press is, of course, on the side of the slaveholders. They are the same fellows who tired the world with their antislave-trade philanthropism. But Cotton, Cotton! . . .

Greetings.
Yours,
K.M.

---

2. The last eight words were written in English.

From letter to Engels (in Manchester)
LONDON, JUNE 19, 1861

Dear Frederick:

. . . Many thanks for your letter about America. Should anything important (militarily) occur, do always write me your opinion about it. According to the picture I have formed of General Scott—now, moreover, seventy-six years old—shaped by the Mexican War (see Ripley[1]), I expect the greatest blunders from him, if the old jackass is not controlled by others. Above all, slowness and indecision. For the rest, I see from the facts reported in the *Tribune* that the North now speaks openly of a slave war and the destruction of slavery. . . .

Your
K.M.

From letter to Engels (in Manchester)
LONDON, JULY 1, 1861

Dear Frederic:

. . . Please write me *at once* what you think of the movements (military) in Virginia. The blunders of the militia officers—Brigadier General Peirce is by trade a "tailor" from the state of Massachusetts—will, of course, be frequently enough repeated by both sides.[1] Is Washington still threatened? Do you believe that the Southern position at Manassas Junction is offensive? Or are the fellows rather in retreat? In Missouri, the defeat of the Southerners seems to be decisive, and there the dreadful "Colonel Börnstein" came to the surface. From a private letter to Weber, it appears that "Colonel Willich" is at the head of a corps from Cincinnati. He has not yet gone into the field.

A closer study of these American affairs has shown me that the conflict between South and North—after the latter has degraded itself by one concession after another for fifty years—has finally erupted in battle (apart from the shameless new demands of the "chivalry") because of the weight that the extraordinary development of the northwestern states threw into the scale. This population, richly mixed with

---

1. Roswell Sabine Ripley, *The War with Mexico* (2 vols., 1849).

1. The reference is to the confused battle at Big Bethel and Little Bethel, Virginia, June 10, 1861. Both the Federal and Confederate troops fired on their own troops and both sides retired in confusion; two men were killed and twenty-one wounded.

new German and British elements, and in addition self-employed farmers, was naturally not as prone to intimidation as the gentlemen from Wall Street and the Quakers from Boston. According to the last census (1860), it grew 67 percent between 1850 and 1860, and consisted of 7,870,869 in 1860, while the total free population of the seceding slave states was only about 5,000,000, according to the same census. These northwestern states delivered the bulk of the victorious party, as well as the President, in 1860. It was also precisely this part of the North which first decided against any recognition of the independence of a Southern Confederacy. Naturally they cannot abandon the lower Mississippi and its estuaries to foreign states. It was also this northwestern population that in the Kansas affair (from which the present war is really to be dated) fought at close quarters with the border ruffians.[2]

A closer look at the history of the secession movement reveals that Secession, Constitution (Montgomery, Ala.), Congress,[3] etc., are all usurpations. Nowhere did they let the people en masse vote. Concerning this "usurpation"—which involves not only the secession from the North but also the strengthening and the sharpening of the hold of the oligarchy of 300,000 Southern slavelords over five million whites— there are characteristic articles that appeared in contemporary Southern papers. . . .

From letter to Engels (in Manchester)
LONDON, JULY 5, 1861

Dear Engels:

. . . In regard to the history of the secession, the matter has been completely misrepresented in the English papers. Except for South Carolina, there was everywhere the strongest opposition to secession.

First: The Border Slave States. In the winter of 1861 there was a Border States Convention to which Virginia, Kentucky, Arkansas, Maryland, Delaware, Tennessee, and North Carolina were invited. These states held individual conventions to choose delegates to the General Convention.

Delaware refused to hold a convention for that purpose.

Tennessee ditto. Its Democratic legislature took it out of the Union through a *coup de main* [sudden attack]. It is true that it held elections

---

2. The pro-slavery elements from Missouri which fought for control of Kansas between 1854 and 1858.

3. The Congress of six Confederate States—Alabama, Florida, Georgia, Louisiana, Mississippi, and South Carolina—sat in Montgomery from February 4 to March 16, 1861, and proclaimed the Confederacy on March 2, 1861, and Arkansas, North Carolina, Tennessee, and Virginia in May, 1861.

later to ratify this invalid act. That took place under a pure reign of terror. More than one-third did not vote at all. Of the rest, one-third was opposed to secession, among them all of East Tennessee, which is presently arming against it.

Kentucky. A hundred thousand for the Union ticket; only a few thousand for secession.

Maryland declared itself for the Union, and has now elected six Union men to Congress.

North Carolina and even *Arkansas* chose Union delegates, the former even with a strong majority. They were later terrorized.

Virginia. The people chose a Union Convention (according to the majority). Some of those fellows let themselves be bought. At the height of the South fever—the fall of Fort Sumter[1]—the Ordinance of Secession was passed *secretly* by a vote of 88 to 55. All other steps —while the Ordinance was still kept secret—for the capture of the federal navy yard at Norfolk and the federal armory at Harpers Ferry were taken in secret. They were betrayed to the federal authorities before their execution. A secret agreement with Jefferson Davis' government was made and large numbers of Confederate troops were suddenly thrown into the state. Under their protection (very Bonaparte-like) only secession was permitted to be voted. Nevertheless, there were 50,000 Union votes, despite the systematic terrorism. Northwestern Virginia, as you know, has now openly broken away from the Secession.

Second: The Gulf States. Genuine popular voting took place only in a few states. In most of them, the conventions, chosen for the purpose of considering the position of the Southern states in regard to Lincoln's election (they later became *their* delegates to the Montgomery Congress), usurped the power not only to decide on secession but also to recognize the Confederate Constitution, Jefferson Davis, etc. How this was done you can see from the following extracts from the Southern papers.

Texas, where, next to South Carolina, the biggest slavery party with the most terrorism was to be found, nevertheless, cast 11,000 votes for the Union.

Alabama. The people voted neither for secession nor for the new constitution, etc. The State Convention passed the Ordinance of Secession with 61 against 39 votes. But the 39 from the northern counties, almost entirely inhabited by whites, represented more free men than the 61; according to the United States Constitution, every slaveholder also votes for three-fifths of his slaves.

Louisiana. At the election of delegates to the convention, more Un-

---

1. April 12, 1861.

ion than Secession votes were cast. But the delegates went over to the other side.

In western Carolina, eastern Tennessee, northern Alabama and Georgia, the mining districts have very different interests from those of the southern swamps.

In the following extracts you can clearly see the December Second character[2] of the whole Secession maneuver (here too the fellows were compelled to initiate the movement to provoke war, which they did under the slogan, "The North Against the South"), how the traitors in Buchanan's administration who stood at the head of the movement —Secretary of War Floyd, Secretary of the Navy Toucey, Secretary of the Treasury Cobb, Secretary of the Interior Thompson—together with the leading Southern senators, were most deeply involved in the *dilapidations*[3] that ran into many millions, as presented to a House of Representatives Committee of Inquiry in 1860. At least for some of these fellows [Secessionists] it was a matter of saving themselves from going to prison. Hence they were the most willing tools of the 300,000 slaveholding oligarchy. Through its cohesiveness, position, and means, it is self-evident that the latter has the capacity at this moment of putting down any opposition. Among a portion of the "poor whites" the slaveholders found their mob, which served as their Zouaves.

Georgia. The *Griffin Union:* "It is mere mockery for the same men who made the Constitution in Montgomery to come back to Georgia and ratify it under the name of a State Convention."

The *Macon Journal:* "The State Conventions . . . called for another purpose . . . assume that they are the people, and under such an assumption of power can appoint delegates to a General Convention without consulting the people. All the acts of the Congress of their Confederacy are passed in secret session with closed doors, and what is done is kept from the people."

The Augusta Chronicle and Sentinel (Georgia's biggest paper): "The whole movement for secession, and the formation of a new government, so far at least as Georgia is concerned" (and Georgia is numerically the largest slave state), "proceeds on only a quasi consent of the people, and was pushed through, under circumstances of great excitement and frenzy—by a fictitious majority. With all the appliances brought to bear, etc., the election of the fourth of January showed a falling off of nearly 3,000, and an absolute majority of elected deputies of 79. But upon assembling, by wheedling, coaxing, buying, and all the arts of deception, the convention showed a majority of 31" (against Union). . . . The Georgia Convention and the Confederate Congress

---

2. Louis Bonaparte had made his *coup d'état,* which overthrew the French Republic, on December 2, 1851.
3. The word is in English.

have gone forward in their work, as none can deny, without authority from the people."

Alabama. The Mobile Advertiser: "The Convention has adopted the permanent Constitution in behalf of the State of Alabama . . . The great fact stands forth that the delegates were not chosen for any such purpose."

The North Alabamian: "The Convention made haste to usurp the prerogative, and ratify the Constitution . . . It is a remarkable fact that the substantial physical force of the country, the hardfisted, hard-working men, expected to do all the fighting when the country calls, were from the beginning opposed to the Ordinance of Secession."

Mississippi. Similar complaints about usurpation in the *Jackson Mississippian* and the *Vicksburg Whig.*

Louisiana. New Orleans True Delta: "Here Secession succeeded only by suppressing the election returns . . . The government has been changed into despotism."

In the State Convention of Louisiana (at New Orleans), old Roselius (one of the leading politicians in the United States) said on March 22, 1861: "The Montgomery instrument [Constitution] . . . did not inaugurate a government of the people, but an odious and unmitigated oligarchy. The people had not been permitted to act in the matter."

Kentucky. In Louisville, Kentucky, Senator Guthrie (proslavery man, and Secretary of the Treasury under Pierce) said on March 16, 1861, that the whole movement was a "plot" and a "usurpation," stating, among other things: "In Alabama a majority of the popular vote was cast against going out, but a small majority of the delegates were for Secession, they took Alabama out, and refused the people any voice in the matter. The vote of Louisiana, too, was against secession, but the delegates suppressed it," etc.

Your
K. M.

From letter to Engels (in Manchester)
LONDON, DECEMBER 9, 1861

Dear Engels:
. . . War, as I have stated in *Die Presse* from the first day, will not break out with America, and I only regret that I did not have the means to exploit the stupidity of the Reuters- and *Times*-influenced Stock Exchange during this fool period. . . .

Your
K. M.

From letter to Engels (in Manchester)
LONDON, DECEMBER 19, 1861

Dear Engels:
    ... In regard to war with America, Pam [Palmerston] may *possibly* succeed in bringing it about, but not easily. He must have a pretext, and it does not seem to me that Lincoln will provide it. A part of the cabinet, Milner-Gibson, Gladstone, *plus ou moins* Lewis, cannot be fooled like John Russell.
    Considered in and by itself, the Americans have not erred, either materially or formally, in English maritime law valid among them. As to the question of material right, the English Crown lawyers themselves have pronounced in the same sense. Hence since they lacked a pretext they have resorted to an error in form, a technicality, a legal quibble. But this is false too. According to English maritime law, two things must be distinguished: whether a neutral ship carries *belligerent* goods and persons, or *contraband of war*, even if the latter consists of goods and persons. In the latter case the ship is to be seized with cargo and persons and brought into a port of adjudication. In the former case—if there is no doubt that the goods have not been transferred to the possession of neutrals (which is of itself impossible in case of persons)—the belligerent goods or persons are confiscable on the high seas, while the ship, etc., goes free. England has constantly asserted this jurisprudence—apart from the authorities—as I have convinced myself by looking up in Cobbett's *Register* all the squabbles with neutrals since 1793.
    On the other hand, since the English Crown lawyers have restricted the question to an error in form, and thus conceded to the Yankees the right of confiscating any British ship that carries belligerents and towing it into a port for adjudication, the Yankees can very easily declare—and in my opinion they will do so—that they are satisfied with this concession, will not violate the *form* in confiscation, etc., in the future, and give up Mason [&] Slidell for the nonce.
    If Pam absolutely wants war, he can, of course, bring it about. In my opinion, that is not his object. If the Americans act in the manner I have supposed, Pam will have furnished stupid John Bull new proof that he is "the truly English Minister." The fellow will then allow himself anything. He will utilize the opportunity to (1) force the Yankees to recognize the Paris Declaration on the rights of neutrals; (2) under this pretext, call upon and make Parliament sanction the resignation from the English maritime law which was signed by Clarendon at

his (Pam's) order, behind the Crown's back and without advance knowledge of Parliament—which he has not as yet dared to do.

Pam is old, and the Russians have tried to force through the Declaration of Paris ever since the time of Catherine II. They still lack two things: the sanction of the English Parliament, and the adherence of the United States. Both of these will be attained on this occasion. The war spectacle seems to me to be merely a theatrical appurtenance, to present to stupid John Bull the definitive resignation of his own maritime law as a victory over the Yankees by the pluck of the "truly English Minister."

Subsidiary reasons for the war spectacle would be diversion from Poland (since even chaps like Conningham of Brighton demand in public meetings the stoppage of further payment on the Dutch-Russian loan) and diversion from Denmark, where Russia is at this moment engaged in pushing aside Glücksburg, the heir presumptive whom it appointed itself.

It is, of course, possible that the Yankees will not yield, and then Pam will be compelled to go to war by his preparations and rodomontades so far. Still, I would bet a hundred to one against it.

Your
K. M.

From letter to Engels (in Manchester)
LONDON, MARCH 3, 1862

Dear Engels:

I would appreciate it if you would send me *this week* (by Friday morning) an article in English on the American Civil War. You can write *quite unconstrainedly*. The [New York] *Tribune* will print it all as a letter of a Foreign Officer. *Notabene:* The *Tribune* hates McClellan, who is allied with the Democratic party and who, so long as he was commander-in-chief of all the armies, prevented all action through *direct intervention* not only on the Potomac (where it was perhaps justified) but also in *all* theaters of operation, specifically in the West. (He was also the soul of the most infamous intrigues against Frémont.)

Furthermore, this Mac, out of *esprit de corps* and hatred of civilians, has protected all traitors in the army, for example, Colonel Maynard and General Stone. The arrest of the latter followed one or two days after Clellan was removed as Commander-in-Chief. Similarly, the shameless Washington "representative" of the *New-York Herald*[1] was

---

1. Malcolm Ives.

arrested as a spy, against McClellan's wishes, the day after he had entertained the latter's whole staff at a champagne breakfast. . . .

From letter to Engels (in Manchester)
LONDON, MARCH 6, 1862

Dear Frederick:
. . . That the Southerners will have concluded peace by July, 1862, does not appear very probable to me. When the Northerners have secured (1) the border states—and these were really at stake from the beginning—and (2) the Mississippi to New Orleans and Texas, there will begin a second period of the war, in which the Northerners will not exert too much military effort, but by quarantining the Gulf States will finally drive them to voluntary reannexation.

[John] Bull's behavior during the present war is possibly the most shameless that has ever occurred.

In regard to brutality on the English side, the Mexican Blue Book[1] surpasses anything known to history. Menshikov appears a gentleman compared with Sir C. Lennox Wyke. This canaille not only develops the most unbounded *zèle* [zeal] in carrying out Pam's secret instructions, but seeks to revenge himself by loutishness for the fact that Señor Zamacoña, a former journalist and Mexican Minister of Foreign Affairs (now out of office), is invariably his superior in the exchange of diplomatic dispatches. In regard to the fellow's style, here are some samples from his dispatches to Zamacoña:

"The arbitrary act of stopping all payments for the space of two years is depriving the parties interested of their money *for that space of time, which* is a *dead loss of so much value to them.*"[2] "A starving man may justify, in his own eyes, the fact of stealing a loaf on the ground that imperious necessity impelled him thereto; but such an argument cannot, in a moral point of view, justify his violation of the law, which remains as positive, *apart from all sentimentality*, as if the crime had not had an excuse. *If he was actually starving*, he should have first asked the baker to assuage his hunger, but *doing so*" (starving?) "of his own free will, without permission, *is acting* exactly as the Mexican government *has* done toward *its creditors on the present occasion.*" "With regard to the *light* in which you view the question, as *expressed*

---

1. *Correspondence Relative to the Affairs of Mexico*, an anonymous volume published in London in 1862.
2. The sentences in quotation marks are from the text in English; the italics are by Marx.

in your above named note, you will excuse me for stating that *it cannot be treated of partially*, WITHOUT *also* taking into consideration the opinions of those who directly suffer *from the practical operation of such ideas as emanating from yourself.*" "I had a full right to complain of having first of all *heard* of this extraordinary measure by *seeing* it in printed bills *placarded through* the public streets." "I have a duty to perform both to my own Government and to that to *which* I am accredited, *which* impels me, etc." "I suspend all official relations with the Government of this Republic until *that* of Her Majesty shall adopt such measures as *they* shall deem necessary."

Zamacoña writes him that the intrigues of the foreign diplomats for twenty-five years are chiefly to blame for the troubles in Mexico. Wyke answers him that "the population of Mexico is so degraded as to make them dangerous, not only to themselves, but to everybody coming into contact with them"!

Zamacoña writes him that the proposals he makes put an end to the autonomy of the Republic and run counter to the dignity of any independent state. Wyke answers: "Excuse me for adding that such a proposition as I have made to you does not necessarily become undignified and impracticable simply *because you, an interested person*" (that is as Mexico's Foreign Minister) "are pleased to say so." However, *satis superque* [enough of this]. . . .

Your

K. M.

From letter to Engels (in Manchester)
LONDON, APRIL 28, 1862

Dear Frederick:

. . . What particularly interests the fellows[1] now is America, and I would appreciate it if you would send me an article on the progress of the war (I mean the battle of Corinth[2]) (this week still); and generally if you would write me every time there is any turn in the military situation. If only to spread in Germany correct views on this important matter. (I have already worked over your former articles for them; they have already been printed.) . . .

Your

K. M.

---

1. On Vienna's *Die Presse.*
2. April 6–7, 1862.

From letter to Ferdinand Lassalle (in Berlin)
LONDON, APRIL 28, 1862

Dear Lassalle:

   . . . The English middle class (and aristocracy) has never disgraced itself more shamefully than in the great war that is now being waged across the Atlantic. On the other hand, the English working class, which suffers most from the *Bellum Civile* [Civil War], has never shown itself to be more heroic and noble. This is the more to be admired if one knows, as I do, all the means used to move them to a demonstration here and in Manchester.[1] The only large organ they still have, the shabby dog *Reynolds's Newspaper*, has been bought by the Southerners, as were also most of their lecturers. But in all vain.

From letter to Engels (in Manchester)
LONDON, MAY 6, 1862

Dear Frederick:

   . . . I shall write again to Dana. I painfully miss contributing to the *Tribune*. This is a mean trick on the part of Greeley and McElrath. From the last numbers of the *Tribune* for March, I have seen two things. First, that McClellan had been accurately informed eight days beforehand of the Confederates' retreat. Second, that Russell of the *Times* availed himself of his sniffing around in Washington during the *Trent* affair to gamble on the Stock Exchange in New York.

   In Prussia, there will be a *coup d'état*, if not a *coup d'éclat*.

   Bonaparte's present maneuvers in Mexico (the affair originally emanated from Pam) are explained by the fact that Juárez recognizes only the official debt to France of £46,000. But Miramón and his gang, through the Swiss banker Jecker et Co., had issued state bonds to the amount of $52,000,000 (on which about $4,000,000 have been paid). These state bonds—Jecker et Co. being only *hommes de paille* [straw men]—have fallen into the hands of Morny et Co. almost for *zéro*. They demand the recognition of them by Juárez. *Hinc illae lacrimae.* [Hence these tears.]

   Schurz is—a Brigadier General with Frémont!!!

Your
K. M.

1. See "English Public Opinion," page 152.

From letter to Engels (in Manchester)
LONDON, MAY 27, 1862

Dear Frederick:

... The blowing up of the *Merrimac*[1] seems to me an evident act of cowardice on the part of the dirty rascals of the Confederacy. The dogs might still risk something. It is wonderful how the *Times* (which supported all the Coercion Bills against Ireland with so much fiery zeal) could wail that "liberty" must be lost in the event of the North tyrannizing over the South.[2] The *Economist* is good too. It declares in its last number that the Yankees' financial luck—the nondepreciation of their paper money—is incomprehensible to it (although the matter is very simple).[3] It had hitherto consoled its readers from week to week with this depreciation. Although it now admits that it does not understand what is its business and had misled its readers on the subject, it now consoles them with gloomy doubts about "war operations" of which it officially understands nothing.

What has extraordinarily facilitated the Yankees' paper operations (the main point being the confidence placed in their cause and therewith in their government) is undoubtedly the circumstance that as a consequence of secession, the West has been almost denuded of paper money, and therefore of a circulating medium generally. All the banks whose principal securities consisted of the bonds of slave states went bankrupt. Moreover, millions in currency, which circulated in the West as direct bank notes of southern banks, were swept away. Then, partly as a consequence of the Morrill Tariff, partly because of the war itself, which largely put an end to the import of luxury goods, the Yankees had a balance of trade and, therefore, a rate of exchange favorable to themselves against Europe during this whole period. An unfavorable exchange rate would have badly affected the patriotic confidence in their paper on the part of the philistines.

For the rest, this comical concern of John Bull with the interest on the national debt that Uncle Sam will have to pay! As if it were not a mere bagatelle in comparison with Bull's national debt; moreover, the United States is now undoubtedly richer than the Bulls were with their debt of a billion in 1815.

---

1. The South's ironclad, *Merrimac*, was blown up in Norfolk harbor on May 10, 1862, to keep it out of Union hands when the city fell.
2. A reference to "The Civil War in America," in the *London Times*, May 27, 1862.
3. A reference to "Extent and Bearing of Federal Success," in the *Economist*, May 24, 1862.

Hasn't Pam got Bonaparte into a pretty mess in Mexico! . . .

Your

K. M.

From letter to Engels (in Manchester)
LONDON, AUGUST 7, 1862

. . . I do not entirely share your views on the American Civil War. I do not believe that all is up. The Northerners have been dominated from the beginning by the representatives of the border slave states, who pushed McClellan, that old partisan of Breckinridge, to the top. The South, on the other hand, acted as a unit from the beginning. The North itself has turned slavery into a military force of the South, instead of turning it against the latter. The South leaves productive labor to the slaves and thus has been able to put its whole fighting strength into the field without hindrance. The South had unified military leadership; the North did not. That there was no strategic plan was already clear from the maneuvers of the Kentucky army after the conquest of Tennessee. In my view, all this will take another turn. The North will finally wage war seriously, adopt revolutionary methods, and overthrow the domination of the border slave statesmen. A single nigger-regiment would have a remarkable effect on Southern nerves.

The difficulty of getting the 300,000 men seems to me to be purely political. The Northwest and New England want to and will force the government to give up the diplomatic methods of waging war which it has used hitherto, and they are now setting the terms on which the 300,000 men shall come forth. If Lincoln does not give way (which, however, he will), there will be a revolution.

In regard to the lack of military talent, the hitherto existing method of selecting generals purely from considerations of diplomacy and party chicanery is hardly designed to bring it forth. General Pope, however, seems to me to be a man of energy.

In regard to the financial measures, they are clumsy, as one would expect in a country where in fact (for the nation as a whole) no taxes have existed until now; but they are not nearly as idiotic as the measures taken by Pitt and Co.[1] The present depreciation of money is to be ascribed, I believe, not to economic but to purely political grounds—distrust. It will therefore change with a different policy.

The long and the short of the story seems to me to be that a war of

---

1. In 1786 Pitt the Younger established a sinking fund to pay Britain's growing national debt.

this kind must be conducted in a revolutionary way, whereas the Yankees have been trying so far to conduct it constitutionally.

Greetings. *Your*

K. M.

From letter to Engels (*in Manchester*)
LONDON, SEPTEMBER 10, 1862

Dear Engels:

. . . As regards the Yankees, I am surely still of the opinion[1] that the North will win in the end; the Civil War can, of course, go through all kinds of episodes, perhaps also including truces, and drag itself out. The South would and could conclude peace only on condition that it retain the border slave states. In that case it would also get California, followed by the Northwest; and the whole Federation, with the exception of the New England states, would again form *one* country, this time under the acknowledged supremacy of the slaveholders. It would be the reconstruction of the United States on the basis demanded by the South. This, however, is impossible and will not happen.

The North, for its part, can conclude peace only if the Confederacy confines itself to the old slave states between the Mississippi River and the Atlantic. In this case the Confederacy would soon reach its blessed end. Interim truces, etc., on the basis of the status quo can at most only entail pauses in the progress of the war.

In regard to the North's conduct of the war, nothing else could be expected from a *bourgeois* republic, where swindle has been enthroned for such a long time. But the South, an oligarchy, is better fitted for war, because it is an oligarchy, where all the productive work is done by niggers and the 4,000,000 "white trash" are filibusters by profession. Despite all that, I will wager my head that those fellows will get the short end of it, despite Stonewall Jackson. It is, to be sure, possible that before that a kind of revolution will take place in the North.

Willich is Brigadier General, and, as Kapp said in Cologne, Stephens is also in the war now.

It seems to me that you are a little too much influenced by the military aspect of things. . . .

Salut. *Your*

K. M.

---

1. Engels to Marx September 9, 1862: "The Bull Run story No. 2, was a splendid little play by Stonewall Jackson, who is by far the best fellow in America . . . It is too pitiful, but the chaps in the South, who know least what they want, appear as heroes, compared to the flabby management of the North. Or do you still believe that the gentlemen in the North will be able to 'suppress' the Rebellion?"

From letter to Engels (in Manchester)
LONDON, OCTOBER 29, 1862

Dear Engels:

. . . As for America, I believe that the Maryland campaign was deci-sive[1] insofar as it showed that even in this section of the pro-Southern border states, support for the Confederacy is weak. The whole struggle turns on the border states. Whoever possesses them dominates the Un-ion. At the same time, the fact that Lincoln issued the forthcoming Emancipation Proclamation [September 1862] at the moment when the Confederates were pushing forward in Kentucky shows that all consideration for the loyal slaveholders in the border states has ceased. The emigration to the South of the slaveholders from Missouri, Kentucky, Tennessee, with their black chattels, is already enormous, and if the war should be prolonged for a while, which is certain, the South will have lost all foothold there. The South began the war for these territories. The war itself was the means of destroying its power in the border states, where, apart from this, the ties with the South are weakening daily because a market can no longer be found for slave breeding and the internal slave trade. In my opinion, therefore, for the South it will now be a matter only of the defensive.

But its only possibility for success lay in the offensive. If the report is confirmed that Hooker is receiving the active command of the Army of the Potomac, that McClellan is being "retired" to the "theoretical" position of Commander-in-Chief, and that Halleck is taking over the chief command in the West, then the conduct of the war in Virginia may also take on a more energetic character. Moreover, the most favorable time of the year for the Confederates is now gone.

Morally, the collapse of the Maryland campaign was certainly of the most tremendous importance.

Regarding finance, the United States knows from the War of Inde-pendence, and we know from observations of Austria, how far one can go with depreciated paper money. It is a fact that the Yankees have never exported more corn to England than they have this year, that the present harvest is again far above average, and that the balance of trade has never been more favorable for them than it has been in the past two years. As soon as the new tax system (a very ridiculous one, at any rate, in the style of Pitt) comes into operation, the reflux of paper money, hitherto steadily emitted, will at last begin. An extension

1. See Marx's article *"On Events in North America,"* page 220.

of the paper issue on the present scale will therefore become superfluous, and further depreciation will thus be checked. What has made even the present depreciation less dangerous than it was in France and even in England, under similar circumstances, has been the fact that the Yankees have never prohibited *two prices,* a gold price and a paper price. The actual mischief of the thing resolves itself into a government debt, for which the proper equivalent has never been received, and into a premium for jobbing and speculation.

When the English boast that their depreciation has never been more than 11½ percent (according to the belief of others, it has been more than double for some time), they conveniently forget that they not only continued to pay their old taxes but that every year they paid new ones as well, so that the return flow of the bank notes was assured from the beginning; while the Yankees actually carried on the war for a year and a half *without taxes* (except the greatly diminished import duties), simply by repeating the issue of paper. In a process of this kind, of which the turning point has now been reached, depreciation is in reality comparatively slight.

The fury with which the Southerners have received Lincoln's acts proves their importance. All Lincoln's acts seem like the mean, pettifogging conditions that one lawyer puts to his opponent. But this does not change their historic content, and indeed it amuses me to compare them with the drapery in which a Frenchman envelops even the most insignificant point.

Like other people, I see, of course, the repulsive side of the form the movement takes among the Yankees; but I find the explanation of it in the nature of "bourgeois" democracy. Nevertheless, the events are world-transforming, and there is nothing more disgusting in the whole business than the English attitude toward them.

Regards for Lupus.[3] *Salut.*

Your

K. M.

From letter to Engels (in Manchester)
LONDON, NOVEMBER 17, 1862

Dear Engels:

. . . It seems to me that you view the American row too much from one side. I have read in the American Coffeehouse a mass of Southern

---

3. Wilhelm Wolff.

papers and saw in them that the Confederacy is in serious straits. The English newspapers have suppressed the story of the Battle of Corinth.[1] The Southern newspapers describe it as the most extraordinary stroke of bad luck that has befallen the South since the outbreak of the rebellion. The state of Georgia has declared the Confederate "Conscription Acts" null and void. Virginia has denied Floyd, the thief and "creature" (literally) "of Jefferson Davis," the right to recruit in that state. Oldham, the representative from Texas in the Congress at Richmond, has protested against the transportation of "picked troops" from the Southwest to the East, that is, to Virginia. From all these disputes, two things emerge quite indisputably:

that the Confederate Government has bent the bow to the breaking point in its efforts to fill the ranks of its army;

that the states are asserting their "states' rights" against the Confederacy as much as the latter did as a pretext against the Union.

The victories of the Democrats, the conservative and blackleg element of the North,[2] I consider a reaction, made easy for them by the poor conduct of the war and the financial blunders of the Federal Government. Besides, in every revolutionary movement there is a sort of reaction, as, for example, occurred in the time of the French Convention, when the reaction was so strong that it was considered counterrevolutionary to suggest submitting the fate of the King [Louis XVI] to universal suffrage; and under the Directory, Mr. Bonaparte the First had to bombard Paris.

On the other hand, the elections will not change the composition of the Congress before December 4, 1864. They merely serve as a sharp reminder to the Republican Administration that the sword hangs over its head. And in any case, the Republican House of Representatives will now make better use of its elected term, if only out of hatred for the opposing party.

As to McClellan, he has in his own army Hooker and other Republicans, who will arrest him any day at the order of the government.

Added to this, the French attempt at intervention,[3] which will bring forth a reaction against the reaction.

Hence I do not see things in such a bad light. What could hurt my viewpoint much more is, rather, the sheeplike behavior of the workers in

---

1. In the two-day battle at Corinth, Miss., October 3-4, 1862, the Confederate troops were defeated and forced to retreat. See "Symptoms of Dissolution in the Southern Confederacy," page 227.

2. In the congressional elections of November 4, 1862, the Republicans lost a number of seats to the Democrats in New York and in the northwestern states.

3. In October, 1862, Napoleon III proposed to Britain and Russia that the three powers break the Union blockade of Southern ports; Russia declined on November 8, and Britain did the same subsequently.

Lancashire. Such a thing has never been heard of in the world.[4] The more so as the rabble of manufacturers do not even pretend to "offer a sacrifice," but leave to the rest of England the honor of keeping their army on its feet, that is, of paying for the maintenance of their variable capital.

In this recent period England has disgraced itself more than any other country, the workers by their Christian slave nature, the bourgeoisie and the aristocrats by their enthusiasm for slavery in its most direct form. But both manifestations complement each other. . . .

Your

K. M.

From letter to Engels (*in Manchester*)
LONDON, NOVEMBER 20, 1862

Dear Engels:
 . . . If only the Mexicans (*les derniers des hommes* [the lowest of men]!) would just once beat the *crapauds*,[1] but those dogs themselves— the presumably radical bourgeois—are now talking even in Paris of *l'honneur du drapeau* [the honor of the flag]!

If Spence does not defeat the Northerners in guerrilla war, nothing will help; not even the bad generalship of McClellan.

Your

K. M.

From letter to Ferdinand Freiligrath (*in London*)
LONDON, DECEMBER 15, 1862

Dear Freiligrath:
 . . . For a few days I was in Liverpool and Manchester,[1] these centers of the cottonocracy and proslavery enthusiasm. Among the great bulk of the middle classes and the aristocracy of those towns you may observe the greatest eclipsus of the human mind ever chronicled in the history of modern times.[2] . . .

Your

K. MARX

---

4. Marx wrote the sentence in English.
1. The French; *crapaud* in French means toad.

---

1. Between December 5 and 13 Marx visited Engels in Manchester and Wilhelm Eichhoff in Liverpool.
2. The last sentence was written in English.

From letter to Engels (in Manchester)
LONDON, JANUARY 2, 1863

Dear Frederick:

Happy New Year!

. . . Burnside seems to have committed great tactical blunders in the Battle of Fredericksburg.[1] He was clearly uneasy about the deployment of such large fighting forces. But basically his asinine behavior was this: (1) He waited for twenty-six days, which clearly implies direct treason in the war administration in Washington; even the New York correspondent of the *Times*[2] admitted that Burnside received supplies, promised for immediate delivery, only weeks later. (2) Despite this, he made his attack, which shows the moral weakness of the man. The worthy *Tribune* began to suspect him and threatened him with dismissal. This paper, with its enthusiasm and its ignorance, did great damage.

The Democrats and McClellanites naturally cried out with one voice, to exaggerate the defeat. The "rumor" that McClellan, "the Monk"[3] of the *Times*, was called to Washington is ascribed to Mr. Reuter.

"Politically," the defeat was good. There was to be no lucky hit before January 1, 1863. The Emancipation Proclamation could have made all this retrogressive.

The *Times* and consorts are completely furious at the workers' meetings in Manchester, Sheffield, and *London*.[4] It is very good that the cataract is removed from the Yankees' eyes in this way. Moreover, Opdyke (mayor of New York and political economist) said at a meeting in New York: "We know that the English working classes are with us, and that the governing classes of England are against us."

I am very sorry that Germany does not make similar demonstrations. They cost nothing and bring in a great deal "internationally." Germany would be justified in making them, as it has contributed more to the Yankees than France did in the eighteenth century. It is the old German stupidity, not to make itself felt in the world arena or to stress what it really accomplishes.

Your
K. M.

---

1. December 11–15, 1862. Burnside's army was defeated by the Confederates under Lee.
2. Probably Charles Mackay.
3. George Monk (or Monck), first Duke of Albemarle.
4. At the end of December, 1862, mass demonstrations in support of the Union were held in these cities.

From letter to Engels (in Manchester)
LONDON, FEBRUARY 13, 1863

Dear Frederick:

. . . The [French] adventure in Mexico is an extremely classical denouement of the farce of the Lower Empire.[1] . . .

In the United States, things go damned slowly. I hope J. Hooker will bite his way out. . . .[2]

Your

K. M.

1. A reference to the empire of Napoleon III, suggesting a decline like that of the so-called Lower Empire of Byzantium.

2. In January, 1863, Lincoln appointed General Joseph Hooker commander of the Army of the Potomac. The President did so with some reluctance, as his memorable letter to Hooker (January 26, 1863) shows:

"General: I have placed you at the head of the Army of the Potomac. Of course I have done this upon what appear to me to be sufficient reasons, and yet I think it best for you to know that there are some things in regard to which I am not quite satisfied with you. I believe you to be a brave and skilful soldier, which of course I like. I also believe you do not mix politics with your profession, in which you are right. You have confidence in yourself, which is a valuable if not an indispensable quality. You are ambitious, which, within reasonable bounds, does good rather than harm; but I think that during General Burnside's command of the army you have taken counsel of your ambition and thwarted him as much as you could, in which you did a great wrong to the country and to a most meritorious and honorable brother officer. I have heard, in such a way as to believe it, of your recently saying that both the army and the government needed a dictator. Of course it was not for this, but in spite of it, that I have given you the command. Only those generals who gain successes can set up dictators. What I now ask of you is military success, and I will risk the dictatorship. The government will support you to the utmost of its ability, which is neither more nor less than it has done and will do for all commanders. I much fear that the spirit which you have aided to infuse into the army, of criticising their commander and withholding confidence from him, will now turn upon you. I shall assist you as far as I can to put it down. Neither you nor Napoleon, if he were to live again, could get any good out of an army while such a spirit prevails in it; and now beware of rashness. Beware of rashness, but with energy and sleepless vigilance go forward and give us victories.

"A. LINCOLN."

"Fighting Joe" Hooker won no victories. Less than four months after Lincoln's letter, Hooker was defeated in the Battle of Chancellorsville (May 1–4), and on June 28 was relieved of his command by General George Gordon Meade, who won the Battle of Gettysburg, which began on July 1.

From letter to Engels (in Manchester)
LONDON, MARCH 24, 1863

Dear Frederick:

... What I consider very important in America's most recent history is that they will again issue letters of marque. *Quoad* [in regard to] England, this will put a quite different complexion on things and under favorable circumstances may lead to war with England, so that the self-satisfied Bull would see, besides his cotton, corn also withdrawn from under his nose. At the beginning of the Civil War, Seward, on his own hook, had taken the liberty of accepting the decisions of the Congress of Paris of 1856 as valid for America *for the time being*. (This came out when the dispatches of the *Trent* affair were published.) The Congress in Washington and Lincoln, furious at the outfitting of Southern pirates in Liverpool, etc., have now put an end to this joke. This has aroused great dismay on the Stock Exchange here, but the faithful dogs of the press naturally obey orders and do not mention the matter in the newspapers. ...

Your

K. M.

From letter to Engels (in Manchester)
LONDON, APRIL 9, 1863

Dear Frederick:

... I attended a meeting held by Bright, at the head of the trade unions.[1] He had quite the appearance of an Independent, and every time he said, "In the United States no kings, no bishops," there was a burst of applause. The workers themselves spoke *excellently*, with a complete absence of all bourgeois rhetoric, and without concealing in the slightest their opposition to the capitalists (whom, moreover, Father Bright also attacked). ...

Your

K. M.

1. On March 26, 1863, the London Trade Union Council held a meeting in St. James's Hall, under the chairmanship of John Bright, to express solidarity with the United States in its war against the Confederacy.

From letter to Frederick Engels (in Manchester)
LONDON, JULY 6, 1863

Dear Engels:
. . . In my opinion, the expedition of the Southerners against the North has been forced on Lee by the clamor of the Richmond papers and their supporters. I consider it a *coup de désespoir* [act of despair]. For the rest, this war will drag on for a long time, and this is very desirable from the point of view of European interests. . . .

Your
K. M.

From letter to Engels (in Manchester)
LONDON, AUGUST 15, 1863

Dear Frederick:
. . . The local philistines are very furious at the *Times,* because the *Times* has taken them in so beautifully with the Confederate loan. These worthies might surely have known that the *Times,* as Cobbett has already revealed to them, is nothing but a "commercial concern" that does not give a damn about how the balance falls, so long as the balance comes out in its own favor. The fellows of the *Times,* like J. Spence— "that man," as the *Richmond Enquirer* says, "whom we have paid in solid gold"—receive the loan scripts partly gratis, and partly at 50 percent discount on the nominal amount. It was thus a fine business to boost it up to 105.

It seems to me very important for the United States to seize the remaining ports, Charleston, Mobile, etc., because it might come into collision with Boustrapa[1] any day. This imperial Lazarillo de Tormes[2] now caricatures not only his uncle [Napoleon I] but even himself. For the "suffrage" in Mexico,[3] as well as that of Nice and Savoy,[4]

---

1. Boustrapa, Marx's nickname for Napoleon III, is made up of the first letters of Boulogne, Strasbourg, and Paris, in all of which he had attempted *coups d'état* at various times.

2. The name of a Spanish picaresque hero in the anonymous novel *Vida de Lazarillo de Tormes y de sus Fortunas y Adversidades* (1554).

3. In June, 1863, the French, after capturing Mexico City, set up an assembly of 215 notables and declared Napoleon III's puppet, Maximilian of Austria, Emperor of Mexico.

4. In 1860, Napoleon III rigged up a plebiscite that gave support to the French annexation of the Italian territories of Nice and Savoy.

whereby he made himself and the latter French, is merely a fine caricature not only of suffrage but also of himself. For me, there is no doubt that he will break his neck in Mexico, provided he is not hanged first. . . .

Your

K. M.

From letter to Engels (in Richmond)
LONDON, MAY 26, 1864

Dear Frederick:

. . . What do you say of Grant's operations?[1] The *Times*, of course, admires Lee's retreats as merely hidden strategy.[2] "It," says Tussy[3] this morning, "considers this very canny, I daresay." I wish for nothing more than Butler's success. It would be beyond price if he took Richmond first.[4] It would be bad if Grant had to retreat, but I think that fellow knows what he is about. In any case, he has the credit for the Kentucky campaign, Vicksburg, and the licking he gave Bragg in Tennessee. . . .

Your

K. M.

From letter to Engels (in Manchester)
LONDON, JUNE 7, 1864

Dear Frederick:

. . . The American news seems to me to be very good, and I was especially pleased with today's editorial in the *Times*, which proves that Grant is being beaten constantly and will possibly be punished for his defeats—by the capture of Richmond.

Salute.   *Your*

K. M.

---

1. The sentence was written in English.
2. Editorials in *The Times* of London, May 25 and 26, 1864.
3. Marx's daughter Eleanor.
4. The third assault on Richmond began in May, 1864, and ended with its capture by Grant on April 3, 1865. General Butler, commander of the Department of Virginia and North Carolina at the time, did not participate in this attack.

From letter to Engels (in Manchester)
LONDON, SEPTEMBER 7, 1864

Dear Frederick:

... In regard to America, I consider, *entre nous* [between us], the present moment as very critical. If Grant suffers a great defeat or Sherman wins a great victory, then all right. What is dangerous is a chronic series of small checks, particularly now at election time. I am entirely of your opinion that so far Lincoln's reelection is a certainty, *still 100 to 1*. But this election period in the model land of the democracy-swindle is so fraught with unforeseen contingencies that they could unexpectedly slap in the face the rationality of events (an expression which the great Urquhart used to consider as crazy as "the justice of a locomotive"). The South seems to have a great need for an armistice, to save it from complete exhaustion. It raised this cry not only in its Northern organs, but also in the Richmond organs, although the *Richmond Examiner,* which found an echo in New York, threw it back at the Yankees with scorn. That Mr. [Jefferson] Davis decided to treat the Negro soldiers as "prisoners of war"—the recent official order of his Secretary of War—is very characteristic.

Lincoln has great resources at his disposal to win the campaign. (Peace offers on his part are, of course, mere humbug.) The election of his opponent[1] would probably lead to a real *revolution*. But with all that, one cannot deny that the outcome of the next eight weeks, when the matter will be decided, will depend much on the fortunes of war. This is absolutely the most critical point since the outbreak of the war. If this is *shifted*, then *old* Lincoln can *blunder on* to his heart's content.[2] For the rest, the Old Man can hardly "make" generals. He can choose cabinet officers better. But the Confederate papers attack their cabinet members just as much as the Yankees attack the ones in Washington. If Lincoln wins this time—which is very probable—it will be on a much more radical platform and under completely *changed circumstances*.[3] The Old Man, conformable to his legal manner, will then find that more radical means do square with his conscience. ...

Your

K. M.

---

1. General McClellan.
2. The italicized words were written in English.
3. The two italicized words were written in English.

From letter to Lion Philips (in Zaltbommel)
LONDON, NOVEMBER 29, 1864

Dear Uncle:

... A few days ago I received a letter from my friend in America, Weydemeyer, colonel of a St. Louis (Missouri) regiment.[1] He writes, among other things: "Alas, we are detained in St. Louis, because, owing to the 'conservative' elements here, military force is necessary to prevent a breakout of the numerous Southern prisoners of war ... The whole campaign in Virginia is a blunder that has cost us hecatombs of men. Despite all this, the South will not be able to hold out much longer: it has sent its last manpower into the field and cannot raise a new army. The present invasion of Missouri, like the incursions into Tennessee, has only the character of a raid, a marauding expedition; a lasting reoccupation of the lost districts does not come into question."

When you think, dear Uncle, that three and a half years ago, at the time of Lincoln's election, the problem was *making no further concessions to the slaveholders,* while now the *abolition of slavery* is the avowed and in part already realized aim, you must admit that *never* has such a gigantic transformation taken place so rapidly. It will have a beneficent effect on the whole world. ...

Your devoted nephew,
K. M.

From letter to Engels (in Manchester)
LONDON, DECEMBER 2, 1864

Dear Fred:

... The worst of such an agitation[1] is that one is greatly bothered as soon as one participates in it. For example, it was again a matter of an Address, to Lincoln, and again I had to draft the stuff (which is more difficult than a substantial work)—in order that the phraseology to which this sort of scribbling is limited should at least be distinguished from the democratic, vulgar phraseology. ...

As the Address to Lincoln was to be handed to Adams, some of the Englishmen on the committee wanted to have the deputation intro-

---

1. Letter from Joseph Weydemeyer to Engels, October, 1864.

1. "Address of the International Working Men's Association to President Lincoln," page 236.

duced by a Member of Parliament, since it was customary. This hankering was defeated by the majority of the English and the unanimity of the Continentals, and it was, furthermore, declared that such old English customs ought to be abolished. On the other hand: M. Le Lubez, like a true *crapaud*, wanted to have the Address made out, not to Lincoln, but to the American People. I have made him properly ridiculous and explained to the Englishmen that the French Democratic Etiquette is not worth a farthing more than the Monarchical Etiquette. . . .

Your

K. M.

Postscript of letter to Engels (in Manchester)
LONDON, FEBRUARY 10, 1865

Apropos. The fact that Lincoln has replied to us so courteously[1] and to the "Bourgeois Emancipation Society" so rudely and purely formally has so angered the *Daily News* that it did *not* print the reply to us. When, however, it saw to its sorrow that the *Times* did so, it had to do the same belatedly in the "Stop Press" section. Levy, too, has had to bite the sour apple. The difference between Lincoln's answer to us and to the bourgeois has made such a stir here that the "Clubs" in the West End are shaking their heads over it. You can understand how much good this does our people.

From letter to Engels (in Manchester)
LONDON, MAY 1, 1865

Dear Fred!

. . . The *chivalry of the South* ends worthily.[1] Lincoln's assassination was the biggest stupidity it could commit. Johnson is stern, inflexible, revengeful, and, as a former poor white, has a deadly hatred for the oligarchy. He will be less ceremonious with the fellows, and because of the assassination he will find the temper of the North adequate for his intentions. . . .

Your

K. M.

---

1. See Charles Francis Adams' reply for President Lincoln, page 239.

1. Marx to Engels March 4, 1865 (a line added at the end of a letter dealing with other things): "It seems to be the end of the Confederacy."

From letter to Engels (in Manchester)
LONDON, JUNE 24, 1865

Dear Fred:
    . . . Johnson's policy troubles me.[1] Ridiculous affectation of severity against individual persons; up to the present, extremely vacillating and weak in substance. The reaction has already begun in America and will soon be greatly strengthened if the flabbiness that has prevailed up to now does not soon cease. . . .

Your
K. M.

From letter to Engels (in Manchester)
APRIL 23, 1866

Dear Fred:
    . . . After the Civil War phase, the United States really is only now entering the revolutionary phase, and the European wiseacres, who believe in the omnipotence of Mr. Johnson, will soon be disillusioned . . .

Tout à vous,
K. M.

From letter written in French to François Lafargue (in Bordeaux)
LONDON, NOVEMBER 12, 1866

My Dear M. Lafargue:
    . . . You will have been as pleased as I was at President Johnson's

    1. Engels to Marx July 15, 1865: "Mr. Johnson's policy strikes me as ever worse. The nigger hatred rises ever more vehemently, and in the face of the old lords of the South he gives up all the power in his hands. If this continues the old Secession rogues will sit in Congress within six months. Without colored suffrage, there is nothing doing, and Johnson leaves this decision to the vanquished, the ex-slaveholders. It is too mad. Nevertheless, one must assume that the matter will develop differently from what the barons imagine. After all, the majority of them are totally ruined and would be glad to sell land to the immigrants and speculators from the North. Enough of the latter will soon come and make some changes. The mean whites, I believe, will gradually die out. Nothing is to be expected of this race; what remains after two generations will merge into an entirely new race. The niggers will probably become small squatters, as in Jamaica. So the oligarchy will finally be broken up; this process could now take place rapidly, but it is being dragged out."

defeat in the last elections.[1] The workers of the North have finally understood very well: labor in white skin cannot emancipate itself where the black skin is branded. . . .

Yours,
KARL MARX

Letter written in French to Auguste Vermorel (in Paris)
LONDON, AUGUST 27, 1867

Citizen:

Two things astonish me in your newspaper,[1] which I respect for its direction, its courage, its good will and its talents.

1. You make your paper an echo of Russian lies (and also Greek, for the Greeks are the tools of the Russians) concerning the so-called revolution in Crete. I take the liberty of sending you an extract from the English press on the true situation in Candia.

2. You print the newspaper scuttlebutt (of Russian origin) that North America will take the initiative against the Turks. You must know that the President of the United States does not have the power to declare war. Only the Senate can make such a decision. Even if President Johnson, a dirty tool in the hands of the former slaveholders (although you are so naïve as to transform him into a second Washington), may want to win some popularity by swaggering abroad, the Yankees are neither children nor Frenchmen. The very fact that the initiative in all these soundings-out emanates from him suffices to nullify any serious effect they are meant to have.

Excuse my taking the liberty of writing these lines to you. We both pursue the same aim—the emancipation of the proletariat. In consequence we also have the right to be candid with each other.

I beg you *not to publish* this letter. I am writing it to you privately and as a friend.

Greetings and fraternity.

KARL MARX
Member of the General
Council of the International
Working Men's Association

---

1. In the congressional elections of 1868 the Democratic party, to which Johnson belonged, was badly defeated. In the Fortieth Congress the Democrats had 49 members in the House and the Republicans 143; the tally was 11 and 42 in the Senate.

1. *Le Courrier Français,* a Paris daily.

Dear Fred:
. . . Apropos! One thing that had puzzled me for a long time: Where, during the three years of cotton famine,[1] did the English get their cotton, even for the diminished scale of production? It has been impossible to find this out from the official statistics. Despite the whole import from India, etc., there was quite an enormous deficit when one calculated the export to the Continent (even occasionally to New England). Nothing, or practically nothing, was left for home consumption. The thing is solved simply. It is now proven (a fact probably known to you, but new to me) that *verbotenus* [literally], at the outbreak of the Civil War, the English had approximately a *three-year supply* (naturally for a diminished scale of production). So what a fine *Kladderadatsch* [smashup] it would have been if the Civil War had *not* broken out!

The exports of yarn and manufactured goods, 1862, 1863, and 1864, amounted to 1,208,320,000 lbs. (reduced to yarn) and the supplies (imports) (reduced to equivalent weight in yarn), 1,187,369,000 lbs. In the first statistic the hidden surplus of manufactured goods was probably overlooked. Despite this, the result comes out the same, that the whole home supply came from existing stocks.

    Salut.   *Your*

                                                         K. M.

Dear Fred:
You will have seen that the cotton estimate is based on a comparison between export and import for 1862, 1863, 1864. The final inference regarding existing stocks of raw cotton, plus cotton manufactures in the United Kingdom, January 1, 1862 (I believe I left out the latter addition in my letter to you), thus depends on the correctness of the premises. The data rest on the Report of Messrs. Ellison and Haywood. The naked figures are as follows:

1. As a result of the Northern blockade of Southern ports during the American Civil War.

Statistics of Cotton in the United Kingdom, 1862, 1863, 1864

Import
(in thousands of lbs.)

	1862	1863	1864	For 3 years
Cotton imported	533,176	691,847	896,770	
Ditto exported	216,963	260,934	247,194	
Available to consumption	316,213	430,913	649,576	
Waste in spinning	53,756	64,637	90,940	
Equal to production in yarn	262,457	366,276	558,636	
Total				1,187,369
Export				
Yarn	88,554	70,678	71,951	
Piece goods, etc.	324,128	321,561	332,048	
Total	412,682	392,239	403,999	1,208,320

Your

K. M.

From letter to Engels (*in Manchester*)
LONDON, DECEMBER 14, 1868

Dear Fred:

. . . In regard to cotton, I have the 1861, etc., list of imports and exports from the Returns of the Board of Trade. The only fact that struck me was what is in any case unheard-of, that during the three years nothing was manufactured for inland. (I mean from the *fresh* raw material *imported* in three years, or only *in substitution for existing stock*.) . . .

Yours,

K. M.

From letter to Engels (*in Manchester*)
LONDON, MARCH 1, 1869

Dear Fred:

. . . After John Bull had compromised himself so nicely by his concessions in the *Alabama* Treaty,[1] Uncle Sam gives him a final kick

1. On November 3, 1868, the representatives of the United States and Great Britain signed a treaty compensation for damage and losses, including the cruiser *Alabama*, suffered by Americans during the Civil War; on April 13, 1869, the Senate, under the leadership of Senator Sumner, rejected the treaty. The so-called *Alabama* claims were finally settled by the Treaty of Washington, May 8, 1871.

in the behind. This is entirely the work of the Irish in America, as I have convinced myself from the Yankee papers. Professor Beesly will learn that the Irish in the United States are not a zero.

Your,

K. M.

Biographical Index

Adams, Charles Francis (1807–1886), American Minister to England, 1861–1868, 112, 125, 126, 131, 147–150, 160, 237n, 239–240, 272–273 & n

Albert, Prince (1819–1861), husband of Queen Victoria, 167–170

Almonte, Juan (1804–1869), Mexican general, Ambassador in Paris, 208

Anderson, Robert (1805–1871), Union general, commanded Fort Sumter, as major, in 1861, xxx, iv, 70

Anneke, Friedrich (c. 1818–c. 1872), Prussian officer, communist, fought in Union Army during Civil War, xxiv

Annenkov, Pavel Vassilyevich (1812–1887), liberal Russian landowner and writer, in friendly contact with Marx when abroad, 36

Applegarth, Robert (1833–1925), English cabinetmaker, member of the First International, 245

Ashburton, Alexander Baring, Lord (1774–1884), British banker and Tory politician, 131, 161

Ashworth, Henry (1794–1880), British manufacturer, member of Parliament, 164

d'Aumale, Henri Eugène Philippe Louis, Duc (1822–1897), son of King Louis Philippe, 84 & n

Bagnagatti, G., Italian member of the First International, 238

Banks, Nathaniel Prentiss (1816–1894), Union general, xxxvi–xxxvii, xxxv

Bastiat, Frédéric (1801–1850), French economist, 16–17 & n

Bazley, Thomas (1797–1885), British manufacturer, member of Parliament, 164–166

Beauregard, Pierre Gustave Toutant (1818–1893), Confederate general, xxv, xxxi, xxxv, xl, 79, 196, 202, 210

Beesly, Edward Spencer (1831–1915), English historian, 278

Bell, John (c. 1836–1875), Union general, xxxiii

Bennett, James Gordon (1795–1872), publisher of the New York Herald, 173, 230

Bentinck, George William Pierrepont, Tory member of Parliament, 180

Berkeley, George Cranfield (1753–1818), British admiral, 155

Bernard, Marie, Belgian house painter, member of the First International, 245

Berry, Hiram George (1824–1863), American general, brigade commander in the Union Army of the Potomac, 201–202

Bierce, Ambrose (1842–1914?), American author and satirist, xii

Bigelow, John (1817–1911), American author and diplomat, xli

Birney, David Bell (1825–1864), American general, brigade commander in the Union Army of the Potomac, 202

Blenker, Louis (1812–1863), German-born Union general, xxiv

Boatner, Mark Mayo, xxxv, xxxvii, xxxviii, xxxix, xl, xli, xliii, xliv, xlv

Bocquet, Jean Baptiste, French member of the First International, 238

Boernstein, Heinrich (1805–1892), German-born officer in the Union Army, 249

Boetticher, Wilhelm Karl (1789–1868), Prussian official, governor of the province of Prussia, 11

Bolleter, Heinrich, German tavern-keeper in London, member of the First International, 238, 242

Bonaparte, Joseph (1768–1844), oldest brother of Napoleon I, King of Naples, 1806–1808, and of Spain, 1808–1813, 233

Bonaparte, Louis Napoleon (see Napoleon III)

Subject Index

Saul K. Padover, Distinguished Service
Professor of Political Science at the New
School for Social Research, in New York City,
did his undergraduate work at Wayne State
University and received his Ph.D. in
Diplomatic History at the University of Chicago.
He has taught political science at the New
School for Social Research since 1949
and each semester he conducts a graduate
seminar on Marx. In addition he was a
Visiting Professor at Wayne State University
for the fall semester of 1971, where he taught
a course on Marx and political Sociology.

Dr. Padover is the author of numerous books,
among them **Jefferson: A Biography;
The Meaning of Democracy;** and **The
Genius of America.**

DATE DUE

DEMCO 38-297